Inti... ...changes

A P...

Alan...

Volu...

Martial Rose Library
Tel: 01962 827306

To be returned on or before the day

D1495134

WINCHESTER

KA 0329577 X

Samuel Fre...
New York – Sya...

© 1985 BY REDBURN PRODUCTIONS (OVERSEAS) LTD

1. *These plays are fully protected under the Copyright Laws of the British Commonwealth of Nations, the United States of America and all countries of the Berne and Universal Copyright Conventions.*

2. *All rights, including Stage, Motion Picture, Radio, Television, Public Reading and Translation into Foreign Languages, are strictly reserved.*

3. **No part of this publication may lawfully be reproduced in ANY form or by any means—photocopying, typescript, recording (including video-recording), manuscript, electronic, mechanical, or otherwise—or be transmitted or stored in a retrieval system, without prior permission.**

4. Rights of Performance by Amateurs are controlled by SAMUEL FRENCH LTD, 52 FITZROY STREET, LONDON W1P 6JR, and they, or their authorized agents, issue licences to amateurs on payment of a fee. **It is an infringement of the Copyright to give any performance or public reading of these plays before the fee has been paid and the licence issued.**

5. Licences are issued subject to the understanding that it shall be made clear in all advertising matter that the audience will witness an amateur performance; that the names of the authors of the plays shall be included on all announcements and on all programmes; and that the integrity of the author's work will be preserved.

    The Royalty Fee indicated below is subject to contract and subject to variation at the sole discretion of Samuel French Ltd.

Basic fee for each and every performance by amateurs in the British Isles	Affairs in a Tent	Code M
	Events on a Hotel Terrace	Code M
	A Garden Fête	Code M
	A Pageant	Code M

    In Theatres or Halls seating Six Hundred or more the fee will be subject to negotiation.

    In Territories Overseas the fee quoted above may not apply. A fee will be quoted on application to our local authorized agent, or if there is no such agent, on application to Samuel French Ltd, London.

6. The Professional Rights in these plays are controlled by MARGARET RAMSAY LTD, 14a Goodwin's Court, St. Martin's Lane, London WC2N 4LL.

The publication of these plays does not imply that they are necessarily available for performance by amateurs or professionals, either in the British Isles or Overseas. Amateurs and professionals considering a production are strongly advised in their own interests to apply to the appropriate agents for consent before starting rehearsals or booking a theatre or hall.

ISBN 0 573 01612 7

INTIMATE EXCHANGES

First produced at the Stephen Joseph Theatre-in-the-Round, Scarborough, on 3rd June 1982 with the following cast of characters:

Celia		
Rowena		
Sylvie	}	Lavinia Bertram
Josephine, Celia's mother		
Irene Pridworthy		

Miles, Rowena's husband		
Toby, Celia's husband		
Lionel	}	Robin Herford
Joe, Lionel's father		
Reg Schooner		

Directed by Alan Ayckbourn
Designed by Edward Lipscomb

Subsequently produced at the Greenwich Theatre on 11th June 1984 and the Ambassador's Theatre on 13th August 1984, with the same cast, director and designer

INTIMATE EXCHANGES
A related series of plays

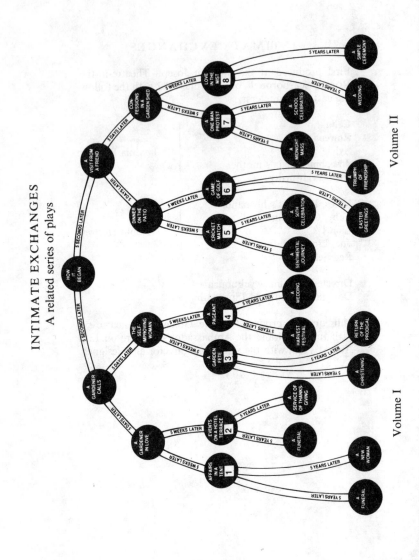

Volume I

Volume II

INTIMATE EXCHANGES

Volume 1

Volume II of *Intimate Exchanges*, containing the four plays on the right-hand side of the plan, is available from Samuel French Ltd.

Scene 1 Toby and Celia's garden
         Five years ago in June
Scene 2 The same. Five days later
Scene 3 Any one of several places
         Five weeks later
Scene 4 A Churchyard. This year

AUTHOR'S NOTE

These plays were written originally for a cast of two. They could of course be performed by a larger cast but the end result would, in my view, be infinitely less satisfying. Similarly with choice of alternatives; it's possible to do just one version but far less theatrically exciting. If, for some unavoidable reason, a decision is taken to mount only one alternative, or one alternative with a larger cast, or even several alternative versions with a larger cast, I would be grateful if the audience could be informed of my original preferences. This would serve (a) to explain why the plays are so idiosyncratically constructed and (b) to let people know what they've missed.

A.A.

A licence issued by Samuel French Ltd to perform this play does not include permission to use any Overture or Incidental music specified in this copy. Where the place of performance is already licensed by the Performing Right Society a return of the music used must be made to them. If the place of performance is not so licensed then application should be made to the Performing Right Society, 29 Berners Street, London W1.

A separate and additional Licence from Phonographic Performances Ltd, Ganton House, Ganton Street, London W1 is needed whenever commercial recordings are used.

INTIMATE EXCHANGES is a related series of plays
totalling eight scripts

This is the First

AFFAIRS IN A TENT

CHARACTERS
APPEARING IN THIS SERIES OF SCENES

Celia
Lionel
Sylvie
Toby
Miles
Irene

HOW IT BEGAN·

Toby and Celia's garden. Since this set will cover all possible seven scenes during the first half of the play, it will vary only in that occasionally we may wish to feature one area more prominently than another. In total, though, it is a well-kept garden which has been left, over the past few years, to go very much to seed. A garden which gives children great opportunities for play and most adults huge feelings of guilt that it isn't tidier. There is a small paved area at one side, the patio, bounded by a low wall which presumably leads directly off the lounge of the house. There is a garden table on this but no chairs. The table, it would appear, has been left out all winter. On it is an empty coffee cup, a packet of cigarettes and a lighter. A lumpy lawn, some of it may even have been flower beds at one time, leads to a garden shed at the bottom of the garden. Beyond that and unseen is a fence. And beyond that again playing fields. From this direction, throughout this scene, occasional shouts of children are heard

All the garden belongs of course to the house, although this is in fact a bungalow. Or sometimes, as it is more grandly known, the Headmaster's Cottage. It is modern, built by Toby's predecessor within the grounds of Bilbury Lodge, Preparatory School for Boys and Girls. It is a mild, sunny June day—in fact, Monday June 14th. The summer term is underway

In a moment, Celia, a rather worried-looking woman in her mid-thirties, comes out of the house. She has on her working-clothes with a scarf tied round her head. She is evidently involved in some heavy domestic cleaning work

Celia (*calling back into the house*) They must be in the shed. I'll have a look. ... Listen, Sylvie, you carry on up in the loft. I'll join you, all right? (*She listens then calls*) Sylvie ...

There is no reply

Celia shrugs, then stands for a moment on the patio to catch her breath. She's obviously been overdoing it more than she realizes. She squints into the sun and breathes the fresh air for a moment. She then looks at herself and cursorily brushes some of the dust off her clothes. She mops her brow with her forearm. Glad of the rest, she now goes to move off towards the shed. Her eyes light on the cigarette packet on the table. She hesitates, stopping in her tracks. She deliberates. Should she or shouldn't she weaken to temptation?

In fact, at this point, we reach the first of our alternatives. Throughout the play, the action will sub-divide as the characters are faced with alternative choices of action. Initially, the choices are smaller. Should she break her rule and have a cigarette before 6 pm?

A GARDENER CALLS

Celia (*weakening*) Oh, what the hell. (*She snatches up the cigarettes and lighter, lights one and perches on the edge of the table. She inhales. It has obviously been some hours since her last cigarette and it is a pleasurable experience*)

The doorbell rings from within the house

(*Irritably*) Oh, no. (*Calling*) Sylvie, could you see who that is? If you're not in the loft. (*She waits*) Sylvie?

The doorbell rings again

Oh. (*She takes a final puff on the cigarette, then calls*) Sylvie. Oh, for heaven's sake. (*She grinds out the cigarette rather crossly, as she says*) All right then, I'll go. I'll go.

Before she can do so, Lionel Hepplewick comes on to the patio from the house. In his early thirties, he has the healthy complexion of a man who spends much of his life in the open air. Whilst being both pleasant and subservient in his manner, he has at the same time a secretive air of someone who knows more about you than he should

Lionel Good afternoon, Mrs Teasdale.
Celia Oh, Mr Hepplewick. Nice to see you.
Lionel (*to Sylvie, presumably somewhere behind him*) Thank you very much. (*To Celia*) I hope this is not inconvenient?
Celia No, no. Sylvie and I were just—er—spring cleaning. Well, something of the sort.
Lionel Midsummer cleaning. (*He smiles*)
Celia (*laughing*) Yes, yes. (*Slight pause*) Heavenly day.
Lionel Oh, yes.
Celia I hope it stays like this.
Lionel Yes.
Celia After that winter.
Lionel Yes. It'll stay like this till Thursday.
Celia Will it?
Lionel You'll get a bit of a cloud then late afternoon, maybe a spot of rain. That'll have cleared up by Friday. A bit breezy Saturday, but Sunday'll be a real scorcher.
Celia Really, really.
Lionel That's just my guess, mind you.
Celia You ought to do the weather forecasts on the television.

Lionel makes a scornful noise

Anyway, excuse the mess. Now what can I do for you, Mr—Lionel, isn't it? Yes, of course it's Lionel.

Lionel I just come round like I promised, Mrs Teasdale.

Celia Like you ...? I'm sorry, I ...

Lionel Oh, you may not remember. A few weeks ago, at the end of last term you may recall, we were talking—yourself, Mr Teasdale and me—and you mentioned then, if I should have any spare time, I should come up and have look at your garden.

Celia Yes, of course. It was a little while ago.

Lionel Now I've got the cricket pitches marked and the outfields mown, I thought I'd just come up and have a look. If that's all right.

Celia Yes.

Lionel Mr Teasdale said it would probably be all right.

Celia (*without enthusiasm*) Yes, of course. Well. There it is.

Lionel Yes.

Celia Neither of us are particularly garden-minded, I'm afraid.

Lionel (*impassively*) No.

Celia We love sitting in them, getting all the benefits. We both loathe any kind of hard work, I'm afraid. Still, what do you think?

Lionel (*after staring for a moment*) That's a useful shed.

Celia Oh, yes. The shed. That's a mess too, I'm afraid. It was put up by our predecessors, the last Headmaster and his wife, Mr and Mrs Cowlishaw. Now he was a very keen gardener, Mr Cowlishaw. He'd have been before your time.

Lionel Oh, yes.

Celia Yes, your father would have been school caretaker then, wouldn't he?

Lionel He would, yes.

Celia He's still well, is he—er—Joe? Is Joe keeping fit?

Lionel Very well, thank you. He's still got his knee troubles but he's a fine old man.

Celia Oh, yes. Is he coping without your mother?

Lionel Just about.

Celia Still, it was a long illness.

Lionel It was a very long illness. It was a relief to see her die, I don't mind saying.

Celia Yes.

Lionel (*holding out his hand and clenching his fist*) She was like that when she died.

Celia Was she? Was she? (*Slight pause*) Like what exactly?

Lionel Like the size of my hand, she was. Fifteen stone woman shrunk down to that.

Celia Oh, dear.

Lionel The size of that.

Celia Yes, yes.

Pause

Well ...

Lionel Yes, we can do something with this, I don't doubt.

Celia Would you like to take a look round?

Lionel Thankyou very much.

Celia I mean, there isn't much. What you see is what we have. I'll make some coffee. Would you like some coffee? Or tea? There's tea.

Lionel Cup of tea would be very pleasant, thank you, Mrs Teasdale.

Celia Right. Tea. I won't be a moment. (*She begins to move inside*)

Lionel Be all right for me to go in the shed, will it?

Celia Yes, help yourself. It shouldn't be locked.

Celia goes into the house

Lionel prowls around the garden, tutting a little, as he examines it more closely. As he reaches the bottom of the garden, he sees someone beyond the hut in the playing field

Lionel (*calling*) Afternoon, Mr Coombes. Very well, thank you. . . . She's just gone in the house. Did you want to speak to her? . . . Right, just as you like. (*He watches whoever it was he was talking to walking away, with a slight look of contempt. He then starts to pace the garden out and appears to be doing calculations in his head*)

Sylvie comes out of the house. She is a young, fresh-faced awkward girl but not unattractive. Like Celia, she is dressed for heavy housework

Sylvie She says do you want sugar in your tea?

Lionel Just a minute, just a minute. Fifteen, eighteen. . . . (*He finishes*) Do I what?

Sylvie Mrs Teasdale, she says do you want sugar in your tea?

Lionel Three, yes. Three sugars.

Sylvie Right, three. (*She begins to go in*)

Lionel You could have told her that.

Sylvie What?

Lionel I say, you could have told her I took three sugars. You know well enough I take three sugars.

Sylvie No, I don't. How should I know you take three sugars? How am I supposed to know?

Lionel Because you do.

Sylvie Nothing to do with me. Take boiled eggs in it as far as I'm concerned.

Lionel You knew. (*He resumes his calculations*) Eighteen times four . . . four eights are thirty-two . . . four ones are four. . . .

Sylvie Seventy-two.

Lionel Carry three. Four and three are seven. Seventy-two.

Sylvie Seventy-two, I said.

Lionel I'm not listening to you. You can't even count sugar.

Pause. Sylvie watches him

What are you up to in there, then? Clearing away the Headmaster's empties, are you?

Sylvie Mind your own business.

Lionel Bet he gets through a few bottles in a week.

Sylvie What are you supposed to be doing anyway?

Lionel I'm going to work on this, aren't I?

Sylvie Can't wait to see that.

Lionel Tidy it up a bit for her.

Sylvie You were going to do my mum's front, you never did.

Lionel It's only two square feet. Not worth it.

Sylvie Still needs doing.

Lionel Concrete it over. Have done with it.

Sylvie Great gardening tip that is. (*She looks towards the field*) Is that Mr Coombes walking along there?

Lionel Yes. Looking for his wife in the bushes, I wouldn't doubt.

Sylvie Who's she with now?

Lionel Anyone's guess. They say at the Squash Club there are more bookings for her than there are for squash courts. Everyone's had her.

Sylvie Have you had her?

Lionel I haven't.

Sylvie Then it's not everyone, is it?

Lionel I don't play squash, do I? If I want her, I've only got to buy a racket. Anyone with a racket can have her.

Sylvie Better buy yourself one.

Lionel Can't afford squash rackets.

Sylvie Yes, you can. You're just mean. You won't spend nothing, will you? Not on anybody. Not even on yourself.

Lionel Not on you, certainly.

Sylvie Wouldn't want you to, don't worry.

Lionel Are you going to get my tea?

Sylvie Two sugars, then.

Lionel Three.

Sylvie We going out Friday or not?

Lionel I don't know.

Sylvie Last week you said we were.

Lionel I don't know what I said last week.

Sylvie Only if we're not, I'd like to make other arrangements, that's all.

Lionel (*unimpressed*) Suit yourself.

Sylvie Are we or aren't we?

Lionel Let you know.

Sylvie When?

Lionel Soon.

Sylvie Because I want to make other arrangements. That's all. I've got arrangements to make.

Lionel I bet.

Sylvie I have. If you don't want to take me, I'll go with someone else. Someone my own age.

Sylvie goes inside

Lionel (*muttering*) Get out of it. (*He resumes his calculations*) Couple of bags of that, then. (*He opens the shed door*) Now, what have we here. . . .

(*Mimicking*) I want to make arrangements, that's all. (*He picks up an implement*) Half a shovel. Better than none. Weedkiller. Need a bit of that round here. Wheelbarrow. No wheel. It's like Kew bloody Gardens in here. (*He picks up an old gin bottle full of some liquid*) Another of his empties. Well, we could start by chucking all that away. (*He comes out of the shed and closes the door*)

Celia comes out of the house with two mugs of tea

Celia It's an awful muddle in there, isn't it?

Lionel Just a bit.

Celia You don't mind a mug, do you? That's yours. Sylvie said you didn't take sugar.

Lionel (*impassively*) Ta.

Celia Well, what do you think?

Lionel I'll need to buy in a bit.

Celia What sort of bits?

Lionel Tools, seed, bit of fertilizer, that sort of thing.

Celia There are tools in the shed.

Lionel Useless.

Celia Really?

Lionel No use at all.

Celia Oh, dear. I don't know what to suggest for the best. It's a problem.

Lionel No problem. You'll have to buy some more, that's all.

Celia No, it's not that. I just don't know, at the moment, if it's going to be worth buying things. You see, it's—well, it's rather awkward, I don't know how to put this. . . .

Lionel If you're a bit short, I could probably get them cheaper.

Celia No, it's not that at all. Though that would probably be welcome. You see, I'm not sure—we're not certain how much longer we're going to be here. There's a possibility my husband may be moving on.

Lionel Moving on.

Celia Yes.

Lionel I see.

Celia It's not certain but . . .

Lionel You'll be moving with him?

Celia Probably. Yes, of course. Possibly. As I say, it's all quite vague.

Lionel I see.

Pause

Celia So. We don't really know. (*A pause*) I wish we did. (*A pause*) I mean, I don't really want to discuss it. Not at all.

Lionel No.

Pause

Celia I mean, I don't think people really appreciate the pressures that a Headmaster sometimes undergoes. I mean, there are the parents. And the children. And the staff. (*A pause*) And his family. They all—mount up. Inevitably. Especially a private school like this. He's also got the Board breathing down his neck. And most of them are—well, they don't understand about teachers.

Pause

Lionel They're dedicated people. Teachers.

Celia They are. They are. (*Slight pause*) Most of them. (*A pause*) It's the family, you see. That's always the first thing to suffer. All the pressures bottle up at work and he brings them home with him and unbottles at home.

Lionel Yes.

Celia (*to herself*) Literally.

Pause

Lionel Well, I——

Celia It's also a terrific strain on me, you see. Because I've so very few people I can talk to. I mean, if you're the Headmaster's wife you just can't afford to be too familiar, you know. Otherwise you get involved in all the politics. School politics, I mean. (*A pause*) So I'm afraid the poor old Headmaster's wife never has much of a shoulder to cry on. (*She laughs*) Still . . .

Pause

Lionel I think you could do with some crazy paving.

Celia I'm sorry?

Lionel Bit of crazy paving would look nice.

Celia Oh, yes. Possibly.

Lionel If it's well laid. You got to lay it well. It's got to be properly laid.

Celia Yes, of course.

Lionel So you don't know if you're going or not then?

Celia No.

Lionel Or if your husband's going or not?

Celia No.

Lionel What do you suggest then?

Celia I don't know. I don't know what to suggest. I don't want you to go to any trouble.

Lionel No trouble.

Celia What do you suggest?

Lionel Me?

Celia What do you think would be best?

Lionel Well. Without particularly knowing all the circumstances, I'd say, perhaps you should take a chance that you'll be staying even if your husband isn't staying. And let me go ahead.

Celia You think so?

Lionel You'll be sorry, won't you, if you're sitting here this time next year looking at the same old mess.

Celia True.

Lionel You'll be glad of me then.

Celia I would.

Lionel I'll come up two or three evenings a week during the summer. Occasional weekend perhaps. Keep an eye on things for you.

Celia Yes, maybe you're right.

Lionel It wouldn't be expensive. Once you've got your tools.

Celia No.

Lionel Just the labour, then.

Celia Quite.

Lionel Sweat's not expensive.

Celia No.

Lionel (*draining his mug*) Good cup of tea.

Celia Thank you. Assam.

Lionel True enough.

Celia All right. So what are we going to do with all this mess?

Lionel Well, I've got a few ideas. If you like, I'll do you a little sketch plan. How it might look.

Celia Oh, splendid.

Lionel You can always chuck it away if you don't like what you see.

Celia No, I'm sure I'll be guided by you.

Lionel I hope so.

Celia I'll just be so grateful if someone can sort it out. I've sat here staring at it day after day. You just carry on.

Lionel It's a joint effort though. After all, it's your garden. You're the one who's going to sit in it.

Celia Yes, of course.

Lionel Your garden. Your money. My sweat. Fair exchange.

Celia Yes. (*She laughs rather nervously*) Well, I hope you don't have to sweat too much.

Lionel Right then. If you'll excuse me, I have the gym to see to.

Celia That your little boy?

Lionel Gymnasium.

Celia Oh, of course.

Lionel Lock it up. I'm not married.

Celia Ah. So when will you start?

Lionel Straightaway, if it suits you. I'll clear out your shed and get that re-stocked. That's the first thing.

Celia You'll keep receipts, will you?

Lionel Oh, yes.

Celia Of anything you buy. For tax. I don't think we can claim back gardening tools. . . .

Lionel You'll get your receipts.

Celia (*confused*) It's not that we don't . . . of course. Well, back to midsummer cleaning. Do you want to cut through that way? (*She indicates past the shed*) Or come through the front?

Lionel (*indicating the former*) That way, if I may.

Celia Of course. Well, goodbye then, Lionel. (*She gathers up their mugs*)

Lionel Goodbye, Mrs Teasdale.

Celia Celia. Do call me Celia, if you want.

Lionel Well, maybe. Maybe.

Celia You don't mind me calling you Lionel?
Lionel No, I don't mind that. Cheerio then.
Celia Cheerio—Lionel.

Celia goes into the house

Lionel stands staring after her for a minute

Lionel (*at length*) Well, now. ... (*He stands in the middle of the garden apparently doing further calculations*)
Celia (*off, angrily*) Look, don't put that on there, Sylvie. Use a tiny bit of nouse, girl. That is clean washing, Sylvie, isn't it?
Sylvie (*off*) Yes, Mrs Teasdale.
Celia (*off*) You know the word clean, do you?
Sylvie (*off*) Yes, Mrs Teasdale.
Celia (*off*) You can be so stupid, stupid, Sylvie. Now look at them. Look at this.
Sylvie (*off*) Yes, Mrs Teasdale.

Lionel listens to this for a second, then, amused, moves away to the bottom of the garden

Celia (*off*) Thank you so much. That's better. Now, will you put that out the back in the dustbins, not on the washing. That will be much more helpful. Off you go.

Sylvie comes out of the house. She is carrying an armload of old paint tins which are very dusty and congealed

Sylvie (*aloud*) Yes, Mrs Teasdale. (*Muttering*) Stupid old cow.
Lionel You do as you're told.
Sylvie You still here?
Lionel Just going.
Sylvie Well?
Lionel What?
Sylvie Have you decided? Are you coming on Friday or are you not?

Lionel considers for a moment

(*Impatiently*) Well?

EITHER he says:

Lionel Well. No, I don't think I am.
Sylvie What?
Lionel I said, I'm not taking you. Sorry.
Sylvie Why not?
Lionel I'm afraid I've made other arrangements.
Sylvie What other arrangements?
Lionel Personal. Sorry.
Sylvie You promised me you were going out with me.

Lionel Then you've been labouring under a false impression, haven't you? Better start sweetening somebody else's tea.
Sylvie Who is she then?
Lionel Never mind.
Sylvie Who is she?
Lionel Bye-bye.
Sylvie Lionel, who is she?
Lionel You'll find out, no doubt.

Lionel goes off round the back of the shed

Sylvie You bet I will. You bet. (*She stands, angry and impotent for a second, still clutching her armful of tins*) I'll bust her bloody head in, too, when I find her.

Sylvie storms off towards the dustbins

The lights fade to a Black-out

To: A GARDENER IN LOVE (page 15)

OR he says:

Lionel Well. I tell you what. I'll come on one condition.
Sylvie What's that?
Lionel You stop messing me about.
Sylvie What do you mean?
Lionel All these other arrangements of yours.
Sylvie I'm free to do what I want.
Lionel Not if you're with me, you're not.
Sylvie I don't have to give up my other friends just because——
Lionel You do if you're with me. Take it or leave it. Only make up your mind because, quite possibly, I'll be making other arrangements of my own.
Sylvie (*sulkily*) You can take a jump then.
Lionel Fair enough. Cheerio then. (*He moves away*)
Sylvie Just a minute then.
Lionel Well?
Sylvie It's two way this, is it? If I don't make other arrangements, then you won't?
Lionel Right.
Sylvie No one else.
Lionel No.
Sylvie All right.
Lionel See you Friday then.
Sylvie Yes.
Lionel (*turning as he goes*) Don't worry. You'll be OK. I got plans for you.

Lionel turns and goes

Sylvie Oh yes? What plans? (*To herself*) What plans? (*She moves thought-fully to the dustbins with her load*)

The Lights fade to a Black-out

To: THE SELF-IMPROVING WOMAN (page 107)

A GARDENER IN LOVE

The same. Five days later. It is the morning of Saturday, June 19th and is another sunny day

There are now two garden chairs by the patio table. On one of them sits Toby Teasdale, a rather crumpled red-faced man in his early forties. He sits with his paper and a cup of tea. He is smoking and coughing as he reads. He also mutters occasionally at various items he comes across. At the other end of the garden there is the occasional clump and bump from the shed. Although, at present, we are unable to see who is in there—whoever it is, is very busy indeed trying to establish some order. The odd item is tossed out into a growing pile of rubbish in the middle of the garden. Toby occasionally glares in the direction of this distraction

After a while, Celia comes out of the house carrying a teapot and a milk jug. She tops up Toby's cup

Celia I wish you'd have something to eat.
Toby (*muttering*) I don't want anything to eat.
Celia A piece of toast. Anything.
Toby I do not require anything to eat at all, thank you very much indeed.
Celia All right.

The sound of a clump from the shed. They both stare

Toby What is he doing in there? Have we any idea?
Celia He's trying to tidy it up.
Toby Does it need tidying up?
Celia Of course it does.
Toby Are we a family in need of a tidy shed?
Celia You can hardly get in there.
Toby When's he going to do something about the garden? I thought we were paying him for the garden. He's been here three days. He hasn't come out of that shed yet.
Celia He has to get organized first.
Toby He's a useless oaf. Not a patch on his father. Do you know, he marked out the first team cricket pitch and made it a yard short. A whole yard. Bloody ball whistling round their ears. Nearly killed the openers.
Celia Well, cricket.
Toby You'd better watch it. If he gets his measurements wrong here, you'll have flower beds straight through your living-room. (*He examines his cup*) What's this?
Celia Tea.
Toby I didn't want any more tea.

Celia Well, you've got it. (*Studying him*) I'm sure half your trouble is you don't eat. I'm sure if you ate, you wouldn't ... you wouldn't feel so awful in the mornings. (*Pause*) What were you doing in the night? You were banging around for hours. (*Pause*) What were you up to?

Toby What?

Celia What were you doing in the middle of the night?

Toby I was answering, if you must know, in polite terms, a call of nature.

Celia Well, you were up for hours.

Toby I do beg your pardon. I didn't realize I had a time limit.

Celia Hours and hours.

Toby Perhaps you could hang a stop watch on the cistern. I'll try and speed things up for you.

Celia Don't be so unnecessary.

Toby If I'm not allowed to spend my leisure in my own toilet ...

Celia God, the quantities you must drink. I dread to think how much useless liquid you take in.

Toby Every bit of liquid I take in is vital. I don't drink any liquid unless it's absolutely essential and that includes this damn tea so take it away.

Celia Gallons and gallons of Scotch and beer and cigarettes. Look at you. The Headmaster.

Toby Is this because I won't have a piece of toast? Is this a sort of verbal version of forcible feeding?

Celia You'll die eventually. You know that, don't you? You'll carry on like this, year in, year out, putting nothing inside you that's remotely good for you and one day, that'll be that. You'll just fall down and explode and drop dead.

Pause

You said you were going to cut back, anyway. You promised Miles. You promised me.

Toby I have cut back.

Celia You have not cut back at all.

Toby I've cut back as much as I intend to.

Celia You had at least three whiskies last night.

Toby Three whiskies? What the hell's wrong with having three whiskies?

Celia Probably more for all I know. You were in the pub before you came home.

Toby All right, I had one there. That's fair enough. That's four.

Celia I bet you had more than one. You never had one.

Toby All right five. We'll call it five then.

Celia Large.

Toby Obviously large. No point in having a small one, is there?

Celia Well, it's too much, Toby. It really is.

Toby I'll be the judge of when it's too much.

Something is lobbed out of the shed to add to the pile

What the hell's he doing?

Celia They won't give you a second chance, you know. The Board of Governors. I mean, Miles really had to argue for you, Toby. He really did. And he's the Chairman. He's not supposed to do that. He's supposed to be impartial. I mean, Miles Coombes is the only really good freind you've . . . They were actually on the verge of voting to advertise for a new Headmaster. That awful Irene Pridworthy. She said really horrid things apparently. About you. Did you know that? Terrible things. I don't want people saying things like that about my husband.

Toby I don't really want to enter into a discussion about Irene Pridworthy's views. I really don't. She's not a woman to be listened to on any topic. Irene Pridworthy should have been held down at a very early age and had rat poison thrust up her nose. That's all I have to say about Irene Pridworthy.

Celia That's precisely what I mean, Toby. Now that's supposed to be a Headmaster talking. You're supposed to be inspiring. You're supposed to lead people. I mean, all this rat poison up noses. It's so negative. You used to be a positive man, Toby, you really did. I mean, when I used to hear you talk in the old days, I was really so excited by you. All your plans and what you wanted to see happen in education, in our own school, in the country. Now you don't seem to want anything except to stuff things up people's noses. What's happened to you, Toby? Is it me? Tell me if it's me. It probably is. It usually is.

Toby I don't think we want to get into all this first thing in the morning, do you?

Celia It's the only time of day when we stand the slightest chance of talking at all. When you're—coherent. I may as well say it.

Toby If we talk, you'll get over-excited. Then I will probably get angry and break something. And then you will start crying and that will make me feel rotten so I'll go off and have another five whiskies. And the only one who'll get any fun out of that little lot will be the chap in the shed.

Celia Do we always have to shout? When we talk.

Toby Apparently.

Celia We didn't shout in the early days, did we?

Toby We didn't talk to each other in the early days. I think that's half the trouble really. If people stopped talking to each other, there wouldn't be any misunderstandings.

Celia We never talk at all. I don't know what you're talking about.

Toby Yes, we do, Celia, we do. Well, we sort of half-talk, that's the trouble. We don't say whole things. We say half things. Because we're frightened the whole thing might be too much for the other one to swallow. So then I go away thinking, what on earth did she mean by that? Did she mean what I thought she said? If she did mean what I thought she said, then I'm deeply, deeply hurt. Only of course, you didn't mean that at all. You meant something completely different. Only you didn't say it. So you'd have been better off saying nothing in the first place.

Celia That's wonderful stuff for the sixth form, Toby, but I'm afraid I haven't the faintest idea what you're talking about.

Toby There you are. Absolutely proved my point. Look, Celia, you go and wash up or something. I'll be off in a minute. I'll get out of your way. I've a staff meeting at eleven.

Celia (*looking at the tea*) You're not going to drink this then?

Toby No.

Celia Sylvie's washing up, anyway.

Toby Sylvie?

Celia Yes.

Toby Does she come on Saturdays?

Celia She missed Wednesday because of her mother.

Toby That's your problem, I think. Nothing to do. People in there doing your washing-up. People out here clearing out your shed.

Celia If I thought you meant half the things you said, I'd pour this tea over your head, I really would.

A clump from the shed

He's working very hard anyway.

Toby He's probably not working at all.

Celia Of course he is.

A clump from the shed

Hark at him.

Toby He's just so stupid, that's him blundering round trying to find his way out.

Celia We've agreed he's going to put a lot of crazy paving down. I hope you approve.

Toby I honestly don't give a damn if he covers the whole bloody area in owl's vomit. I'm not going out there anyway.

Celia sniffs

Oh God, Celia, don't start.

Celia I do try, Toby.

Toby Yes, I know, I know, I know.

Celia (*openly weeping*) It really is all over, isn't it? It really is.

Toby I don't know.

Celia I'm going to have to go away. I'll have to.

Toby If you think that's best.

Celia I'll take the children somewhere for a bit. Probably finish up at my mother's. God, what an awful thought.

Toby I thought you got on well with her.

Celia Yes, I do. But I don't really want to sit listening to her telling me how history repeats itself. And then we'll start discussing whether it is that the women in our family all marry men who are drawn to drink or whether it's we that drive them to it.

Toby Look, I don't want to hurt your feelings again unnecessarily, Celia, but there are a whole load of more important reasons than you and your mother, why a man should turn to drink, I can tell you.

Celia Yes, all right. You tell me, what are they?

Toby OK. You want a few? You want just a few of them? Here we go.

Number one: I think the whole of life has become one long losing battle, all right? That's the first reason I'm drinking. Number two: I find myself hemmed in by an increasing number of quite appalling people all flying under the flags of various breeds of socialism, all of whom so far as I can gather are hell bent on courses of self-reward and self-remuneration that make the biggest capitalist look like Trotsky's Aunt Mildred. Number three: On the other hand, we have the rest of the country who don't even have the decency to pretend that they're doing it for the benefit of their fellow men. Ha ha. They're just grabbing hand over fist the most they can get for the minimum of effort by whatever grubby underhand means they can muster. Number four: We have half the men going around looking like women and half the women looking like men and the rest of us in the middle no longer knowing what the bloody hell we are. Number five: And the few remaining women who don't look like men are busy ripping their clothes off and prancing around on video cassettes and soft porn discs trying to persuade us that sex can be fun. Fun, for God's sake. So can World War Three. Number six:—are you still with me?—We now have a police force that according to my paper anyway, is more dishonest than the people we're paying them to arrest. Don't, for God's sake, ask them the time, just hang on to your watch. Number seven: They've started this filthy floodlit cricket with cricketers wearing tin hats and advertisements for contraceptives on their boots. Number eight: You can no longer walk through the centre of any town anywhere in this country without being set upon by thousands of bald tattooed Neanderthals. Number nine: You can't get a hotel room in London for love nor money because they're all booked up by hordes of bloody foreigners in black berets busy wiring up suitcases full of bloody explosives to blow the rest of us up. And Number ten: whisky very, very shortly is going to be ten quid a bottle. Have I made my point, Celia?

Celia I don't know what to say when you get like this. I just don't know.

Celia hurries indoors

Toby stares at his paper for a second and then slams it down

Toby I'd suggest they brought back hanging only they'd be sure to hang all the wrong people. (*He rises*)

Sound of a clump from the shed

Toby walks down the garden and dodges an item, an old chest expander, which is thrown out onto the pile. He then leans into the shed

I say, Hepplewick. (*He coughs because of the dust inside*) It's all right, don't come out. I hate to tear you away from our shed. When you're finished, I'd like that second eleven outfield mown. We've a first round house match on it on Monday. I don't want them wasting hours hunting for the ball around leg slip. Just get it mown, all right? (*He moves away and examines the pile of rubbish finally picking up the chest expander*) Do you know, I think this used to be mine. (*He tests it, but finds it altogether far too heavy-going*)

Sylvie comes out of the house with a polythene bag of rubbish from the kitchen pedal bin

Toby stops as he sees her

Sylvie (*with a slight smirk*) Morning, Mr Teasdale.
Toby Morning, Sylvie.

Sylvie passes him, Toby is as unimpressed by Sylvie as Sylvie is by Toby

Sylvie (*indicating the chest expander*) I didn't know you went in for that, Mr Teasdale.
Toby I don't. It's my wife's.
Sylvie Oh.

Sylvie moves off to the dustbins

Toby crosses to the patio and picks up his paper

Toby (*calling*) Celia. Celia, I'm off now. Cheerio. (*Muttering*) If you can hear me or not. And I'm sure you don't give a damn anyway. (*He moves back down the garden, passing Sylvie on his way*)
Sylvie Goodbye, Mr Teasdale.
Toby Goodbye, Sylvie.
Sylvie Mind how you go, won't you?

Toby looks at her suspiciously, then goes off round the back of the shed

Sylvie stops by the pile of rubbish and studies the contents

Clattering from inside the shed

Didn't see you at the dance last night then?

More clattering from inside the shed

I went with Pete Bartlett. (*Pause*) Well, he asked me. Couldn't refuse.

Another clump

I take it your other arrangement, so called, didn't include the dance then? Doesn't whoever it is dance, doesn't she? Eh? Got a wooden leg, has she?

A piece of junk flies past her

Maybe she's very old, is that it? Your age, is she? Can't get about without her sticks, poor old thing. Never mind. You'll be good company for each other. Darby and Joan Hepplewick. (*She picks up the chest expander*) Here, try this, I should. Do you good.

Lionel comes out of the shed, very hot and grimy

Lionel What you on about?
Sylvie Morning.
Lionel Wouldn't try that. You'll get them caught in the springs.
Sylvie At least I got something.
Lionel Bloody mess in there.

Sylvie Well, I'm busy. Can't hang around here.
Lionel Bye-bye.
Sylvie Bye. (*She moves towards the house*) I'm going out again with him, you know. Pete Bartlett.
Lionel Good.
Sylvie He's got a car.
Lionel He can run you over then, can't he?
Sylvie You'll be sorry. You will. You'll be sorry.
Lionel (*with mock alarm*) Ooh, ooh.
Sylvie You wait.

Sylvie goes into the house

Lionel looks after her amused. He picks up the chest expander. He does a few workouts with it. Unlike Toby, he's clearly very fit and quite strong. Pleased with himself, he tosses it down

Lionel goes off behind the shed and returns in a second, with a couple of pieces of broken paving. He puts these down. He goes back for some more

Celia comes out of the house with a mug of tea

Celia Lionel.

Lionel returns with more paving

I wondered if you wanted some more tea.
Lionel Wouldn't mind. Warm work.
Celia We seem to have a lot left in the pot. That the paving?
Lionel Yes.
Celia Very nice.
Lionel He unloaded it outside the gate there. I told him to put it inside. Just too damned lazy. Typical.
Celia Dear. Here. (*She hands him the tea*)
Lionel Ta. I'll get it moved in. Have to level it first though.

Lionel sets the cup down and exits for some more paving stones

Celia Yes, it'll need to be level. We don't want anything too crazy.

Lionel returns with more paving stones

Celia hovers, reluctant to go back into the house

Heavy work.

Lional grunts

Yes, my husband was just saying he thought the paving would look marvellous. He definitely approves of our scheme.
Lionel Glad to hear it. (*He picks up the mug*)
Celia You—may have heard him just now.
Lionel I didn't hear nothing.
Celia Oh. I felt sure you had. He—gets a little excited occasionally. He—feels deeply about some things.

Lionel No harm in that.

Celia No. I think depth of feeling is a good thing. I mean, I don't think there's enough of it these days. Is there? All terribly superficial. Awful.

Lionel True.

Pause

Celia Nice to see your father the other day. In the village.

Lionel Oh, yes.

Celia Do you often go shopping together?

Lionel Occasionally. If he feels like a push round, I push him round.

Celia He looked very fit.

Lionel Oh, yes.

Celia How old will he be now?

Lionel Just coming on seventy-two.

Celia Oh, really very young.

Lionel Not so bad. (*He drinks his tea*)

A silence

Celia I'm sorry, you obviously don't want me chattering round you while you're working.

Lionel That's all right.

Celia I'm afraid I do rabbit on a bit. You're—er—you're not a great talker, I'd have guessed. From talking to you.

Lionel I can talk a bit.

Celia Oh, yes. No, what I meant was, you prefer not to. Talk. Do you?

Lionel (*amiably*) Want to talk now, do you?

Celia No, no.

Lionel Like to hear me talk?

Celia No, I—er——

Lionel Now. What would you like to hear me talk about? Music? That interest you at all? Music?

Celia No, I'm sorry, I didn't really mean this. . . .

Lionel (*ploughing on*) What sort of music do you like then? Do you like music, do you?

Celia Me? Oh yes, very much. I'm afraid I'm mostly, I'm afraid——

Lionel Afraid what?

Celia I'm a little bit square, I'm afraid. I prefer the classical sort of music really.

Lionel You don't like pop music?

Celia Well, some of it. Some of it I find very interesting. Obviously exploring new—new sounds.

Lionel I don't like any of it. It's rubbish.

Celia Oh.

Lionel You like Sibelius?

Celia Oh, yes. Very much. Very much indeed.

Lionel Jean Sibelius. Eighteen sixty-five to nineteen fifty-seven. His violin concerto's very good, isn't it?

Celia Marvellous. And all the . . . all those swans and things.

Lionel Swan of Tunella.

Celia Wonderful, wonderful.

Lionel Do you know Nielsen? Carl Nielsen. Eighteen sixty-five to nineteen thirty-one.

Celia No, no.

Lionel Danish. He's not dissimilar. You ought to listen to him. I think you'd like him. Carl Nielsen.

Celia Yes, I will. I will. That's something to remember.

Lionel (*warming*) It's a little bit like, you know, a lot of people now, they go for Mahler. . . .

Celia Oh, yes, Mahler, yes.

Lionel Gustav Mahler. Eighteen sixty to nineteen eleven. A lot of people know him but what they don't know is Bruckner. Now I prefer Bruckner.

Celia (*getting very lost*) Do you?

Lionel To my mind, he's superior. Somebody once said "Mahler spent his life looking for God but Bruckner had found him." I think that was Wilhelm Furtwangler.

Celia He found Wilhelm Furtwangler?

Lionel No, God.

Celia Oh, I see. Yes, I'm sorry. Bruckner had found God. That's very good, isn't it? Very good.

Lionel Anton Bruckner. Eighteen twenty-four to eighteen ninety-six.

Celia Yes, I'll certainly remember him. I've heard of him, of course, but I'll certainly remember him.

Pause

The film was very good, wasn't it? Mahler. Did you see it?

Lionel No.

Celia Interesting man. Got very grumpy and wore glasses. (*Pause*) Very long.

Lionel The film.

Celia No, his music. You really do need an evening, don't you?

Lionel He took his time.

Celia Yes. (*Pause*) Well, we have music in common. As well as gardens.

Lionel Yes.

Celia My husband's not musical.

Lionel No?

Celia So we let the children have the record player. And of course, they play all this dreadful stuff.

Pause

Look at all this rubbish. If there's anything you want, just help yourself. (*She picks up the chest expander*) Heavens, look at this. It's one of those — things, isn't it?

Lionel Chest expander.

Celia Yes.

Lionel Build your muscles up.

Celia I shouldn't think you need this, do you? All this exercise. Still, if you know anyone who . . . Do you have any brothers or cousins?

Lionel No.

Celia I have two brothers, actually. One's in Canada. He's doing frightfully well. He's a lawyer. Married a Canadian. He's got four children. Then my younger brother's in Scotland. He's something to do with the Forestry Commission and he's just got divorced. I see him now and again. Joey. But I hardly ever see my elder brother, Derek. I haven't seen him for years. I'm always meaning to fly over and visit them but ... my mother's still alive. Very hale and hearty. Well, she's quite young. Not yet sixty. My father's dead but ... Yes.

Pause. Lionel continues to look at her. Celia remains strangely embarrassed

I used to work for a firm that organized conferences. You know, for businesses and so on. Booking hotels and travel, you know. I love travelling. That's how I met my husband. Well, he was at a conference. That was when he was in industry. Before he came back to teaching. Then I had children. I was his second wife. So. That's me, really.

Lionel Very interesting.

Celia You're looking very thoughtful and rustic.

Lionel Thoughtful. Not particularly rustic.

Celia Oh, I didn't mean that rudely.

Lionel I live in the middle of a council estate that's got two trees left alive on it. And I went to school round the back of the shoe factory. That doesn't exactly make me rustic, does it?

Celia No, no.

Lionel The closest I get to nature is pull-starting the school mower. I suppose that's fairly rustic.

Celia No, I'm sorry, I was pigeon-holing. I shouldn't do that. It's very wrong to pigeon-hole people. They're themselves.

Lionel Right.

Celia Right.

Slight pause

Lionel What's yourself then?

Celia Well, I—I've told you all about me.

Lionel No, you haven't. You've told me about your brothers. You've told me about your mother. You've told me about your father, your husband and your job. You haven't said anything about you.

Celia Well. I'm not rustic. Certainly. What do you think I am? You tell me. Be as rude as you like. I don't mind. I'm rather used to it. Go on. Pigeon-hole me.

Lionel Well. I'd say you were just a little bit short on self-confidence just at the moment.

Celia Yes, that's possibly true. Very shrewd of you.

Lionel You're a bit like a woman who's just fallen off her bicycle.

Celia How do you mean?

Lionel You've skinned your knees, got a bit nervous. Only thing to do in those cases is to get re-mounted. Right?

Celia Yes. Yes.

Lionel Get pedalling again. Get your legs working. Get your thigh muscles aching.

Celia Well.

Lionel Only way. Can't spend the rest of your life lying on your back in a ditch now.

Celia No.

Pause

I think I've rather lost the thread of this.

Lionel You know what I mean.

Pause

Celia Extending this bicycle thing a bit further, I mean where am I pedalling to? I mean, am I just pedalling for the sake of pedalling or am I supposed to be pedalling towards something?

Lionel Depends which direction you're pointing in. Two things can start happening when you start pedalling. Certain things can get nearer and other things can get further away. And if you pedal hard enough, they'll disappear altogether.

Celia But then I suppose if I pedal too hard, I could risk falling off again?

Lionel Maybe.

Celia Finish up flat on my back in a ditch again, wouldn't I?

Lionel At least it'll be a different ditch ... different bit of sky to look at ... different cow parsley.

Celia Same position, though. No better off in the long run.

Lionel Probably not.

Celia Not at all.

Lionel If you feel like that, I should put your bike away in the garage if I were you.

Pause

Celia (*fanning herself*) It's very warm now, isn't it? This has been a marvellous spell, hasn't it? (*She looks into the shed and picks up an old tea mug from inside*) Oh, you've done a marvellous job in here. That's so much clearer. (*She turns and smiles at Lionel*) So much.

Lionel smiles back

This is ridiculous, isn't it? I mean, it just doesn't happen. Well, it does happen. It's ridiculous. It's like Lady ... (*She checks herself*)

Lionel Lady Chatterley? I can read as well.

Celia I'm sorry, that's terribly rude again.

Lionel Wouldn't mind being him. Not really.

Celia Yes, I know. But I mean there, there was a vast class and social difference. She had a title and he was a gamekeeper. I mean, I'm straight middle class. Middle middle class. Not even upper. My father was a chemist. I mean, that's middle, isn't it? Manager of a chemist's. Nothing very grand. And you're a ...

Lionel I'm an ordinary working-class lad. My dad was a sheet metal worker till he became caretaker/groundsman of that place, after his accident. My mother worked in a laundry and I'm a master baker.

Celia A what?

Lionel Baker. I trained. I got certificates.

Celia How amazing. A baker. And you gave it up?

Lionel That's right.

Celia Why?

Lionel They closed the bakery. I was looking round for other outlets and then Dad retired so I thought, bugger baking so I took his job. It doesn't pay nothing like but then we don't need much. I can eat up at the school.

Celia It's a great shame, though. I'm sure there's a huge demand for good baking. In this area. There really would be. I mean, look how far you have to go for a decent loaf. Absolutely miles.

Lionel Oh, there's scope. You open a good bakery round here, you'd clean up.

Celia Why did they close it?

Lionel Old man Wallace trained me. When he died, his sister sold up. It was where that clothes shop was. The one that closed as soon as it opened.

Celia Oh, yes, the boutique. So the shop's empty.

Lionel Yes. Ovens are still there at the back. Haven't been touched.

Celia You ought to take it.

Lionel Take it? What with?

Celia You could get a loan.

Lionel Get away.

Celia From the bank.

Lionel What with? The only security I've got's my Dad's wheelchair.

Celia Well, there must be ways. I mean, I know there are. I could probably—I mean, not personally but ... I have contacts. No, I'm not being silly. I mean, it would be a proper business proposition. We'd be partners. You'd bake and I'd——

Lionel Take.

Celia No, that's not fair. I wouldn't. I'd work as well. I'd run the shop. Oh, it would be heavenly. I do adore the smell of fresh bread.

Lionel I wonder if you would at six o'clock in the morning.

Celia (*carried away*) And then we could have doughnuts and cakes ... Do you bake cakes?

Lionel I bake all sorts of things.

Celia And fruit scones. And fresh baked pies. And apple turnovers—I adore apple turnovers.

Lionel Don't get too carried away, will you?

Celia No. Well?

Lionel I'd need to think.

Celia Yes, of course but don't you think it'd be exciting? I mean, supposing I managed to raise the capital, which I think I could do actually, quite easily. We could buy the lease on the property which I suspect wouldn't be that much and then do it up and renovate it and run it. Together, as partners. I'm sorry, I realize I'm chattering on here, rushing ahead. You probably think I'm slightly mad or something, but the whole thing suddenly seems to be terribly exciting. Doesn't it to you? It must do a little.

Lionel Oh, yes.

Celia I mean, it probably isn't quite the same feeling for you because you haven't—well, you haven't had to cope with what I've had to cope with but, you see, if you have reached a point in your life as I think I have where everything does seem to have come to a terrible halt, like someone's stopped the film with their thumb or something and it all seems to be over and finished, then if suddenly, a little like your bicycle ride, you come over the hill and everything's endless again, well, it's just so nice to have somewhere to go. (*She dabs her eyes*) Sorry, you can see what sort of state I'm in. Really. I don't think I realized myself. I think we could—excuse me a minute. (*She goes into the shed*)

Lionel looks slightly puzzled. The sound from within of Celia blowing her nose. A slight pause. She comes back, controlled again

I do beg your pardon. I really didn't realize quite how much I'd let things get on top of me.

Lionel Been lying in the ditch too long.

Celia (*laughing*) Yes. Oh, dear. I wish I wasn't a woman sometimes.

Lionel Why not?

Celia I don't know. I sometimes think life might be easier.

Lionel I'm glad you are.

Celia A woman?

Lionel Yes. Makes it worthwhile being a man.

Celia Thank you. (*She opens and closes her mouth*) I'm sorry, I think I'm going to have to go indoors. Lie down or something. Have a cold bath. Wash my hair. I don't know. Would you excuse me?

Lionel Of course.

Celia goes indoors

Lionel starts picking up some more paving. He completes another trip, and is turning back to the shed to go off for yet another when someone appears to shout at him from the field

(*Cupping his hand to his ear*) What's that ... right ... right you are, Mr Teasdale ... yes ... yes, I will ... right. (*He moves back towards the house and calls*) Mrs Teasdale. Mrs Teasdale ... I got to go. Mrs—(*he shrugs and gives up and moves back past the pile of paving stones. He picks up the chest expander and extends it to its full extent in a sort of triumphal flourish*) Ha!

Lionel throws down the expander and rushes off past the shed. If we could but see it, he clears the garden fence as he goes

Sylvie (*speaking as Lionel exits*) Lionel? Lionel?

Sylvie comes hurrying out. She is in mid-housework as usual. She runs to the end of the garden

Lionel. (*She glares at his retreating figure*) Where are you off to now, you

rotten bugger? I'll break her bloody neck if I find out who she is. I really
will. I turned down all my best offers for you, Lionel bloody Hepplewick.
... (*She turns away*) Rotten bugger. Knows he can twist me round. (*She
starts to cry leaning against the shed*) Bloody Lionel bloody Hepplewick. I
bloody will. I'll bloody kick him round the bloody. ... Too bloody right.
Right up his stupid bloody ... bloody will. (*She sits in the shed doorway*)

After a moment, Toby comes round the shed into view

Toby (*glaring back in Lionel's direction, muttering to himself*) Stupid oaf. I
bet he doesn't check the petrol. (*He moves on past the shed and, seeing
Sylvie, stops*) Hallo, what are you doing there?
Sylvie (*overcome with grief, says by way of an answer*) ... not—bloody isn't
fair ... I give him bloody ... not fair ... all I done ... I gave him ... he
just don't ... he don't give a bloody monkey's. ...
Toby I'm sorry. Could you say that again?
Sylvie (*rising angrily*) You bloody wouldn't understand, would you?

Sylvie rushes in the house

Toby Extraordinary. (*He looks into the shed to see if anyone else is in there*)
How could anyone be that fond of Hepplewick. Quite extraordinary. (*He
sees the chest expander and is tempted to have another go with it. He looks
round and since no one appears to be watching, he picks it up again. He tries,
with great effort, to work it*) Oh, God. Oooh. (*He stops, breathless*) I really
must be a spot out of condition. (*He puts the expander down again*) Hadn't
realized quite how much I—(*He trips on the paving stones*) What the hell
...? Crazy paving, that's all we need. Next step, barbecue. That'll be the
beginning of the end. Middle-classes living it rough. Standing out in a
light drizzle setting fire to four hundred quid's worth of fillet steak.
Everything tasting of meths. Tremendous.

*Celia comes out of the house with a cardboard box. As she sees Toby, she
stops*

Celia Oh, it's you.
Toby Apparently.
Celia Where's Lionel Hepplewick?
Toby Lionel Hepplewick is hopefully just starting to mow the outfield of the
second-eleven cricket pitch. All eighteen and a half yards of it.
Celia He was doing our paving.
Toby Getting on like a house on fire, wasn't he? The Egyptians could have
done with him when they started pyramids. Got him on the job they'd still
be burying Nefertiti.
Celia I thought you had a meeting.
Toby I did and it's over.
Celia Already?
Toby Senior prefects' meeting, that's all. Suggestions for the improved day-
to-day running of the school. Didn't take long. They made suggestions. I
vetoed everything and sent them packing. That's democracy. Not having

thirteen-year olds telling me how to run my life. I wanted a word with you.

Celia Oh, yes. (*She puts the cardboard box down by the rubbish that Lionel has thrown from the shed*)

Toby Have you been crying?

Celia No. Hay fever, I think.

Toby You look as if you've been crying.

Celia Would it be so surprising if I had?

Toby No.

Celia Well.

Toby Then have you?

Celia What?

Toby Been crying.

Celia No. I said, no. Can't you take no?

Toby Sylvie was.

Celia Was she?

Toby Just now. When I came back. Crying her eyes out. Sitting there muttering rural incantations.

Celia What was the matter?

Toby I don't know. Putting a curse on our shed perhaps. No, I think it was Hepplewick.

Celia Oh.

Toby Fancy crying over Hepplewick. Doesn't leave you much emotional reserve when something really important happens to you. I mean, how the hell's she going to behave when she gets a flat tyre on her bike.

Celia What?

Toby Bike.

Celia Oh.

Toby You all right?

Celia Yes.

Toby Well, I'm glad you are because you look absolutely ghastly.

Celia Thank you so much, Toby. That's so morale raising.

Toby No, I meant you looked as if you'd recently been used as a footbridge or something. I think you're in need of a break.

Celia Oh, my God.

Toby Look, I came back ...

Celia Why? (*She starts to put some of the rubbish into the cardboard box*)

Toby Because. Well, because. Because I say a lot of things some of which I wish I hadn't said when I've said them. To you. But then I've always said a lot of awful things to you. Let's face it. The mainstay of our whole relationship is based on it. Me saying awful things to you and you accepting them. I can't quite think how it started, but it always has been like that, hasn't it? Walking across the field there, you know, I was trying to remember the first time I was ever rude to you.

Celia What an extraordinary comment on our relationship, isn't it? Most couples I know, when they suddenly feel nostalgic, they bring out the wedding photos. Or they remember their honeymoon. Or when he proposed. You want to remember the first time you were ever rude to me.

Toby No, I was just trying to remember why it all started.

Celia It started, Toby, because at one stage I don't think you actually meant all the things you called me. When you called me a grimy old insole or whatever, it was presumably meant as a joke. Now I think you mean it.

Toby I never called you a grimy old insole, did I?

Celia Toby, you say the most awful things to me. I don't think you realize.

Toby Really?

Celia Really. I mean, that new dress I wore the other day for the school concert, just as we were getting into the car, you said I looked like a baboon in drag.

Toby laughs

No, it's not funny, Toby. It's very hurtful. I mean, it would be very different if I was terribly glamorous and confident. Then perhaps I could take it but I'm not. I mean, some nights I get home, I look at myself and I wonder if you're right.

Toby Now you know I didn't mean that. You don't look like a baboon. Not from this angle anyway. No, you don't. Sorry. Anyway, that's why I came back. To say I was sorry. And it's quite the most marvellous day out there so I was going to ask you for a walk.

Celia A walk.

Toby Yes.

Celia Where to?

Toby I don't know. To the pub, if you like. (*Seeing her face*) No, not the pub. Just a walk. A totally publess walk. That way. There are no pubs at all that way.

EITHER she says:

Celia Toby, listen.

Toby Uh-huh.

Celia I have something to say to you.

Toby Fire ahead.

Celia I think I may have to go away for a little while, Toby. Away from you.

Toby Ah.

Celia I'll take the kids. I won't leave you with them but—you see, I think I've been walking along this path, possibly of my own choosing, I don't know, which has been getting gradually narrower and narrower. In fact, I didn't realize quite how narrow it had got till I nearly fell off it.

Toby What happened?

Celia It's not important. The point is, if I stay here I'm probably going to finish up needing psychiatric treatment and that would be awful for all of us.

Toby Look, Celia, we've talked about this before and each time we come round to the——

Celia Yes, I know we do. Only this time, I mean it. I really mean it, Toby.

Toby Where are you going?

Celia I don't know precisely. Yet. I think I want to get involved with something. Maybe open a shop or something.

Toby (*blankly*) A shop.

Celia Yes.

Toby A greengrocer's, that sort of thing?

Celia That sort of thing.

Toby Extraordinary idea.

Celia Just something that would get me *active* again. Get me pedalling.

Toby Pedalling?

Celia Yes.

Toby You mean, pedalling greengroceries.

Celia No, no. Pedalling a bicycle.

Toby You're going to open a bicycle shop.

Celia Oh, Toby.

Toby I don't know what you're talking about, Celia.

Celia You're deliberately not understanding me. Anyway, that's what I'm going to do.

Toby What are you going to do?

Celia I'm going to get involved. In something new. In something exciting.

Toby (*after a slight pause*) Well, I'm sorry, Celia. I know you asked me not to call you any more names but if you ask me, you're rapidly going about as loopy as a punch-drunk panda in an old string vest.

Celia (*grimly starting to tidy up*) We shall see, Toby, we shall see. You can laugh but we'll see. She might just surprise you, this punch-drunk panda. (*She picks up the chest expander and in a sudden defiant gesture, thrusts her arms above her head, extending it fully*) Haaaaaaahhh!

Toby is impressed

The Lights fade to a Black-out

To: AFFAIRS IN A TENT (page 35)

OR she says:

Celia Toby, listen.

Toby Uh-huh.

Celia I think you should know, Toby, that this morning I came within a very inch of leaving you.

Toby Oh, Celia.

Celia Yes, I know it's something we've said before in the heat of the moment but this time, it was quite considered and—fairly calm. I do think if we carry on like we are, then I'll probably collapse on you or something. And that would be a fat lot of use to either of us. And as for the children—well, I don't think they'd enjoy it, seeing their mother carted off somewhere.

Toby I think you're being slightly melodramatic.

Celia No, I'm not, Toby, honestly. I don't know what it takes to make you realize. There are some mornings, things look so bleak and meaningless, I just want to lie there in bed and never get up again.

Toby That's natural. So do I some mornings.

Celia You know perfectly well, Toby, that the reason I can't get up and the reason you can't get up are vastly different. Now don't change the subject.

Toby You're probably tired.

Celia Yes, I am. But it's not that either and you know it. So something's got to alter.

Toby Yes. I think the evidence is pointing to me, isn't it?

Celia In part.

Toby Perhaps a holiday would be nice. Would you fancy that?

Celia Yes, of course I would. I've been begging you to take one for ten years.

Toby Well, then let's do that. Just the two of us. Park the kids. Have a holiday. Go somewhere exciting.

Celia Abroad.

Toby Yes, even that if you like.

Celia Oh, I forgot. You don't like abroad very much, do you?

Toby Not much. Still if you want to go——

Celia No, this country. I'll be quite happy. Let's go somewhere where we'll both be happy.

Toby Somewhere exciting.

Celia Yes, there must be somewhere in this country.

Toby Oh, there is.

Celia I do want us to stay together, Toby. I really do. We have awful times occasionally and at times like that, I just want to grab my things and run. But then again. ... You know, a few minutes ago I suddenly got this picture of what it might be like living without you and I don't think I want that.

Toby We'll make it work then. I promise. We'll make it work. We'd better go for that walk. It may rain later.

Celia Oh, no.

Toby Possible. (*He picks up an old bottle from the pile and sniffs it*) I don't think I can cut this out, you know. Don't ask me to do that. But I'll try not to let it make me too—obstreperous in future. (*Moving to the house*) I'm just going to get some more sensible shoes on. Hang on there.

Toby exits

Celia (*picking up the bottle he has discarded*) Oh well. I suppose that's the best offer I've had so far. (*She tosses the bottle into her box. A thought occurs to her. She moves towards the house calling*) Sylvie? Sylvie? Are you still there, Sylvie? Oh, heavens, I think she's gone home. Silly, silly child. Really. (*She turns back and looks at the garden, then prepares to go into the house to tidy up for her walk*)

In the distance, from the field, Lionel's voice is heard

Lionel (*calling, off*) Mrs Teasdale. Mrs Teasdale.
Celia (*turning, startled*) Lionel? Lionel, what is it?

Lionel runs on and pulls up short by the shed

Lionel (*breathlessly*) I just wanted to say—I left the mower running so I can't stop a minute—I just wanted to say, yes, Mrs Teasdale. That's all. Yes.
Celia Yes?
Lionel Yes to the shop. Yes to anything you like. Partners.
Celia Oh.
Lionel And one other thing, Mrs Teasdale—Celia—and this is a promise, you're not ever going to fall off your bike again because I'll make damn sure you don't—I'm going to be right there with you, I promise. I know what you were trying to say to me earlier and I think you understood what I was saying to you. So. OK. That's all I want to say. OK.
Celia Lionel, I'm afraid I don't think it is.
Lionel What?
Celia OK. I don't think it can be. Not realistically.
Lionel I don't quite follow you. A minute ago——
Celia Yes, but thinking about it realistically, Lionel, it was absurd, wasn't it?
Lionel (*blankly*) Absurd?
Celia Well, all these wild dreams, granary loaves and apple turnovers. I'm sorry, it's probably my fault. I'm in a rather unpredicable state at the moment. Up and down like one of those ping pong—things. Please, I beg you to forget everything I said. I behaved hysterically and irresponsibly. All this crazy paving and the heat, I'm sorry. Now, you go back to your mower and I'm—I've got to go out.

Lionel continues to stare at her

All right? See you later then. I hope. Bye-bye.

Celia goes into the house

Lionel stands for a moment, taking in this new situation

Lionel (*shaking his head, softly*) Oh, no. You don't get rid of me that easy. Not that easy. I'm not bloody taking second bloody place to any bloody body. (*He raises his voice*) You wait. Just you wait. I love you. (*He raises his voice, to a shout*) Do you hear me, Celia? I love you, Mrs Teasdale!

Lionel runs off

Almost immediately, Celia comes back, having heard something. She looks round the garden slightly puzzled and seeing nobody, frowns, shrugs and goes back into the house

The Lights fade to a Black-out

To: EVENTS ON A HOTEL TERRACE (page 73)

AFFAIRS IN A TENT

A small marquee pitched in the Bilbury Lodge School grounds. Five weeks after. It is 3.30 pm on Saturday, July 24th

Outside, Sports Day is in progress. The sounds of children's voices, occasional adult ones, starting pistols and the odd amplified announcement are heard. Inside the tent, where we are, all is relatively calm. This is the area designated as the V.I.P.'s tea tent. It is furnished in expectation of a small, select gathering. There is one longish serving-table to one side covered with a long white cloth reaching to the floor and beneath this, though unseen at present, a long oilskin undercloth. In addition, there are about five other smaller tables scattered about with three or four chairs around each. These latter tables still await their cloths. There are two entrances to the tent itself. One, the "service" entrance is apparently where everything is loaded and unloaded; the second is the main entrance that evidently looks out on to the main sports field. The tent is at present deserted

After a second or so, Celia enters from the service entrance. She appears harrassed and flustered and is in the process of unloading provisions and equipment. She is carrying a box of cutlery which she places on the main table. She pauses briefly for breath and then, glancing at her watch, hurries out again to fetch something else

A second after she's gone, Miles Coombes comes sauntering in through the main entrance. He is a lean, rather sad man about the same age as Celia

Miles (*surveying the lay-out*) Yes. Yes. (*He nods*) Good.

    Celia hurries back with a box of tablecloths

    Ah, Celia.

Celia (*distractedly*) Oh, hallo, Miles. (*She dumps the box on the table*)

Miles Busy?

Celia Yes.

Miles Doing it all alone, are you?

Celia Yes. I'd have thought that seemed fairly obvious, Miles.

    Celia goes out

Miles (*lamely, after her*) Sorry. (*He wanders around to see what's what and looks into a box*) Cutlery, eh? Yes. What are these? Tablecloths.

    Celia returns with a stack of sideplates, also in a box

Celia (*irritably*) Oh, do get out of the way, Miles, please.

Miles (*stepping aside smartly*) Excuse me, Celia, I'm sorry.

Toby (*off, over the loudhailer*) And now we have event number seven on
your programmes. This is the first of three eliminating heats for the nine-
year-old girls' one hundred metres. Would the girls in Heat Number One
please assemble by Mr Hogg at the starting line. All girls in Heat Number
One.

Miles, hearing this, meanders back to look out of the main entrance

*Celia stands catching her breath. When recovered she starts counting the
sideplates*

Miles (*looking out of the tent and speaking over the end of the announcement*)
Ah. Start of the girls' hundred metre heats. Lord. There's a frightfully
tubby little thing at the back. Will she make the finals, I wonder? Will she
even finish the course? Looks doubtful. She's out of breath just crouching
there.

Sound of a distant starting pistol

Celia loses count

And they're off! Come on, little thing. You can do it. God, she's miles
behind. Come on, come on. You can do it. Jolly good, she's done it. She
nearly came last in the next heat as well but she's done it. Crash, down she
goes. God, she's completely knackered. Is that the Bell girl?
Celia Sounds like it. Sylvie's sister, Rachel.
Miles Rachel Bell. Of course. She's the brainy one. Very large, isn't she?
Celia Puppy fat.
Miles Really? Never seen a dog that shape.
Celia (*looking round irritably*) Well, I don't know where he is, I really don't.
Miles What?
Celia Lionel Hepplewick. He's supposed to be here. He was supposed to be
here at two. What's the time now?
Miles (*consulting his watch*) Er—it's—er. . . .
Celia (*consulting her watch*) It's twenty to. It's twenty to. Just look at all
this. Where is he? I mean, where is he? In half an hour's time, I have
twenty people coming in here for tea.
Miles It's about eighteen and a half minutes to.
Celia Nothing's ready. Is it? Look. Look.
Miles Now, there's plenty of time. You mustn't get——
Celia There is not plenty of time. (*She starts to unload the tablecloths*)
Miles Celia, may I have a wee word in your ear?
Celia No, I'm sorry, Miles. You couldn't possibly. I've got mountains to
do. (*She begins to spread cloths over the small tables*)

Miles follows Celia attempting to keep out of her way as he does so

Miles All I'm saying is I think you can afford to take things just a fraction
more calmly, Celia. Do you really need to rush about quite so much? I
mean, it's a lovely day. I just hate to see you getting quite so flustered.
Celia You'd be flustered. Excuse me.

Miles (*stepping aside*) Sorry. I mean, School Sports Day, one always hopes everyone's going to let their hair down, have a bit of fun.

Celia Fun?

Miles That's been the tradition that we've tried to——

Celia It may be fun for some.

Miles I realize they also entail a lot of hard work.

Celia They certainly do.

Miles As Chairman of the Board of Governors, I'm extremely aware of this. Of course I am. And we're deeply grateful. The thing is, though, when we, that is to say, the Board, when we agreed to you personally providing the teas for the V.I.P. tent, we really didn't envisage—I don't think any of us—that you were going to take it all quite so seriously.

Celia You can hardly take them lightly, can you?

Miles There was, I admit, in the back of our minds a financial consideration. It was generally felt that Fletchers, the regular caterers, were—even allowing for inflation—getting pretty steep or, as the Reverend Fognorth put it, providing unacceptably high teas.

Miles laughs. Celia doesn't

I thought that was quite good. So, when you came along with your offer, we were obviously very attracted. And interested. Toby was dead against it, as you probably know. But the Board overruled him.

Celia Toby has been opposed to this from the start. What really irks him is the thought of my doing anything at all on my own. Something that doesn't exclusively revolve around him. That couldn't possibly be important, could it?

Miles You're really going into this catering line quite seriously, then?

Celia Naturally.

Miles (*dubiously*) Good.

Celia We were all set to buy the old bakery, you know.

Miles What, the Wallace place?

Celia Yes.

Miles Good job you didn't. It's in a shocking state.

Celia We were all set and then it fell through.

Miles The roof?

Celia No, the money. Anyway, we're undeterred. We're still going ahead.

Miles You and—er—Lionel Hepplewick?

Celia Yes.

Miles He's—(*cautiously*)—he's—er—rather an odd choice for a business partner, isn't he, Celia?

Celia So everybody keeps on and on saying. We shall see, won't we?

Miles Well, he is, you know.

Celia I disagree. Lionel is just one of those people who since he was a child has never been given the slightest encouragement by anyone.

Miles No. Well, I suppose there's a chance there's nothing there to encourage.

Celia Of course there is. What a terrible thing to say.

Miles Sorry.

Celia That's appalling, Miles. Everybody has something in them to encourage. No, Lionel's like me. I've never been encouraged. Never.

Miles No?

Celia No, not at all. People treat me like an idiot to my face and then laugh at me behind my back.

Miles Oh, come now.

Celia Of course you do. I've seen you do it. Well, you wait. When my little firm gets going, you'll be laughing on the other side of your face, won't you?

Miles I don't laugh at you, Celia. I'm very fond of you.

Celia We've even got a name for it.

Miles For what?

Celia Our firm. We've thought of the name.

Miles Really, what's that?

Celia We're calling it Tea Service.

Miles Tea Service.

Celia Good, isn't it?

Miles Tea Service.

Celia I think it's brilliant. It's a play on words, you see.

Miles Yes, I see. I see.

Celia We spent hours, Lionel and me, going through dozens of combinations. None of them seemed right. You see, we needed something simple, yet catchy. Something people would instantly remember. Then we thought of that.

Miles Super, yes.

Celia I think it's brilliant.

Miles Oh, yes.

Celia My idea, actually.

Miles Was it?

Celia I'm very pleased with it.

Miles Yes. What was it again?

Celia (*acidly*) Tea Service.

Miles Tea Service. Yes, very good. What does it do exactly?

Celia Well, the idea is, you see—you're sitting at home, suddenly you feel like tea and you can't be bothered so you just lift the phone, order what you want and round we come in a jiffy.

Miles Good Lord.

Celia You see?

Miles Wouldn't be quicker just to put the kettle on, would it?

Celia No, I'm not talking about someone on their own. If you have people round, say, and you don't really want to be bothered with baking and sandwich-making and homemade jams, you just phone us and round we come. Lay it all out, everything homebaked, everything fresh and there you are. As soon as you've finished, we'll whisk it all away again.

Miles (*still unconvinced*) Yes.

Celia We'll do everything except pour the tea for you. That's our catch-phrase. It's based on an American idea.

Miles American.

Celia Yes, Lionel showed me an article. In the States, apparently, they do it all the time.

Miles I didn't think they had tea. I thought they went straight through.

Celia No, well, with them, it's dinners mainly. Awful junk hamburgers, I'm sure. But it's the principle.

Miles Let's get it straight. I pick up the phone.

Celia Yes.

Miles And call you.

Celia Yes.

Miles At teatime.

Celia Yes. Well, just before. Give us time to get there.

Miles What if you're already out?

Celia How do you mean?

Miles Serving tea somewhere else?

Celia Ah, well. We have an answering machine.

Miles Oh, God. Not one of those things.

Celia Please state your order. That's what it says. And then we, if we're out, we can phone in to see if there's any messages. We can dial in, you see. Then we can phone you.

Miles Terribly complicated.

Celia Not at all.

Miles I mean, you'll have to keep stopping to phone in, won't you?

Celia Not all the time.

Miles And then, hang on, while you're phoning in to find out if anybody's phoned, nobody else can phone. So you could be losing business.

Celia You're just making objections.

Miles No, I'm not. I'm being objective. By the time I've phoned your answering machine and you've phoned your answering machine and then phoned me, I'm probably having dinner.

Celia It's typical. I've had no encouragement from anyone at any stage.

Miles Celia, I'm sorry. It just sounds to me frightfully impractical. I mean, with all due respect, the prospect of you two careering round the countryside with a car load of cream cakes hunting for phone boxes seems to me a dubious proposition.

Celia Well, we've bought a van, so there.

Miles A van? What sort of van?

Celia Er—oh, what do you call it? A transient.

Miles A Transit.

Celia Transit, yes.

Miles In which Gloria was once sick. (*He laughs*)

Celia What?

Miles Nothing. *Sic transit gloria*. Nothing.

Celia I don't know what you mean. It was second hand.

Miles Is it the one parked out the back there?

Celia Yes. We're going to paint it. Once we've designed a logo.

Miles Logo, yes. Who did you buy it from?

Celia Jack Wrigley.

Miles Is he one of the Wrigley brothers?

Celia Yes.

Miles Oh, Celia, they're a load of crooks.

Celia Lionel looked the vehicle over very carefully. He's a trained mechanic. We didn't rush into it blindly.

Miles No?

Celia We got a bargain, believe me.

Miles From the Wrigley brothers?

Celia Yes.

Miles Unlikely. They're the only people I know who can sell you vehicles that have fallen off the back of other vehicles.

Celia It's a nice little van. Quite nippy.

Miles Probably used in a bank raid.

Celia He didn't even want to sell it to us.

Miles No?

Celia He was going to give it to his wife for her birthday.

Miles What, a Transit van?

Celia Yes.

Miles What's she getting for Christmas? A bulldozer?

Celia Laugh away. We're cleaning it up, respraying it.

Miles You'd better before the police trace it.

Celia We're putting the logo on the side—a steaming cup of tea. In blue.

Miles Blue tea?

Celia No, the cup.

Miles You'll look like Meals on Wheels.

Celia Not at all.

Miles You'll have old age pensioners chasing you through the streets demanding free biscuits.

Celia I wish you'd go away, Miles. How can I concentrate here with you snuffling round?

Miles All right, I'm sorry. I wanted to see you were coping, that's all. (*He saunters to the door*) I'll wander off then. If I can't be of any help. (*Slight pause*) You know me by now, Celia. I always want to look out for you when I can.

Celia (*irritably*) Isn't Rowena with you?

Miles Yes, she's—she's around. Warming up for the Mothers' Race, I think.

Celia (*coolly*) Really? Then perhaps you ought to look out for her, then.

Miles Right, I'll see you later. I'll look in again around four fifteenish before I bring all the Governors in.

Celia We'll be ready. Don't worry.

Miles Fine. Fine. Only we've got the Countess of Smailes with us.

Celia Yes, I know. I know.

Miles She's a very charming woman.

Celia Yes, I know her terribly well.

Miles Marvellous, the interest she's taken in the school, isn't it? I mean, Prize-giving and School Concerts. . . .

Celia (*fiercely*) Oh, Miles, just go away.

Miles (*retreating*) Right. Do take care, Celia, won't you?

Miles leaves the tent

Celia Dear heaven, how am I expected to do anything when people—I mean, how am I expected to? Really. (*She surveys her handiwork so far*)

An improvised fishing rod consisting of a stick and a school tie is pushed through the tent doorway. It hovers over the trophy table. Celia sees it, startled

(*Catching sight of someone just outside the tent door*) What do you want, Rutling? What are you doing with that stick? Well, you keep right away. This is the Headmaster's tent. Strictly out of bounds. Now run along and do up your plimsolls before I give you lots of—marks. Minus marks. Go on. (*She mutters*) Horrid little boy. (*Seeing someone else*) Hallo, good afternoon, Mrs Rutling. Yes, they do, don't they? All sorts of mischief at that age. Yes. (*She laughs, then, watching her go*) No wonder he's like he is with a mother like that. Dreadful skirt. Now then. (*She returns to her tables*) What we need desperately now is food. I mustn't forget the flowers.

Lionel enters from the service entrance with a cardboard box

Oh, thank God. At last. Lionel, where have you been?
Lionel Took a bit longer, Celia. Sorry.
Celia Longer? We're due to start tea in twenty minutes.
Lionel Now, now, now. You just remember a poem my dad once wrote.

> While other folk are flapped and flurried
> A master baker can't be hurried.

Celia Yes, well, I'm getting a little weary of your father's inane poetry, Lionel. It seems to do nothing but preach the doctrine that nobody should do anything at all.
Lionel No, he reckons they should do it. But very, very slowly.
Celia Well, frankly, it's a fat lot of use.
Lionel Well, what's the matter with that? It's good very, very slowly, isn't it?
Celia That's quite enough of that, if you don't mind.
Lionel (*laughing delightedly*) Aha! She's away. Off she goes.
Celia Well . . .
Lionel Mind your heads. Tin hats on.
Celia I just don't like that sort of talk, Lionel. I never have. Now, what have you made that's taken you all this time?
Lionel Ah, well. It was my domestic oven at home that did me. Took longer.
Celia Of course.
Lionel Should have allowed.
Celia You certainly should. (*Excitedly*) Well, come on, let's have a look. Our first loaf.
Lionel Yeah. (*He produces a rather strangely shaped brown object*) There she is.
Celia Oh.
Lionel (*laying it down on the table reverently*) There.

Celia Yes.

A pause while they stare at it

It's a—it's a very curious shape, isn't it?

Lionel It is.

Celia Is that—meant?

Lionel Oh yes.

Celia Oh. I've never seen—I've never seen a loaf of bread quite that shape before.

Lionel I hope not. I hope you haven't.

Celia No?

Lionel There'd be trouble if you had. Every master baker, you see, he has his own trademark. That's mine. That's the way I bake. That's the way it falls under my hands.

Celia Oh.

Lionel Now another baker, he'd look at that loaf and he'd know straight-away. He'd say, that's a Hepplewick loaf, that is. We all recognize each other, mostly.

Celia But does it have to be ... I mean, I've got to make sandwiches. It's going to be very difficult.

Lionel Well. Yes. It's not an ideal sandwich loaf, I'll give you that.

Celia It certainly isn't. I don't quite know where to cut it. Are they all this shape?

Lionel Mostly, yes.

Celia (*circling the loaf with a knife*) Well, I'll ... I'm sure this can't be right.

Lionel Hey, hey, hey. That's enough of that. Don't you start criticizing.

Celia I'm sorry.

Lionel Thought we were partners.

Celia We are. Right. Here goes then. (*She attempts to cut the bread. It is an enormous struggle*)

Lionel Blunt knife, is it?

Celia Lionel, it's like—it's like concrete.

Lionel Firm. You want a firm texture for a sandwich. Don't want a soggy loaf, now do you?

Celia (*struggling vainly*) No, no.

Lionel Nothing worse than a soggy sandwich, I say.

Celia (*giving up*) Dear God, Lionel, I'm sorry. I don't know if I've got the strength. What on earth's it made of?

Lionel A little yeast, a little flour, a lot of know-how.

Celia It's completely uncuttable. We can't expect people to eat that.

Lionel Why not?

Celia Because—because, well, frankly, it's inedible.

Lionel You think so?

Celia Lionel, it's awful. I mean, look at it. (*She bangs the loaf on the table*) Listen to it. I can't serve this up to the Board of Governors. There's a Countess out there as well. They can't eat this. Some of them are quite elderly with—with dentures. They couldn't cope with that.

Lionel No, I'll grant you. That's very much a young person's loaf, that is. It's not for the elderly.

Celia I don't know who it's for, Lionel. Frankly, I'm very disappointed. I mean, what are we going to do? I don't know. Look at the time. Well, we'll have to give them just cake. Let's have a look at the cakes. Where are they?

Lionel Ah, now. I'm afraid I got all behind with them.

Celia Behind?

Lionel 'Fraid so. I had to stop and cook my dad's dinner, you see.

Celia How far behind did you get?

Lionel I didn't make them.

Celia You made no cakes?

Lionel 'Fraid not.

Celia No cakes?

Lionel The bread, you see, that took up all the time.

Celia You mean, we've got nothing at all to give them?

Lionel We've got some tea.

Celia (*in rising panic*) What are we going to do? What are we going to do?

Lionel All right, Celia, calm down.

Celia We have the Countess of Smailes, we have Colonel Malton, we have Irene Pridworthy, we have all of them coming here for tea in ten minutes.

Lionel Well, you could try them on the bread.

Celia Lionel, I could—I could strangle you. I could really just take you by the neck and——. Look, I'm going to the corner shop. I'll try and get a sliced loaf or something and a few cakes. They'll be those awful wrapped things, dear God. I've told everyone it was fresh-baked. Lionel, I could kill you. Wait here for me. Don't let anyone in.

Lionel It'll be OK.

Celia Just wait. I'll take the van. Have you the keys?

Lionel (*producing them*) Now, you may have a bit of trouble starting it.

Celia (*impatiently*) I can drive, I can drive, you know. I'm not totally inept.

Lionel I think it's just that it's flooded. I'll be able to——

Celia (*hurrying out*) I'll be back.

Celia goes out through the service entrance

Lionel I think I know what it is. I'll be able to fix it. Nothing serious. Soon get that fixed. Can check the suspension at the same time. (*He examines the loaf*) Don't know what she's complaining about. Good bread that. (*He bangs it down*) Listen, mum, you can hear the goodness. (*He wanders to the main entrance and calls*) Afternoon, Mrs Coombes. Limbering up there, are you? Good luck in the Mothers' Race. I've got some money on you. What's that? . . . Me? . . . (*obviously something complimentary*) Well, thank you. Yes, I keep myself fit. What's that? Well, depends who I'm running after, doesn't it? (*He laughs, then watches her move away and mutters*) I could have her. Any old time I could have her. If I wanted her. Only got to give her the nod. Might do that one of these days. I fancy a bit of that. I'll think about it. Let her know. (*Returning to his loaf*) Nothing wrong with this bread. (*He saws away at it*) Bloody hell fire. (*He manages to cut a piece off with difficulty*)

Irene Pridworthy, a large woman in her early sixties, enters. She pulls up short as she sees Lionel

Irene Ah.

Lionel Afternoon, Mrs Pridworthy.

Irene Who the blazes are you?

Lionel Lionel Hepplewick, Mrs Pridworthy.

Irene Oh, are you the caterer?

Lionel Yes.

Irene Getting our tea, are you?

Lionel Right.

Irene Yes. I was hoping for an early nibble but ... (*She looks round disappointedly*) Is—er—Mrs Teasdale about?

Lionel She's just stepped out.

Irene I see. You're helping her, are you?

Lionel I'm her partner.

Irene Oh, you're Hepplewhite.

Lionel Hepplewick.

Irene Yes. (*Looking about her again*) Not much of a spread, is it?

Lionel Not yet. It will be.

Irene I hope so. I'm getting very peckish. Watching all these brats running about takes it out of you.

Lionel Stayed fine.

Irene What?

Lionel Weather's stayed fine.

Irene Yes. (*After a pause she stares at him*) Haven't I seen your face before?

Lionel Possibly. Possibly you have, Mrs Pridworthy.

Irene Wait a minue, weren't you——? Yes, of course, you were—you were the school caretaker, weren't you?

Lionel I was.

Irene Made a right pig's ear of that, didn't you?

Lionel Well.

Irene Blew up the boiler, I hear.

Lionel There was a fault in the system.

Irene A fault in your bloody head by the sound of it. What are you up to now, then? Going to poison us all with your tea, are you?

Lionel (*laughing heartily*) I hope not. I hope not, Mrs Pridworthy.

Irene Poison that Countess woman if you want to. She's a pain in the B.T.M. She's a gusher. I hate women who gush at you. Either spit it out or put a cork in it. One of the two.

Lionel Well, it's not for me to pass judgement.

Irene So. You and Celia Teasdale have gone into partnership, have you?

Lionel Correct. We're opening a little business.

Irene I see. Nothing mucky going on, is there?

Lionel Mucky?

Irene With you and her.

Lionel Oh, no. Nothing like that. I've far too much respect for Mrs Teasdale to start anything like that. She's a very dignified and gracious woman.

Irene She's a tip.

Lionel Pardon?

Irene She's an emotional rubbish heap. Cracking up. I know the signs. Beware. My sister went the same way. Fifty-seven years old. Took all her clothes off in Hamley's toy shop. Tragic. It's glands, you know. They play tricks. Particularly women's. Celia Teasdale's a mass of glands, so be careful. Or you'll get yourself into something you'll regret. (*She discovers Lionel's loaf*) What the hell's that?

Lionel That's bread.

Irene Bread?

Lionel Home baked.

Irene Looks like hippo droppings.

Lionel Fresh, that is.

Irene Who made it? Celia Teasdale?

Lionel I did.

Irene You did?

Lionel Yes.

Irene I thought you were a caretaker.

Lionel I'm a master baker first and foremost.

Irene A what?

Lionel Master baker.

Irene Oh, a master baker. Are you? Splendid. You can recommend this, then?

Lionel I certainly can.

Irene May I try a bit?

Lionel Of course. Let me get some butter.

Irene No, I'll have it as it is. Don't want to spoil my tea. (*She chews some bread*) Grief.

Lionel All right, then?

Irene (*having difficulty with her speech*) It's a good ... it's a good ... it's a very good chew.

Lionel Oh, yes. It is.

Irene I don't think I've had anything like this since Nanny died. She used to make parkin rather similar. Used to stuff it about our person. Then later on, we'd skim it across the lake. Used to go for miles. Killed a duck with it once. Hell to pay. No, it's not bad at all, this.

Lionel Thank you very much.

Irene Keep you regular.

Lionel Oh, yes.

Irene Good roughage. I'll take the rest with me if I may? (*She picks up the remainder of the slice*)

Lionel My pleasure.

Irene Make sure the Countess gets a good sized slab, won't you? Might shut her up for a bit. See you later.

Irene exits

Lionel Goodbye, Mrs Pridworthy. (*He glares after her*) Yes, you wait. You'll be the first to go. Blow her up for a kick-off. Get a bit of dynamite from somewhere. Bang. Teach her. Talking to me like that. (*He picks up a piece of bread*) Your time will come. (*He chews*) Christ, she must have jaws like an industrial shredder. She'd have probably eaten my doughnuts and all. (*He moves to the main door of the tent and throws the bread out through it*) Look at him then. Terry bloody Hogg. Fancies himself, he does. Open to all-comers down to his navel. Swinging his starting pistol. All he needs is an eye-patch and a parrot. (*Suddenly excited*) Hallo. They're starting the Mothers' Race then. I've got to see this. I've got money on this. Don't want to miss it. Not after last year. Be a cracker.

Lionel goes out of the main entrance

Toby (*off, over the loudhailer*) Ladies and gentlemen, we're still very short of entries for the Mothers' Race. Could we please have more volunteers for this very popular event. Come along now, there is a very attractive prize of some bath crystals donated by Mrs Granary. So hurry along, please, all you fleet-footed mothers.

Sometime during this, Celia returns through the service entrance. She is clasping one half of a sliced loaf and a small packet of jam tarts

Celia (*distraught*) Lionel, the van wouldn't start and when it did start, it went ten yards and then it stalled. I thought you'd fixed it, Lionel. Lionel? Oh no, where is he? Where is he? (*Rushing to the main door*) Lionel? He can't just have walked away. I really don't believe it. (*She yells*) Lionel! (*As someone replies*) No, nothing. It's all right, Terry. Nothing. (*Turning away*) I do wish Terry Hogg would button his shirt up. It's quite obscene. All that—hair.

The bread is thrown back into the tent, hitting Celia

Why do people do this to me? Why? Do they do it, deliberately? I think they do, you know. It's not fair. You work your heart out and nobody. . . . No one. It's just not fair.

Toby enters angrily

Toby Celia, what's that bloody van of yours doing parked across the cinder track?
Celia It stalled on me. I can't get it to start. There's nothing I can do about it.
Toby Well, you can't leave it there. We're trying to run the Mothers' Race.
Celia What am I supposed to do? I can't do anything. Ask him. Ask Lionel. He's supposed to have fixed it. Talk to him. Why me? What does everyone blame me? (*Feverishly, she starts to open her packet of bread and locate the butter from a box*)
Toby (*realizing her state*) All right, all right. Don't get excited. We'll move it.
Celia What do you mean, don't get excited?

Toby (*calling*) Hogg? Terry! Organize a crew to give it a shove, will you? Come on, you lot. Anyone who failed to qualify in the opening heats help push the van. Come on. That includes eliminated high jumpers. Now, get on with it. (*He turns back to Celia*) Where is he, anyway?

Celia Who?

Toby Your—Hepplewick. Where's he gone?

Celia I don't know. I wish I did. He was here a minute ago.

Toby (*looking out of the tent*) There he is. Over by the Mother's Race finish.

Celia What on earth's he doing there?

Toby I don't know. Ogling, I should imagine. He's a great little ogler.

Celia You can hardly blame him if Rowena Coombes is running again.

Toby Running? She's the hot favourite.

Celia Well. I only hope she doesn't tuck her dress into her—underwear like she did last year. Quite unnecessary.

Toby Gave her a good turn of speed though. Mind you, that was probably because half the fathers were chasing after her.

Celia I'd have thought that would have slowed her down.

Toby Do you want me to call him? Hepplewick?

Celia No, I'll manage without him. I'm better off alone as usual. (*She puts out ten saucers very quickly. Teaspoons fly*)

Toby (*watching her*) Celia, don't overdo it, will you?

Celia Why does everybody keep saying that to me?

Toby Well, probably because——

Celia Because you've told them to say it.

Toby Because you don't look ... you don't seem awfully fit really.

Celia I'm perfectly fit.

Toby Well, take it easy. It's difficult enough running a house and kids but trying to do all this as well. ...

Celia I know your feelings on the matter. You'd be perfectly happy to see me at home chained to the sink.

Toby Ah now, come on, Celia.

Celia You would.

Toby Now, you've got the wrong man to say all that to, you really have. You know I don't give a stuff if you're washing-up or driving a fork-lift truck so long as it keeps you happy. ...

Celia You say that.

Toby It's true.

Celia It doesn't work that way, though, does it? You know it doesn't. You need to be fed.

Toby No, I don't. I never eat. You know that.

Celia The children need to be fed.

Toby Well, tell them to get on with it and get their own.

Celia What, James? Who tried to make us early morning tea in the percolator? No, thank you very much.

Toby The thought was there.

Celia So was the mess. Took me all Sunday to clear up.

Toby Anyway, you know what I mean, Celia.

Celia You don't believe I could start something on my own, go ahead with it and see it through. Now I'm doing just that and you're worried. You're even a little bit jealous, aren't you?

Toby Jealous?

Celia Yes.

Toby Of you?

Celia I think you are.

Toby My God. It's terrifying, isn't it? All these years, how little we know about each other.

Celia That's true, at least.

Toby (*discovering Lionel's loaf*) What's this?

Celia Nothing.

Toby Has its owner been informed?

Celia What are you talking about?

Toby I thought it was something you'd run over in the road.

Celia It's bread.

Toby Bread?

Celia It's an experiment. It didn't work.

Toby A cottage loaf?

Celia Probably.

Toby Presumably part of the fireplace.

Celia Look, Toby, I shall get very angry in a minute.

Toby Celia ...

Celia I will, really.

Toby Can I help you?

Celia Help?

Toby Yes.

Celia You?

Toby Yes.

Celia Why?

Toby Because I'm really worried about you. Genuinely.

Celia Don't be silly. I know you think I'm a frail creature that can't possibly cope with two things at once but you're wrong.

Toby I never thought that, Celia. You may be short on certain characteristics but energy certainly isn't one of them. All I'm saying is there are limits even to super-woman.

Celia You can sneer. We women are about to show you.

Toby Oh, God, don't start all that. Don't bring sex into it.

Celia Sex! I'm not talking about sex.

Toby I mean, sexual politics. I don't care what sex you are. I'm worried about you as a person. Male or female, what's the difference?

Celia I don't think you notice what I am half the time.

Toby You're quite right, I don't. I hope we're past all that rubbish.

Celia What rubbish?

Toby All that kissing goodnight and patting each other's rumps.

Celia You speak for yourself.

Toby I'm speaking for both of us. You've always secretly loathed it too. Right from the early days you hated me even holding your hand. We used to sit there on your sofa like two stuffed gerbils. I'd put my arm round your shoulders and you'd stiffen up as if you'd just swallowed a broom handle. Both of us ticking off the minutes till we could decently get off down to the pub for a quick one.

Celia If you want to do something, finish buttering those.

Toby OK. Is this all the bread there is?

Celia Yes.

Toby There's twenty of them.

Celia I know. It's Saturday. The shop was sold out. That was his own personal supply. I had to beg him.

Toby Right.

Pause

Celia unpacks some little flower vases for the tables

Anyway, they don't need sandwiches. They can get straight to the cake, can't they? That's what they've all come for.

Celia Yes.

Toby You've got some cake, I take it?

Celia Yes.

Toby Where?

Celia (*pointing to the packet of jam tarts*) There.

Toby Ah. (*Slight pause*) You don't think ...

Celia (*shrilly*) That's all he had left. They'll have to put up with it.

Toby Yes. (*After a pause*) We'd better save the strawberry one for the Countess, hadn't we?

Celia (*shakily*) It really wasn't my fault.

Toby No, it doesn't matter. It really doesn't matter at all.

Pause

Celia unwraps some small flowers and arranges them in vases

We can split the lemon curd one into ten. I'll tell them it's part of the economy measures.

Celia The flowers are nice, anyway.

Toby Yes. We can always finish off with those.

Celia Toby.

Toby Sorry.

Celia I had it all planned.

Toby I know. I know.

Celia (*irritably*) Look what you're doing.

Toby What?

Celia You're buttering it on both sides.

Toby Oh, Lord, sorry.

Celia Oh, go away. You're useless.

Toby Right. What are you putting in them? Grass?

Celia There are some tomatoes and cucumber in my bag.

Toby (*wandering to the entrance*) What's happening out here? Aha, at last. The Mothers' Race is coming under starter's orders.

The next section partially overlaps, up to Celia's exit

Celia Where's my bag? I've lost my bag.

Toby (*still looking out*) Pretty big field today.

Celia I've lost it. Toby, I've lost it.

Toby (*abstractedly*) I'll help you look in a second.

Celia I can't have lost it. I really can't have lost it. That would be too much. (*She hunts around feverishly*)

Toby Where's the favourite, then? Where's Rowena Coombes? Ah, there she is. Jostling in the throng. Good God, what on earth is she wearing?

Celia It's not here. Where is it?

Toby Somebody's school shorts. They certainly aren't hers. Somebody in the fourth form by the size of them.

Celia I don't believe this.

Toby And what's Thompson G. wearing? Grief, he's got her skirt on. She's got his shorts and he's got her skirt. My God, there's going to be trouble about this.

Celia I had it when I went to the van. . . .

Toby There's a lot of money resting on this, you know.

Celia Toby, please help me.

Toby Mmm? (*He remains fixed on the race*)

Celia I drove the van across the cinder track. Then it stalled.

Toby Mrs Ramsbottom's looking pretty sharp. Colonel Malton's got a tenner each way on her.

Celia I got out of the van with the bag on my arm. . . .

Toby I'm sticking with Rowena Coombes. Look at those legs. Built for speed.

Celia I know I had it then. And I tried to open the bonnet and I must have put it down.

Sound of a distant starting pistol

Toby They're off!

Celia That's right! I put it down on the cinder track while I ran to the shop.

Toby Come on, Rowena.

Celia I just took my purse to the shop.

Toby Come on, girl. Look at her go.

Celia So it must still be there.

Toby What the hell's that in the middle of the track?

Celia (*with a cry*) My handbag!

Celia rushes out of the main entrance

Toby Well, it's a damn silly place to put your handbag. Right in the middle of the . . . whoops, Mrs Thompson's fallen over it. Mrs Burke's fallen over Mrs Thompson. Mrs Walker's fallen over Mrs Burke. Mrs Ramsbottom's fallen over Mrs Walker. Good. Mrs Jones has fallen over Mrs Ramsbottom. Mrs Hackett has fallen over Mrs Jones. So has Mrs Wilson. So has Mrs Studemore. They've all gone. No, they haven't. There she goes. Rowena Coombes is clear. She's jumped the lot of them. She's got to do it. There's no one in the race. She's going to do it. She's nearly done it. She's done it. Bravo! Thompson G.'s shorts appear to have split but what the hell? God, look at all those mothers. There's an absolute mountain of writhing stockinged feet. I think I'm staying in here.

Celia returns with her bag. It is now muddy and flattened

Celia Look at it. Look at it. (*She displays her bag*)
Toby Yes. It was a damn silly place to leave it, Celia, it really was. I mean, look at the damage it's caused. Half those damn women there have probably broken their legs. I may have to go round shooting them.

Celia removes a squashed bag of tomatoes from her bag

What's that?
Celia Tomatoes for the sandwiches.
Toby Oh, thank God. I thought it was human.
Celia (*producing another squashed bag*) Cucumber.
Toby Yes.
Celia Why didn't they look where they were running?
Toby I don't think you can honestly blame them, Celia.
Celia They ran over them deliberately.
Toby No one did it deliberately. You're running a race. You're Sebastian Coe. You're coming round your final bend. You don't expect to step in a bag of mixed veg, do you?
Celia What am I going to do?
Toby You put it in the sandwiches. It doesn't matter.
Celia What this? It's revolting.
Toby It's going to look a damn sight worse when they've finished chewing it. Go on, what's it matter? So long as you and I know not to eat it.
Celia It's not fair. It really isn't. The hours I've put into this. And no one, no one even begins to understand. All the effort and the organization.
Toby All right, all right.
Celia (*shouting*) Don't stand there saying it's all right. It's not all right.
Toby Look, Celia, for God's sake stop screaming.
Celia (*still loudly*) Why shouldn't I scream?
Toby (*equally loudly*) Because everyone's staring at us. (*Shouting out of the main entrance*) Go away. Go on, buzz off!
Celia (*distraught*) What am I going to do?
Toby (*angrily and violently*) Look, I tell you what you do. You take your damn tomatoes here—(*He grabs a handful of bag and tomato*)—and you stuff it on your bloody awful bread—(*He does so*)—and then you take another piece of your bloody awful bread and you jam it on the top—(*He does so*)—and then you bang it down like that. (*He slams his fist down on the sandwich*) And there you are. One tomato sandwich. And nobody bloody knows the bloody difference. What more do you want?

Celia sobs

(*Holding out the sandwich*) There you are. What's wrong with that? Perfectly good sandwich. Delicious.
Celia (*more quietly*) Toby, put it down, please.
Toby Right. I'm just trying to help. (*He puts down the sandwich*)

Celia I don't need help, thank you. I can manage. Leave me alone, please.

Toby (*a little puzzled by her quiet manner*) OK. What about tea? Do you want me to tell them to ...

Celia We'll have tea very soon, don't worry. Everything's under control.

Toby Yes, righto, Celia. All right. You give us a call. Fine. We'll run a few more heats before tea. You're not to worry. I'll send you your—Lionel chap.

Celia I don't want him, thank you.

Toby You need someone, Celia.

Celia I don't need anyone. Nobody.

Toby OK, old thing. OK. Just as you like.

Toby goes out of the main entrance

(*Off*) All right, there's been a bit of a hitch with the tea but we'll soon be having it. ... (*His voice fades away*)

Celia (*surveying the marquee*) They will have tea when I tell them to have tea. And not before. They will sit where I tell them to sit and they will have proper table manners or they won't be allowed in. (*She indicates a chair*) Mrs Pridworthy can sit here and Colonel Malton will sit here. And they can have half a cake each and no more. The Reverend Fognorth can sit here and the Countess and Miles Coombes over here. Rowena Coombes can sit outside. Right. And they can have one piece of bread here. Teddy will sit here next to Lucy Ragbags and Dutch Doll here. And I'm going to put Rabbit here and Mr Fuzzyperks here next to me. And I will pour tea because it is my tea party. Would you like a cup of tea, Teddy? (*In a gruff voice*) Thank you very much. I'd love a cup of tea. (*As Celia*) Good. Then you pass your cup. (*In a squeaky voice*) Could I have a cup of tea, Celia?

Miles Coombes enters during the next speech and stands looking puzzled

(*As Celia*) No, you cannot. You wait your turn, Rabbit. And take your paws off the table. (*In a squeaky voice*) Sorry, Celia. (*In a gruff voice*) Celia, Dutch Doll's eating all the biscuits. (*As Celia*) That's naughty, Dutch Doll, you mustn't do that. (*As Dutch Doll*) I want to eat the biscuit. (*As Celia*) Well, you can't. (*In a squeaky voice*) Can I have a biscuit? (*As Celia, fiercely*) No. Nobody can have a biscuit. Why don't you do as you're told? Why are you doing this to me? You're doing it deliberately. Now I'm going to pour Teddy's tea. And if anyone else misbehaves, they'll sit out there with naughty Rowena Coombes. Good. Now, that's better. Just look at Mr Fuzzyperks. He's being very good. (*She sings a little children's song*)

Miles Er—Celia.

Celia Hallo, it's Mr Coombes.

Miles Hallo.

Celia (*as Teddy*) Hallo, Mr Coombes.

Miles I beg your pardon?

Celia Say hallo to Teddy.

Miles Yes. Hallo, Teddy.
Celia (*In a squeaky voice*) Hallo.
Miles Hallo.
Celia (*as Dutch Doll*) Hallo, Mr Coombes.
Miles Yes. Afternoon.
Celia Sit down, then.
Miles Who, me?
Celia Go on.
Miles Right, yes. (*He goes to do so*)
Celia (*screaming*) Not on Mr Fuzzyperks.
Miles Sorry. Sorry, Mr Fuzzyperks.
Celia (*in a squeaky voice*) Naughty man.
Miles I'm frightfully sorry. Look, Celia, I think I'm just going to fetch Matron.
Celia Matron can't come to tea. She's not invited.
Miles Ah, no, isn't she?
Celia Sit down.
Miles Yes. (*He looks at the seat apprehensively*) Is it OK here?
Celia Yes, you can sit there.
Miles (*sitting*) Jolly good. Look, Celia, I maybe should invite the others to ...
Celia Have you washed your hands?
Miles Oh yes, you bet. Look, perhaps you'd like a stroll outside.
Celia Eat up.
Miles (*looking round at the empty table*) Yes. What shall I—er ...?
Celia Pass Mr Coombes a sandwich, Teddy.
Miles Ah.
Celia (*as Teddy*) Want a sandwich, Mr Coombes?
Miles Right, yes. One of these. Delicious.
Celia (*fiercely*) Not those. Those are the cakes.
Miles Sorry.
Celia How many times do I have to say it? You don't eat the cake until you've finished the bread.
Miles Yes, I didn't realize there was still some left.
Celia You know what happens to people who eat cake first.
Miles (*nervously*) No. No ...
Celia Well, I've told you enough times. They get bitten in the leg, that's what happens to them. They get bitten for being bad. Grrrr! (*She goes down on her hands and knees, crawls swiftly round the table, and sinks her teeth into Miles's leg*)
Miles No, no, Celia. Come on. Come on, for God's sake.
Celia (*clinging on grimly*) Grrr!
Miles Aaaah! That's my leg! Please. Celia, these are new trousers. Please. Come on, come on, you're hurting me now.

Miles attempts to prise her away but her teeth are apparently embedded in his leg as she continues to growl

God, this is agony. Celia, Celia.

Miles finally topples over. They roll about. He pulls Celia free and temporarily overpowers her

(*Panting*) Now, that's enough. Enough, all right?

Celia appears to have grown calmer and Miles releases his hold slightly. Celia goes for his throat. Miles finds he is fighting for his life

(*Shouting vainly*) Help, help, help! Somebody, please. . . . Oh, God. Celia, Celia.

In the struggle, Miles pulls part of the long tablecloth off the serving table revealing the oilcloth beneath it. He manages to wrap Celia in the table cloth and, in this way, stifles her struggles. Mummy-like, he bundles her under the table. He kneels exhausted for a moment, breathing heavily

Oh, dear heaven. (*He gulps for air, then calls faintly*) Help, please. Could somebody help me. (*He pulls himself weakly to his feet and attempts to reach the entrance. He collapses almost immediately clutching his leg*) Aah! I think she's bitten through the hamstring or something. (*He talks to Celia under the table*) Celia. Celia, can you hear me? Now, lie still. Just lie there. No one's going to hurt you, Celia. I'm going to get some help. I'm going to get someone to look after you, you see. Now, lie still, Celia. There's a good girl. I won't be a moment. I'm leaving Teddy here with you. And Mr Thing and everybody else. They're all here. So don't be lonely. We're all here, aren't we? (*In Teddy's voice*) Yes, we're all here. (*In a squeaky voice*) All here. (*As Miles*) There you are. Did you hear that, Celia? They're all here.

Behind him, Irene Pridworthy enters

(*As Teddy*) I'll look after you, Celia. (*As Miles*) There you are, Celia, do you hear that? Teddy says he's going to look after you. Isn't that jolly nice of Teddy? Three cheers for Teddy. Hip hip—(*In a squeaky voice*)—hooray. Hip hip—(*In a squeaky voice*)—hooray. Hip hip . . . (*He sees Irene*)—ha ha.

Irene Who the hell are you talking to?
Miles Ah, Irene. Look, there's been an emergency.
Irene Who, you?
Miles No, Celia Teasdale. She's—she's had a collapse.
Irene Where is she?
Miles Er—under the table.
Irene Under the table?
Miles It's OK. She's quiet at the moment. But she—she needs medical help. Could you possibly keep an eye on her while I . . . I'll just. . . . (*He moves to the door*)
Irene (*lifting the oilcloth and staring under the table*) My God, is that her?
Miles Yes.
Irene Looks like Nefertiti. Can she breathe?
Miles Yes. I wouldn't—I wouldn't unwrap her. She bites.
Irene Bites?

Miles Yes. Quite nastily.

Irene Are you sure about this, Coombes? You haven't done something to her, have you?

Miles Me? Of course not.

Irene Well, you never know. You read some odd things. Innocent looking little rabbit suddenly turns on a woman. You have to watch it these days.

Miles (*loftily*) I think you can consider yourself perfectly safe, Mrs Pridworthy. I won't be a moment. (*He limps to the entrance with dignity*)

Irene Hey, Coombes.

Miles Yes.

Irene Tell your wife to put her skirt on again, there's a good chap.

Miles Oh, God.

Irene Doesn't look so good in front of the Countess, does it? Running around in her drawers.

Miles (*going*) Why does she do this to me?

Miles goes out

Irene I know what I'd do with her. I'd tan her backside with a tent pole. That's what I'd do with her. Only way to treat women like that. (*Speaking under the table*) I say, Celia? Mrs Teasdale? Are you all right? Can you breathe under there? I don't think you can really, can you? Hang on, I'm going to heave you out. Don't panic. But I'm warning you, if you start trying to bite me I won't stand any nonsense. So don't try it. I'll do the same to you as I do to all animals that try to bite me. I won't tell you what that is but, believe me, they don't forget it in a hurry. I don't think you'd like it anyway. Right, out you come. (*She heaves the totally enclosed bundle—a live stand-in for Celia—out from under the table*) By God, you're a big girl, aren't you? Right, I'll tell you something. I've got terrible gut-ache, too. I think its that damn bread. There we are. Still alive then, are you? (*She prods the bundle*)

The bundle squirms

(*Straightening up*) Good. That's all that matters. (*She looks out of the main entrance*) Ah. Here they come. Reinforcements.

EITHER Toby enters:

Toby (*as he enters*) Sorry, I was just——(*He sees the bundle*) My God, is that her?

Irene Coombes wrapped her up.

Toby Is she all right? Can't we . . .?

Irene Better not. She's been nipping people. Probably safer to leave her wrapped up till we get a professional.

Toby Yes, Matron's on her way. She's just dealing with the last of the mothers.

Irene Any of them broken?

Toby One suspected fracture. Mrs Jarvis. Mrs Studemore fell on her.

Irene Poor thing.

Toby (*kneeling beside Celia*) Celia . . . Celia. . . . It's Toby, can you hear me?
Is she all right? I can't hear her breathing. (*He listens again*) Oh yes,
there's something. Look, do you think while we're waiting, we could put
her into a chair or something? Rather than just leaving her lying around
here. Would you mind?

Irene Not at all.

They prepare to pick her up

Ready?

Toby Yes.

Irene Hup.

Toby Hup.

Irene Two, three, there you go.

They sit Celia in a chair, still swathed and helpless in her tablecloth

Toby Thank you very much.

Irene I hope to heaven she's the right way up. Otherwise she must be in
agony.

Toby Well, don't let me detain you, Irene. If you want to get back to the
fun.

Irene I'd hardly describe it as fun. It's like Culloden out there. See you later.
I hope we're going to get some tea. I'm starving.

Irene goes out

Toby sits down beside Celia

Toby Celia. Celia, I don't know if you can hear me but—er—this is—God,
this is difficult. I hope I—don't worry. I've been—I've been remiss, Celia.
I've not been a good husband, I know that. Frankly, I've been a wash-
out, Celia. But it's going to change, I promise you. As from now. So don't
worry. You're not to worry. I'm here, Celia, and I'm going to be here
always, you see. So. Eh? (*He pats her on the knee*) Oh, dear God, she is the
wrong way up.

The Lights fade to a Blackout

To: A FUNERAL (page 59)

OR Lionel enters:

Lionel How do you do? Spot of trouble, is there?

Irene You could say that.

Lionel (*seeing Celia*) God, what's that?

Irene That's your partner.

Lionel Mrs Teasdale?

Irene 'Sright.

Lionel What's she doing then?

Irene Relaxing. What do you think she's doing, you oaf?

Lionel Is she all right?

Irene No, not at all. She's blown her stack. Lost a screw.

Lionel Has she?

Irene Coombes wrapped her up for safekeeping. She was starting to bite people. Told you it would happen. Still, could have been worse. Could have been Hamley's. Where's her husband? Is he coming?

Lionel In a minute. He's still untangling the mothers.

Irene Mothers?

Lionel After the race. Quite nasty. I won a tenner though. Hogg owes me.

Irene Good for you. I lost the lot. Blew it all on Mrs Studemore. Fifty to one outsider.

Lionel Mrs Studemore? She fell over the starting line.

Irene I know she did. Stupid old fool. She looked quite good in the paddock. Well, that's racing for you. Wait there, I'll see if I can get some help.

Irene exits

(*Off*) Matron ...

Lionel Right. (*He stares at the bundle on the floor*) Mrs Teasdale?

The bundle squirms

Lionel sits down beside it

OK, Mrs Teasdale. It's all right. Don't panic. It's only me. Lionel. Everything's under control. You just lie there. Take it easy. Now, can you hear me? Celia? Now listen. You're not to worry. You've just fallen off your bike again, Mrs Teasdale. But you mustn't lose heart. We'll soon have you back in the saddle, never fear. We'll have you pedalling before you know it. I won't desert you. Trust me. You can trust old Lionel.

Lionel pats what he believes to be the bundle's cheeks. They are, in fact, its feet. This is made even clearer as it bites him in the leg. Lionel yells in agony. He stands and attempts to move to the door calling for help. The bundle clings on grimly and drags along behind him

The Lights fade to a Black-out

To: A NEW WOMAN (page 65)

A FUNERAL

A Churchyard. This year

The church door is closed. A gravel path leads away from it to an unseen road. A variety of gravestones border the path

We hear a church bell signifying a funeral and, in the silence that follows, only a few rooks from the vicarage trees

After a short pause, the church door opens and Celia appears looking frail and feeble. She is accompanied by Toby upon whose arm she leans heavily for support. Both are dressed in black. Toby closes the church door and as he does so Celia stumbles slightly

Toby (*steadying her*) Easy now. Easy does it.
Celia All right, all right. Just give me a moment.
Toby Do you want to sit down?
Celia Yes, yes. I think I need to just for a second.
Toby (*guiding her to the bench*) Here we are then. Carefully, that's it. (*He seats Celia*) All right?
Celia I think so.
Toby I don't think you should have come out, you know. You're still not very strong, are you? I thought things were getting better only. . . . (*He stares round the churchyard rather gloomily*) As soon as we get home, I'd better pop you back into bed. Make you some hot milk and honey. Just in case.
Celia (*feebly*) Oh, Toby, you don't have to . . .
Toby Can't be too careful. (*He stands patiently waiting for her to recover*)
Celia I'll be all right in a moment.
Toby Take your time. Take your time.

Pause

Celia Lovely service.
Toby Yes, it was. Well, as lovely as a funeral can be, I suppose.
Celia Oh, yes.
Toby Goodbye, Joe Hepplewick. Still, at least there's the consolation that he won't write any more poetry. Though knowing that local paper, they'll probably reprint all his old stuff as a tribute. Bring out a colour supplement. (*After a pause*) Lionel looked well. Did you talk to him?
Celia No.
Toby He looked—affluent.
Celia Did he?
Toby I hear he's doing pretty well. Amazing, isn't it? I mean, I think most of

us wrote him off completely. You were right, you know. You said he'd go places, didn't you? Remember, you said he would? Clever thing. (*After a pause*) Er—it just occurred to me, before the new term starts, if you're feeling better next week, I wondered if we might have a little break. Go away somewhere. Might do you good. It's out of season now, of course, so it won't be too noisy for you. I know you won't want noise. Nor will I. What do you say? See how you feel?

Celia Well ...

Toby Don't decide now. Not this instant.

Celia Remember the last time, though.

Toby I do.

Celia We had to come straight back home.

Toby True.

Celia Because I wasn't up to it.

Toby That was three years ago, though, Celia. That was our last holiday. All twenty-four hours of it. I mean, the point is, I think I personally could do with a break as well. I mean, I feel pretty good. Getting shot of the drinking helped and, of course, not smoking. Well, hardly. Not in the house, anyway. Not since it upset you. But I just feel I could do with a little holiday. I mean, all this rushing home at lunchtimes and so on. ...

Celia Not every lunchtime.

Toby No. A lot of them. Most of them. Still, I wouldn't have it any other way. Not if it—helps you. But that and trying to run the school ... gets a bit heavy, sometimes.

Celia Poor Toby.

Pause

Toby You see, I was chatting to this travel agent—well, it's young White-head's father. You know, Jack Whitehead and apparently there's a cancellation next week. Benidorm. Five days. So. Thought I'd mention it.

Celia You hate holidays.

Toby Well. ... Nice to have a change. (*After pause*) So. Possible, is it?

Celia (*without holding out much hope*) Possibly. (*She coughs*)

Toby I hope you'll soon be better, Celia.

Celia Well, as the doctor said, it's not going to happen overnight, is it, Toby?

Toby No, no. It's just one hoped after five years, you might ...

Celia If you want to go off on your own ...

Toby No, no.

Celia ... I'd probably manage.

Toby No, no. (*After pause*) No, no. I couldn't leave you. You want to stroll on yet?

Celia In a moment.

Toby Right. Don't get chilly, will you?

Celia No. (*After a pause*) Perhaps you could fetch me the rug from the car. Would you mind doing that?

Toby Of course. Of course, I will. Hang on.

Toby hurries towards the road

Toby (*turning back and looking at her hopefully*) You're looking a lot better, you know, Celia.

Celia (*smiling faintly*) Well, that's a start anyway, isn't it?

Toby (*gloomily*) Yes.

Tony exits

Celia (*singing softly*)
        Oh, God our help in ages past
        Our hope for years to come,
        Our shelter from the stormy blast,
        And our eternal home ...

It was a lovely service. (*After a pause*) I don't know what I'll have for tea. I think I'll ask Toby if he'll toast me a teacake. If we've any left. We should have some left. He can always pop out. Or one of the children. And strawberry jam. Yes. (*Pause*) And some of that homemade cake. We certainly have some of that left. And a nice strong cup of tea. (*Pause*) He must let the pot stand longer. Otherwise it's too weak. I keep telling him that, he doesn't listen. I do like my tea nice and strong. He's impossible. It's the same with the toast in the morning. Lightly browned, I keep saying. Does he ever listen ...?

The church clock chimes

Where on earth's he gone to? I could be freezing to death out here.

The church door opens and Lionel appears. He is dressed rather trendily

Lionel (*softly*) Mrs Teasdale?

Celia continues to frown to herself and mutter, not hearing him

Lionel Mrs Teasdale? Celia ...

Celia (*seeing him*) Oh. Lionel.

Lionel Afternoon, Mrs Teasdale.

Celia Good afternoon.

Lionel Saw you coming out the back way here. Hoped I might catch you. Just to say thank you for remembering Dad's funeral.

Celia Well ...

Lionel Appreciated that. Really did.

Celia I managed to make it, anyway.

Lionel I'm glad.

Celia coughs. A pause

You've—er—been a bit under the weather, I hear.

Celia Yes. Just a little.

Lionel Course I've been that busy. Been a little out of touch. I haven't seen you for—well, how long? I don't know. Three, four years, is it?

Celia Yes.

Lionel I'd been meaning to come and see you but ...

Celia I haven't been seeing very many people, to be honest.

Lionel No, quite.

Celia Too many people. Too much noise, you know.

Lionel Yes. I can see that. Been a long one, then, this illness?

Celia Five years, yes.

Lionel Well, I hope it's not too much longer for you.

Celia (*smiling bravely*) I'm afraid it's more or less permanent, Lionel.

Lionel Is it?

Celia One never really gets over that sort of thing. The body heals but the mind ... well, of course, we still know so little about it.

Lionel True, true. Still, you've got Mr Teasdale to look after you.

Celia Oh, yes.

Lionel I saw him scuttling round.

Celia Yes.

Lionel That's the way, eh? Keep him busy. Out of mischief. (*He laughs*)

A silence

Celia I must say, you're looking prosperous.

Lionel Thank you. I owe that to you, really, I think. You set me on the road.

Celia Me?

Lionel You put me on to catering. I've never looked back. Fast food. All the rage, you see.

Celia Fast food?

Lionel You know, microwave takeaway, that sort of stuff. Kids go for it. Quick, cheap, no hanging around. Got three branches now.

Celia Heavens. Are you still doing teas?

Lionel Teas?

Celia Yes.

Lionel No. Jacked them in, I'm afraid.

Celia Didn't they catch on?

Lionel Oh, they caught on. Surprisingly. No profit, though, was there? All work, no profit. What sort of business is that? In the food industry you want low overheads, fast turnover, minimum wastage. After I—after I bought you out, you know, like—I had a look round and went straight into that. Never looked back. Still hard work but as long as I don't have to eat it myself, I'm not complaining. (*He laughs*) Joking, of course.

Celia Yes.

Lionel Well, the wife's waiting. Gets hopping mad if I keep her hanging around.

Celia Yes, I haven't met her, have I?

Lionel No, she's—I don't know how you'd take to her, Celia, frankly, but she's a good woman. Good for me. Got her head screwed on. I call her the Human Calculator.

Celia Really?

Lionel Feed in the figures, out they all come, tick, tick, tick. Don't know how she does it. Still, it's a good arrangement. She does all the business side, leaves me to be creative. Nice to have met you, anyway, Mrs Teasdale. I know Dad would have appreciated it, too.

Celia Good.

Lionel If you're passing through town ever and you feel like a bite ... you know, chicken in the basket ... nice juicy hamburger, french fries ... come and look us up, won't you?

Celia I will.

Lionel Discount to friends.

Celia Thank you.

Lionel Give us a ring. Let us know you're coming. Kwickieburgers. That's what we call ourselves. We're in the book. Under K. 'Bye.

Celia Goodbye, Lionel.

Lionel goes into the church

(*Muttering*) Where's he gone with my rug? I wanted it ages ago. Ages and ages and ages. He doesn't care about me. He really doesn't. I can sit here and die as far as he's concerned. Well, if I feel ill tomorrow, I shall just have to stay in bed and it will be his fault and serve him right. (*Pause*) I think I'd like some boiled fish for supper. I know we've some in the fridge. With parsley sauce. I'll get Toby to boil me up a bag of that. With brown bread and butter. And maybe a little rice pudding to follow. Yes. I'll get him to do the sausages for breakfast. With a few grilled tomatoes. And maybe a slice of bacon. But it must be lean bacon. The last lot he got was disgusting. They'd never have sold that to me. And then we'll have the roast lamb in the evening. Lovely. With the beans. And peas.

Toby reappears carrying a rug

Toby Sorry.

Celia Where have you been?

Toby Sorry, I met Irene Pridworthy. Couldn't get away. She was rabbiting on. Sent her love. Hoped you were feeling better.

Celia Well, I was until I was left sitting out here.

Toby Yes, I'm sorry. You know what she's like though. Here's your rug.

Celia I don't want that now. It's far too late. The best thing I can do is hurry home to bed.

Toby My God, you're not feeling worse?

Celia Just a little throaty. Probably isn't anything. I'll just have to take it quietly for a couple of days.

Toby Ah. Then perhaps we shouldn't be thinking about next week.

Celia Next week?

Toby This Benidorm business. I mean, I——

Celia I don't honestly think so, Toby. It would be so foolish for me to——

Toby Oh, yes.

Celia You go. Don't let me stop you.

Toby No, no.

He helps Celia get up

Up you come. I'll stay with you. Be no fun without you, would it?

Celia Perhaps next year.

Toby Yes, yes.

Celia See how we feel. Time for tea.

Toby Yes. Your appetite's still pretty good, anyway.

Celia It's going to take time, Toby, it really is.

Toby Oh, yes.

Celia (*stumbling*) Careful.

Toby (*steading her*) Sorry.

Celia You know what Dr Burgess said. The only thing that will finally cure me is time, Toby.

Toby Oh, yes.

Celia (*as they go*) It's all a question of time. All in good time . . .

As they go out to the road the Lights fade to a Blackout

A NEW WOMAN

A Churchyard. This year

The church door is closed. A gravel path leads away from it to an unseen road. A variety of gravestones border the path

We hear a church bell signifying a funeral and, in the silence that follows, only a few rooks from the vicarage trees

Celia is pacing about in the churchyard. She looks very smart and businesslike. She glances at her watch with a certain impatience

Celia (*noting the time*) Oh, Lord. (*She paces about some more*)

In a second, Toby, dressed for a funeral blunders out of the church, closing the door behind him. He fails to notice Celia. He is obviously a little the worse for wear. He stands breathing heavily for a moment

Toby (*trying to clear his head*) Oh, dear God. (*He takes one or two more deep breaths*)

Celia watches him silently

(*Recovering slightly*) Oh, well . . . (*He turns to go back into the church and sees Celia. He speaks disbelievingly*) Celia? (*After a pause*) Celia?

Celia Hallo, Toby.

Toby Oh, thank God for that. I thought I actually had passed on. Is it really you?

Celia Yes.

Toby Terrifying. Every time I go to a funeral and I seem to go to more and more of them these days, I get the sneaking fear it's going to be mine. Only they haven't bothered to tell me. In case it upsets me.

Celia You're looking as well as ever.

Toby Not so bad.

Celia You look frightful.

Toby I feel frightful.

Celia Isn't Mrs Bartlett looking after you?

Toby Sylvie? Oh well, she's—she's all right. She's picking up the empties anyway.

Celia My God, Toby, why do you do it? I always thought it was me who used to drive you to drink.

Toby No, no. Anyone can do it. I'm not at all choosy. Sylvie Bartlett will do just as well.

Celia Look, if Sylvie's no good, Toby, let me know and I'll get you someone else. I mean, I'm paying for her, not you. I don't want to waste my money on someone who's useless.

Toby She's all right. She would be if it wasn't for her bloody silly husband. Lazy oaf. Anyway, it's been a long time.

Celia It certainly has.

Toby I get news of you through the children when they do their monthly shunt.

Celia Yes, they keep me informed about you, too.

Toby I'm sure they do.

Celia No, they're always very loyal.

Toby Are they?

Celia Much more than you deserve.

Toby I didn't realize you were here today.

Celia I'm not officially. I'm on my way somewhere else.

Toby Why the hell didn't you come in for the service? Standing outside like this, it's ridiculous.

Celia He was Lionel's father. Nothing to do with me. I hardly knew him.

Toby You knew him as well as I did.

Celia More to the point, I loathed the sight of him. It would be a little insincere of me, surely. Standing in a church mouthing platitudes about a man you're absolutely delighted to see the back of.

Toby He wasn't that bad, Joe Hepplewick.

Celia He was appalling. (*After a pause*) Anyway, this has worked out quite well. I'm on my way to a meeting and since it was in Brighton, it meant Lionel could stop off for the service and then drive me on afterwards.

Toby Doesn't he get the day off, then? For his father's funeral.

Celia He never asked for one.

Toby Conscientious.

Celia Yes.

Pause

Toby And you're still doing well?

Celia Amazingly. Considering.

Toby (*without great enthusiasm*) Jolly good.

Celia Well, people always need to eat, you see, don't they? However depressed things get, they still want food. In fact the worse it gets, the more they want to eat to forget it. Particularly at the luxury end of the market. Never any shortage of money there it appears.

Toby No.

Celia They gobble it faster than we can produce it. And with these continual advances in freezing techniques, one really can deep-freeze very sophisticated dishes with hardly any loss of quality at all.

Toby Bloody expensive, though.

Celia Oh, yes. But then look at the ingredients. Everything's fresh.

Toby Or it was before you froze it.

Celia You know what I mean.

Toby Anyway, it's a damn sight too expensive for me. Can't afford that on a schoolmaster's salary.

Celia I'll send you some if you're interested.

Toby Don't bother.

Celia You never ate at all when I was with you. Don't tell me you've taken it up again.

Toby Yes, I'm heavily into cheese sandwiches and vinegar crisps.

Celia Well, eat a little now and again, Toby. Or we'll be burying you. (*She glances at her watch*) Where on earth has he got to? What's keeping him?

Toby He's at his father's funeral, Celia. You'll have to be a little tolerant. It's very much a one-off occasion.

Celia So's my meeting. I have an important contract to sign. You won't believe this but we've actually achieved the breakthrough. We're going to start exporting cordon bleu cookery to the French.

Toby You are?

Celia Quite a coup.

Toby As they say.

Celia What?

Toby Nothing.

Celia And how's the school?

Toby Knocking along. They're still trying to get rid of me. Only I won't let them. Their latest one was to suggest to me that they thought the Headmaster really ought to be a married man. So I told them I was married. I just didn't have a wife any more. That thoroughly confused them. Are you—on your own?

Celia Very much so. Don't the children keep you posted?

Toby No, they're loyal to you as well.

Celia Why do you ask? Did you think I would be?

Toby I thought you might be living with Lionel.

Celia Oh, Toby ...

Toby What?

Celia Come on. I hoped you thought a little more of me than that. Really. With Lionel? No, I've had offers but I haven't really—seen anyone suitable. You?

Toby No, none at all. Women come round and knock on the door occasionally, ask if I'm interesting in setting up house but I pack them off pretty sharpish. What do I want with six-foot Swedish blondes with big chests at my time of life?

Celia You could put your name down for Rowena Coombes.

Toby Rowena? Heavens, no. They've left.

Celia Both of them?

Toby Yes.

Celia Miles as well?

Toby Abroad. Australia. Suddenly upped and off.

Celia How extraordinary. So you've lost your friend, too.

Toby Yes.

Celia Poor Toby. Have you got their address?

Toby No.

Celia Oh, really. I'd like to send them a postcard.

Toby Or a chicken dinner for two. Well, I must get back in.

Celia Lovely seeing you.

Toby Yes, awfully nice.

Celia I know as the years go by, Toby, we have less and less in common but then as you always used to say, we never had very much when we lived together. But I'm still fond of you, Toby. And I still think of you.

Toby Yes, that's absolutely super.

Celia You still feel bitter, don't you? It was my health that suffered, Toby, not yours. I was the one who was ill, for God's sake. I was the one who spent a year and a half in hospital. And who was it who came to see me? Lionel. You hardly came near.

Toby Because you didn't want me to.

Celia How do you know?

Toby You more or less said so.

Celia I was ill, Toby. I was terribly ill.

Toby Well, maybe we both were. (*After a pause*) Too late now.

Celia But you still feel bitter towards me, don't you? Because I didn't come trotting home. You still feel badly about that.

Toby I don't feel a damn thing, Celia, I really don't. Sorry. Wish I could oblige you. That's the way it is these days. It's really a first-class feeling. I thoroughly recommend it. Bang your head, you no longer feel it. Lose your wife, you have a good laugh about it. Terrific feeling. Excuse me.

Toby goes into the church

Celia (*calling after him*) Goodbye, Toby. Do try and eat something, won't you?

The church door closes

Oh, what's the use?

The church clock chimes

Celia glances at her watch impatiently. She takes a small executive-type personal recorder from her handbag

Celia (*switching it on*) Belinda, this is to a Colonel Malton, The Close, Green Road, Bilbury. On personal paper. No typed signature. Dear Jack, I've just heard from Toby that Miles and Rowena Coombes have left the district. Stop. Presumably he is no longer Chairman of the Board of Governors? Question mark. I'd hate to lose touch with them altogether and I wonder whether they left a forwarding address with you? Question mark. Para. I hear they've gone to Australia. Full stop. Heavens! Exclamation mark. What will they make of that? Question mark. Particularly Rowena!! Two exclamation marks. I hope you and the dogs are all in good health and that I'll run into you sometime when I'm next down. Stop. With every good wish. And, Belinda, would you also arrange to send a family moussaka, a bœuf bourgignon and a chicken tandoori, no, better make that chicken à la crème—he'll never eat tandoori—to my husband with a compliments slip, no charge. Finally, to Donald Jefferson in Manchester. Dear Donald, I was extremely disappointed to hear from your secretary on Wednesday . . .

Lionel comes hurrying round the corner of the church. He is dressed in a chauffeur's uniform

Lionel Sorry, Mrs Teasdale.

Celia That's all right, Lionel. There's absolutely no hurry. Was it a pleasant service?

Lionel Very nice. Very tasteful. It was all arranged very well. The Reverend Fognorth spoke very nicely and then my cousin, that's the one who arranged it, Harry, he read some of Dad's poetry. So it was a really good occasion. I was very moved.

Celia Lovely.

Lionel I hope I haven't kept you waiting. I had to chat a little bit, you know.

Celia Not at all. Lovely to see the old village again. Are you fit now?

Lionel Oh, yes. Brighton next stop, is it?

Celia Yes, I'll be about an hour. No more. You can have a look at the sea if you like. And then I want to go straight back to London for this dinner tonight. So home to change and you can drop me in the West End for nine. Then you can take the rest of the evening off. I can easily get a cab home from there.

Lionel Oh, thank you very much, Mrs Teasdale.

Celia But I shall need you first thing in the morning, I'm afraid.

Lionel Right, Mrs Teasdale.

Celia I'll have to go out to Slough and talk to those wholesalers personally. I think it's time for strong words. Is it unlocked?

Celia exits

Lionel follows her hurriedly, putting on his cap

Lionel (*as he follows her*) No, I'll do that, Mrs Teasdale. I'll do that. Careful how you go. Mind your step now.

He goes. The lights fade to a Black-out

**INTIMATE EXCHANGES is a related series of plays
totalling eight scripts**

This is the Second

EVENTS ON A HOTEL TERRACE
preceded by *How It Began* (page 3);
A Gardener Calls (page 5) and *A Gardener
in Love* (page 15)

CHARACTERS
APPEARING IN THIS SERIES OF SCENES

Celia
Lionel
Sylvie
Toby
Miles

EVENTS ON A HOTEL TERRACE

A seaside hotel terrace. Five weeks later. 4 p.m. Saturday, July 24th. It is a sunny teatime

Distant piano music can be heard from the hotel lounge, playing popular medleys from long ago operettas and there is the squawk of the odd seagull

There are some five or six tables in view with their attendant chairs and umbrellas. All are empty save one where Toby and Celia sit amidst the debris of a tea they have recently finished. They stare out over the low wall that bounds the terrace and past the flight of steps leading to the gardens and road. They appear to have run out of conversation. There is a long silence

Toby Well, I must say this is absolutely terrific. (*After a pause*) Sensational. (*After a pause*) I mean, I couldn't have had a better holiday if I'd planned it myself.

Celia I wish you had.

Toby I mean, what an exciting place this is. How on earth did you find it? All this—activity. People rushing hither and thither. The laughter of vivacious diners at the crowded tables mingling with the gay sound of passionate gypsy music.

Celia All right.

Toby The dizzy riot of colour as the giddy throng swirls first this way and then that. (*After a pause*) It's like the first act of *Carmen* out here, isn't it? (*A pause*) The glint of sunlight on the twinkling spokes of passing wheel-chairs. The merry clatter of walking frames mixing with the cheery whistle of howling hearing aids, and the clatter of dentures closing around stale angel cake.

Celia (*very irritably*) All right.

Toby I didn't realize you'd brought me here to die. I'd have packed my dark suit.

Celia I brought you here to rest. That's all. Rest.

Toby In peace.

Celia One week. That's all we're doing. One week. Consider yourself lucky. The doctor wanted it to be longer. If he had his way ...

Toby Well, he didn't. I don't know what we're doing here at all quite honestly. Waste of time. All I did was fall over. I just fell over.

Celia You didn't just fall over.

Toby What's wrong with falling over? It isn't the first time I've fallen over——

Celia I know that.

Toby ... won't be the last.

Celia I'm sure.

Toby Well then.

Celia This was a rather different sort of falling over, wasn't it? I mean, you weren't.... Well, it doesn't normally happen to you in morning assembly. I don't know why you're moaning. At least you've had a warning. A little heart tremor that says be careful. Some people don't get a warning at all. Louis Southerwick didn't. Just fell out of his chair playing Scrabble. Dreadful for his wife.

Toby She probably had a word with three Zs.

Celia No warning or anything. I think you've been terribly lucky.

Toby We don't even know mine was a heart thing.

Celia Doctor Windsor said quite categorically that he was ninety-five per cent certain that he was almost sure ...

Toby Windsor is absolutely hopeless. We should have had Burgess.

Celia Burgess is on holiday.

Toby You know what Windsor's like. He can't even get his bloody bag open.

Celia Oh, don't be so stupid.

Toby It's perfectly true. I was lying there stretched out on a couple of benches, there was Windsor rolling around on the parquet trying to get his bag open. I could have been breathing my last for all he knew. He can't even get at his stethoscope.

Celia He came round in a great hurry. He slammed his bag in the car door. Perfectly natural thing to happen.

Toby Oh yes, happens every day. Pass by any hospital car park, hundreds of doctors slamming their bags in doors. (*After a slight pause*) Anyway, all we've got is his guess.

Celia It isn't a guess.

Toby Of course it's a guess. He didn't have any equipment. He even had to guess my bloody temperature. No, as far as I can make out, all this is his word against mine.

Celia What else could it have been?

Toby It could have been any one of a dozen things. It could have been the heat. Becomes extremely warm sitting in a hall with two hundred small children. It could have been the Reverend Halliwell's bone-grindingly boring "Thought for the Day", which appeared to go on for a week, which finally got to me. It could have been Hawker's piano playing. It could have been Matron's B.O. There are dozens of very sound reasons why a man should faint during school assembly. I'm amazed I hadn't thought of it before (*He looks behind and tries to catch someone's attention in the lounge*) Waiter—wait—oh, God.

Celia What do you want? More tea?

Toby No, I wanted a paper.

Celia A paper.

Toby Yes, a newspaper. Just because we've landed here in this geriatric Valhalla doesn't mean we can't keep in touch with the rest of the poor mortals. Besides I can't miss my paper. They get more fascinating to read as days go by. Filled with people all attempting to justify their own appalling behaviour, right from the Prime Minister down to the chap who strokes the boiler. All desperately wanting me to see their point of view. Well, I think as you get older you have to choose. You either become very broad-minded and try to see everyone's point of view, like dear old, soggy old Miles Coombes always does, or you become extremely narrow-minded like me and see nobody's point of view at all. Which I think is safer.

Celia You certainly never see mine. Otherwise you wouldn't sit here going on.

Pause

Toby (*trying again*) Waiter. Oh. (*He gives up*) We could read that the school's blown up. You never know your luck. (*He calls*) Waiter! . . . Do you think he's just ignoring us on purpose?

Celia I don't think he heard you.

Toby He's not used to us mad young things. Do you honestly mean to say you couldn't find anywhere livelier than this?

Celia Not at this time of year. Not at that short notice.

Toby (*sighing*) Oh, well.

Celia Would you like to go for a walk?

Toby No.

Celia We ought to do something now we're here.

Toby We are. We're sitting here waiting to go home again.

Celia Yes, you always were hell on holiday. I remember that from the dim, distant past. On our last one. Ten years ago or whenever it was. This is no more fun for me, it really isn't. I don't want to be here. I'd much sooner be at home.

Toby Perhaps you're missing Lionel Hepplewick.

Celia Oh, don't start that.

Toby He's probably missing you.

Celia (*smiling*) You have to laugh.

Toby I'm not laughing. Bloody cheek. One of the reasons I sacked him.

Celia Really? It wasn't? Because of me? If I thought you'd got rid of Lionel because of me, I really would be——

Toby No, I didn't.

Celia You didn't?

Toby No.

Celia Promise you didn't.

Toby No. I got rid of him on the strength of what he, as school grounds-man, had done to our first-team cricket pitch.

Celia He tried his best.

Toby His best was an act of vandalism on a scale unrivalled since the Visigoths first went off on a works outing.

Celia So long as it wasn't me, that's all.

Toby You're glad he's gone, though, aren't you?

Celia Well . . .

Toby Oh, come on.

Celia Yes.

Toby The man absolutely plagued the life out of you.

Celia Yes. Yes, he was a nuisance.

Toby Banging on the bedroom windows in the middle of the night.

Celia He didn't know you'd be there.

Toby You mean you'd have let him in if I hadn't been?

Celia No, of course not.

Toby Shouting through the letter box at crack of dawn.

Celia I know, I know.

Toby That nearly did kill me. I was just picking the rate demand off the doormat. . . .

Celia Yes, I know.

Toby I don't know why you're defending him, you nearly called the police.

Celia Well, he did get obsessive.

Toby He was a lunatic. Absolute cock-eyed fixation. If I ever see him again, I'll. . . . It must be a serious mental disorder, mustn't it? It wasn't as if you encouraged the man, was it? (*After a pause*) Was it?

Celia No.

Toby You never encouraged him.

Celia I said, no.

Toby No, he's one of those people. Quite common. They just sit down one day and pick someone out of a phone book. Ring them up, tell them they've just got engaged to them. Some poor bloody woman doing her morning wash finds herself engaged to a chap on the end of a phone she's never met.

Celia He was quite harmless though.

Toby A man who did what he did to a cricket pitch is capable of anything.

Celia I mean, I wasn't frightened by him or threatened. I did get irritated, I suppose, but—well, there were nice touches. I got quite fond of the little bunches of flowers in the milk bottles.

Toby You didn't feel that at the time. Whenever I came home, I always found you crouching under the sofa in case it was him.

Celia (*sadly*) He never finished my crazy paving either. Still, I suppose in retrospect it's quite pleasant. I mean to feel one has created quite such a depth of feeling in someone, however misguided.

Toby Yes, I'm sure Mussolini felt much the same way. (*After a pause he looks at Celia*) What's the matter?

Celia Nothing.

Toby You're sitting there looking like a stuffed puffin.

Celia I was just surveying life ahead and it rather depressed me.

Toby At least you've got some. According to you and the bag-wrestling medic I've hardly any left at all. (*He rises*) Look, I'm going to get a paper. These waiters are obviously trained not to respond to vocal sounds or hand signals. Short of rolling coins on the floor in front of him, I can think of no other way of attracting his attention. Now when I come back—hang on to the table because here's an exciting bit—we will go for a walk.

Celia Oh, so now we are going.

Toby We'll stroll along the promenade, very gently in case I fall down, then we'll stroll back again and if you're very good, we'll sit down in the lounge and wait for dinner while we both enjoy not having a drink. Then we'll slip up to the Arctic suite and so to bed. That's not too exciting, is it?

Celia It's no more fun for me.

Toby I'm relieved to hear it. I'm not suffering alone. See you in a minute. (*He moves to the hotel door, then turns to Celia*) This is the sort of music that makes you want to jump up and dance the night away, isn't it? Ha-cha-cha!

Toby goes into the hotel

Celia (*muttering*) It's no more fun for me. In fact it's worse for me. I have to sit and listen to him. Much sooner be at home. (*After a pause she gets up and moves to the corner of the terrace. She holds out an arm to test for breeze*) No, it's very mild. (*Suddenly, with frustration*) Oh, it's not my fault. It's always got to be my fault. Silly man. (*She returns to her table and lights a cigarette. She wanders along the terrace. She looks over the edge of the wall*) Ah, croquet, that's nice. (*She stands, brooding*)

A waiter, Lionel, appears

Lionel I say, I say.

Celia What?

Lionel Mrs Teasdale?

Celia (*incredulously*) Lionel?

Lionel It's Lionel, Mrs Teasdale.

Celia Yes.

Lionel You haven't forgotten me, have you? Lionel.

Celia Of course I haven't. Lionel.

Lionel Lionel, Mrs Teasdale.

Celia What are you doing here, Lionel?

Lionel Sssh, Mrs Teasdale, I can't talk now. They're watching me.

Celia They are?

Lionel They watch every move you make, you can't do a thing.

Celia Who are these people?

Lionel Mr Hobjay.

Celia Mr Hobjay?

Lionel The assistant manager. Him on duty. He's watching us.

Celia Oh, I see.

Lionel He's just in there on the trolley. Look, I must talk to you, Mrs Teasdale.

Celia Lionel, I don't know how you got here or what you think you're doing. . . .

Lionel Please, Mrs Teasdale.

Celia It won't do any good, Lionel.

Lionel It's a matter of life and death, Celia.

Celia Oh, Lionel.

Lionel It is, I swear it. Please, Mrs Teasdale. I'm not joking. Not with Mr Hobjay in there, I promise. I must see you urgently, please. I must talk to you alone. (*He turns to respond to someone in the lounge*) Yes, I'm coming, sir, I'm just coming.

Celia Lionel, we simply can't——

Lionel Please, Mrs Teasdale. (*He starts to move back inside*) Yes, sir. I'll be right with you, sir.

Lionel goes back in the hotel

Celia Oh, heavens. (*She walks about a little*) Oh, Lord. (*She walks about a little more*) Oh, God. Now that's——Now what do I do? Well, we can't stay here, we'll have to. . . . (*She goes to the door of the hotel and waves as if trying to catch someone's attention*) Toby—Toby. Oh. (*She gives up, then in reply to someone*) No, it's all right, I'm just calling my husband. (*Loudly*) Calling my husband . . . yes . . . yes, it is, lovely . . . oh, hell. (*She moves away and sits thoughtfully at a different table*) I don't know what to do.

Toby returns with a paper

Toby Here we are. *The Evening Chronicle*. A journal as packed full of incident by the look of it as the town it serves. Local man's hat blows off. Story and pictures inside. Want to look.

Celia No.

Toby Why have you moved?

Celia I haven't moved.

Toby Oh no, nor you have. It's just the tea things that have moved, you've stayed where you are. Are we off then?

Celia Just a minute.

Toby What?

Celia I've just . . .

Toby Just what?

Celia Nothing.

Toby You all right?

Celia Yes, yes, yes.

Toby Coming then?

Celia Change your shoes.

Toby What?

Celia Those are your indoor shoes.

Toby Indoor shoes?

Celia You know perfectly well they are. I bought them for you to wear in the hotel.

Toby You want me to go up to the Arctic suite?

Celia Yes.

Toby And change into another set of shoes?

Celia Please.

Toby You realize you're talking to a man with a suspected heart tremor.

Celia Yes.

Toby And if Windsor had ever got his bag open, it could have been definite.

Celia Yes, all right.

Toby And you're proposing to send me up three flights of stairs to change from one perfectly sound pair of shoes into another.

Celia Go in the lift then. Use the lift.

Toby The lift is jammed full of old ladies joy-riding. You can't get into it. You know that. All right. Want to look at this?

Celia No.

Toby No. Seen one hat blow off, you've seen them all. I'll stick it upstairs. (*He moves away and then turns back*) You know, we're going to hit a snag here.

Celia Oh, Toby, do hurry up.

Toby When I change from this identical pair of shoes into the other identical pair of shoes, I'm going to have to walk downstairs in the outdoor shoes in order to reach outdoors. Now is this permissible?

Celia Go away.

Toby You don't want me to carry them? Or is the great Cobbler in the Sky going to hurl aside his last and show his displeasure by raining stick-a-soles upon the Grand Hotel.

Celia (*weakly*) Please, Toby.

Toby (*as he goes*) That's what life's all about really, isn't it? Changing shoes. And one man in his time wears many shoes. . . .

Toby goes indoors

Celia Oh, it's impossible . . . I can't . . . it's impossible. He's impossible. Everything's impossible. (*She goes and fetches her handbag from her original table and because that is rather cluttered, hurries across to sit at a third clear table where she can write. She sits down, takes out a small notebook and pencil*) Oh, it's absolutely impossible. I can't. It really is . . . (*She starts to write, muttering as she does so*)

Lionel returns carrying a tray of tea for one

Lionel Tea, madam?

Celia Oh. (*She covers the piece of paper*)

Lionel (*loudly*) Lovely afternoon, madam.

Celia Lionel, I don't want tea. I've had some.

Lionel Have some more, Mrs Teasdale. It's the only excuse I've got to be out here.

Celia But I can't drink any more.

Lionel Please. (*He lays out the tea for her and says loudly*) Here we are, madam. Cake, there.

Celia I don't want any cake, it's disgusting.

Lionel (*softly*) I need to see you, Celia, it's urgent. It's very urgent indeed. I wouldn't be troubling you like this if it wasn't urgent.

Celia Look, Lionel, here is a note I have written to you—look, let me finish it, then I'll give it to you.

Lionel I can't have a note. It has to be personal. Let me pour you the tea.

Celia I don't wany any tea. (*She lays her hand on the teapot before he can pour*)

Lionel Celia, I decided last night, I just wanted you to know, I'm going to kill myself.

Celia You're not going to kill yourself, Lionel, don't be silly. Not for me, I'm not worth it.

Lionel I am.

Celia Nobody's worth killing themselves for.

Lionel (*moving away dramatically*) I'm going to drown myself off the edge of this terrace.

Celia That is the croquet lawn, Lionel. Now come back and behave yourself.

Lionel (*tearfully*) Please, Mrs Teasdale. Celia, please.

Celia (*anxiously, with a glance towards the hotel*) Lionel, people are watching. Now come along.

Lionel Please.

Celia Yes, all right, all right. Pour the tea.

Lionel I love you, Mrs Teasdale.

Celia Yes, I know, Lionel. I realize.

Lionel Just so much, it's——

Celia Yes, it's awful, Lionel, it's awful. I know how you feel.

Lionel, sniffing, slurps tea into her saucer

In the cup, please, Lionel, in the cup.

Lionel I'd give my life for you, you see, Mrs Teasdale.

Celia Yes, but there's no need to. There's no point.

Lionel Please don't give me a note, Mrs Teasdale.

Celia No, no, I won't give you a note, I promise. We'll have a proper talk. Now that's a promise. But Lionel—Lionel, are you listening?

Lionel Yes.

Celia You'd better keep busy. They all seem to be watching us in there. Clear that table there.

Lionel Right. I will. Thank you, Mrs Teasdale. (*He goes over to the other table and starts clearing it*)

Celia Can you hear me?

Lionel Yes.

Celia Now, listen—I wish that old man wouldn't keep staring at me—now, Toby's had—my husband's been a little ill, Lionel.

Lionel Yes, I know.

Celia And the doctor has said that he must take things quietly. It's dangerous for him to become excited. . . .

Lionel (*hopefully*) How excited's that?

Celia So I'd be grateful if you wouldn't let him see you.

Lionel Well, I'll try.

Celia Please, Lionel, not here.

Lionel No, Mrs Teasdale.

Celia You mustn't let him see you here. Promise?

Lionel I promise, I promise. Would you like a sandwich?

Celia No, I do not want a sandwich. I've had a sandwich. I've had several.

Lionel Please eat, Mrs Teasdale. Otherwise Mr Hobjay will get suspicious.

Celia Oh, to blazes with Mr Hobjay. All right. (*She takes a sandwich*)

Lionel Thank you, Mrs Teasdale. Those are very nice.

Celia Now my husband's coming back here and then he's going for a walk so please keep out of the way till he does.

Lionel Yes, Mrs Teasdale. I'm very grateful, Mrs Teasdale.

Celia Lionel, do blow your nose.

Lionel Yes. (*He takes a paper napkin off the tray*)

Celia Don't let people see you like that.

Lionel No, right.

Lionel goes back into the hotel

Celia What are they all doing in there? They're all lined up by the window. Shoo. Go away. Yes, you. Mind your own business. (*She pulls a face*) To you, too. What an unpleasant old woman. (*To herself*) I don't want all this tea. What am I going to do with all this tea? (*To someone off in the lounge*) What? No, I don't know what's the matter with the waiter. I think he's Italian probably. They're always very emotional. (*She laughs*) Perhaps I under-tipped him. Yes. (*She laughs*) Oh, what the hell. (*She eats a sandwich and drinks her tea*)

Toby returns. He stops as he sees Celia at another table, eating and drinking

Toby Ah, you're having tea.

Celia Er—yes.

Toby Thought you were. (*After a pause*) Doesn't time fly in this carnival atmosphere? It seems like only ten minutes ago since we were last having tea.

Celia I felt like some more.

Toby Did you?

Celia Yes.

Toby Doesn't sound like you.

Celia I'm on holiday. I want to be different.

Toby Oh, is that what people do on holiday? Be different. Right. Hang on, I'll just put my shoes on the other feet.

Celia ignores this

So you're not ready for a walk?

Celia No, you go on.

Toby Go on?

Celia Yes, I'll be a little while.

Toby Why?

Celia Because I want to finish my tea.

Toby I see. Are you—are you going to make a habit of this? Double meals.

Celia I don't know.

Toby Only if you intend eating two dinners this evening, I think I'll just join you for the second one if you don't mind.

Celia Please, you go on, Toby, you go on.

Toby (*pulling Celia's note from under the plate*) What's this?

Celia Nothing.

Toby What is it?

Celia Nothing. It's private. Give it to me.

Toby (*reading*) You can't keep choosing—no, it's not—chasing after me . . .

Celia Would you mind giving that to me, please? It's very private. Strictly. Private.

Toby What the hell is it?

Celia (*after a slight pause*) It's a poem.

Toby A what?

Celia I thought I'd—it's silly—I thought I'd just try and write some poetry. That's all.

Toby Because we're on holiday.

Celia Yes.

Toby Thank God we're only here for a week.

Celia That's all.

Toby Otherwise I'd finish up with a twenty-four stone poetess. I had you marked as a prose woman, you know.

Celia Well, there you are.

Toby If you are home first, please put gas on mark four and boil kettle. That sort of thing. There you are, totally wrong. Just as you settle for being married to Jane Austen, you find all along you've been living with a closet Edith Sitwell.

Celia I'll catch you up.

Toby What's the matter with this one then, Edith? You've got a bit stuck with it, have you? You can't keep chasing after me—er—I've started on my second tea. How am I doing?

Celia Do go away.

Toby With any luck I'll get one free. Well, it's a start. Set you on your way, Edith. Any help?

Celia Toby!

Toby Poems. I don't know what the hell you're up to, Celia, and I don't really want to know. I just wish to God you'd pay me the compliment of not treating me like a complete imbecile. I'm going for a walk. I'll leave you to your stanzas.

Toby goes off towards the sea

Celia (*shouting after him*) Oh, go on. Go away. And good riddance. I hope you fall in the sea. Nasty, sarcastic, conceited man. (*Then in the direction of the lounge*) Enjoying it, are you, dear? Good. (*She pulls another face and mutters*) I don't know why I bother. I book hotels. I make all the arrangements. I persuade mother to look after the kids. I bribe the kids so they'll behave. I do everything for him. All he has to say is thank you. One little tiny thank you. All he does is complain. Well, that's it. That's it. That's finally it. That is it. If he drops dead, it's not my fault. I wash my hands of him. So there. (*She rises and moves to the wall to look after him*) Which way is he going?

Lionel comes out on to the terrace. He has another tray loaded with tea

Lionel (*speaking loudly as he comes*) Tea for one, then, was it, madam?

Celia No, it was not.

Lionel Thank you, madam. Over here. (*He sets the tea-tray down on yet another table, and starts to lay it out, speaking quietly*) I have to keep bringing them out, Mrs Teasdale, otherwise they ask what I'm doing out here.

Celia But, Lionel, I don't want any more tea. It's ridiculous.

Lionel No, you see, the point is, as long as there's tea coming out here and dirties going back, he won't be curious, you see, Mr Hobday.

Celia But he can see there's nobody else out here but me.

Lionel Ah no, he can't, you see, because he's just round the corner there with his trolley. He has to stay by his trolley because the old ladies pick at the cakes. So long as I let him catch a glimpse of me now and again—(*He steps back in line with the windows and speaks loudly*) Oh yes, indeed, madam. Those there are cucumber and those are tomato. (*He moves back towards her quietly*) That will have fooled him, you see, Mrs Teasdale. That will have fooled him. Sit down, Mrs Teasdale, have one of these.

Celia This is the first hotel I have been in where the meals are compulsory. (*She takes a sandwich*) This is going to cost us a fortune, isn't it?

Lionel That's OK, Mrs Teasdale. I'll fix it so that it's on somebody else's bill, don't worry.

Celia Somebody else? They can't pay for my tea. Teas.

Lionel Some of these old folk staying here, Mrs Teasdale, money to burn, money to burn. (*He pours her some tea*) There we are, madam.

Celia I don't know why we're the only ones out here anyway.

Lionel Most of them prefer it in the lounge so they can hear the music, you see.

Celia Yes, that's why we came out here.

Lionel Yes, it's not quite Sibelius, is it, Mrs Teasdale? Now I haven't much time. . . .

Celia No, neither have I.

Lionel But you must listen. Listen to me now, Celia. The fact is, I love you.

Celia (*impatiently*) Yes, we know all this, Lionel. The truth is we——

Lionel Please, please, please. (*Then more quietly*) I love you. I love you to a degree I never thought possible. I need you and I want you and I mean to have you. I love your voice. I love your eyes. I love your hair. I love your body. I love your hands and feet. I love all of you. I dream of you, Celia. I wake up and I am hurting because I'm thinking of you so hard. It's a pain when I'm not with you. Nobody should be in that sort of pain, nobody. Not for love. So I am asking you please. Please. Because I'm not going to stop following you ever. You're more than just important. You're everything. You're the north, south, east and west of my life. You're just—the universe, Mrs Teasdale. (*He stops, breathless, staring at her*)

Celia, who has heard nothing like this in her life for some considerable time, if ever, is deeply moved

Celia Oh, Lionel. (*After a pause*) Oh, dear Lionel. Nobody's ever said anything as beautiful as that to me, ever. (*After a pause*) I don't know what to say. I just don't know—what—to say.

Lionel You say: yes, Lionel. Yes, please.

Celia No, it really isn't as simple as that. It isn't. I wish it was. I'd love to be your universe, I really would.

Lionel All you have to say is yes, that's all.

Celia That's not all. I have a husband, Lionel. I've got children.

Lionel Husband. He doesn't love you. I've watched him. He doesn't love you. He doesn't care about you at all.

Celia Well, he does, Lionel. I think he does. . . . He just doesn't make a great show of it.

Lionel If I were married to you, whenever you stepped through that front door every morning, every evening—I'd be there to kiss your feet.

Celia Yes, well, that's not awfully practical, Lionel, not when you're married.

Lionel He doesn't love you. You tell me honestly that he loves you.

Celia Well, he——

Lionel Honestly. Can you swear that he loves you?

Celia (*after a slight pause*) No. Not now. I don't know that he does.

Lionel Right. Have a sandwich.

Celia (*taking one*) Thank you. (*After a pause*) What about the children? I've got two children. I couldn't abandon them.

Lionel We can look after them.

Celia Lionel, they're terribly expensive. They're worse than a car. They need paying for endlessly. I mean, even if I worked, we'd need to——

Lionel We could. We could do it.

Celia You mean, you'd honestly take on two children that weren't even yours?

Lionel I could cope. I'm good with kids.

Celia You're mad.

Lionel Simple. (*He moves away*) I better clear this table. (*Loudly*) Yes, we had a little rain earlier in the week, madam, but we've been very lucky these last couple of days. (*He begins to clear the table*)

Celia (*softly*) It's ridiculous, Lionel. You can't.

Lionel (*loudly*) Is that a fact, madam, I didn't realize that.

Celia (*softly*) No, really, we couldn't. (*She laughs*)

Lionel (*loudly*) Oh, that's very good, madam, I hadn't heard that one.

Celia (*softly*) You know, nobody's ever said—ever. Not to me.

Lionel (*loudly*) Is that a fact?

Celia (*softly*) I'll say one thing, it's awfully nice to feel wanted.

Lionel (*loudly*) Yes, you want to look at the Aquarium, madam, when you've got a minute.

Celia Oh, dear God, I don't know what I'm doing any more.

Lionel (*loudly*) Then there's the Botanical Gardens.

Celia I've a husband down there with a heart condition, Lionel.

Lionel (*loudly*) I should take him to see the dolphins, madam.

Celia And I'm walking out on him.

Lionel (*loudly*) And you'll have a great time.

Celia Mind you, he'll probably outlive us all. Do you know, I'm suddenly feeling terribly happy. Most peculiar. I'm probably getting hysterical. You may have to slap me, Lionel.

Lionel I couldn't do that, Mrs Teasdale. Not to a guest.

Celia I'm just terrifically excited. It's all so—dangerous.

Lionel I might get away with kissing you, if you like.

Celia No, I don't think you would, Lionel. We mustn't start that. Not here. Not in front of an invited audience.

Lionel (*gazing through the windows*) Oh, them. Never mind them. Would you have another one of these, then?

Celia (*taking a sandwich*) Lord, I suppose so. How did you know we'd be staying here?

Lionel I found out.

Celia How?

Lionel Sylvie told me.

Celia Sylvie? Is she still talking to you?

Lionel There was nothing promised there. There never was. Only what she invented. She'll be all right. She'll find someone her level. She's a very shallow person. Stood next to you, Celia.

Celia Well, she's much younger. She's quite a little bit younger.

Lionel I don't think she'll ever get much older either. She's a narrow girl with narrow ideas who wants a narrow life. Which she'll no doubt get. But not from me.

Celia Poor Sylvie.

Lionel Would you mind finishing that sandwich, Mrs Teasdale.

Celia Lionel, I'm bursting.

Lionel Just one or two more.

Celia Look, I think I'll have to put some in my bag.

Lionel And if you could manage a swig of tea as well, I'd be grateful.

Lionel goes in

Celia Well, I'm certainly not pouring that in my bag. (*She loads several sandwiches into her handbag. As she is doing so, she is aware of being watched from the windows. She nods and smiles at the windows*) That's right. I keep a big brown rat in here. He gets very hungry. (*She mutters*) Nosey old bitch. (*She gets up and moves to the wall, looking out for Toby*) No. No sign of him, thank God.

Lionel comes out from the hotel with another tray

Lionel (*loudly*) Would you like to take a seat over here, madam? There's just one table spare over here.

Celia Oh, no.

Lionel It's all right. He doesn't suspect. He just congratulated me. We've never done such a good trade on the terrace. He's very pleased, Mr Hobjay.

Celia Well, hooray for Mr Hobjay.

Lionel Please, Mrs Teasdale. You wouldn't want to get me fired. Not if I've got the kids to support.

Celia Now, look.

Lionel Please, just sit here, would you? And try looking like somebody else.

Celia Well, I'll sit down but I'm sorry, Lionel, I physically can't drink any more. I can actually hear it sloshing around inside me.

Lionel I'm sorry, Celia. It'll only be a mintue or two longer. Just while we arrange our plans. (*He pours her some tea*) There you are, madam. Nice cup of tea. Bet you're just about ready for that. (*Softly*) Sorry, Mrs Teasdale. They enourage us to chat with the guests. Gives it a family feeling.

Celia It appears to be full of grandparents.

Lionel (*serving her sandwiches*) Couple of these, madam?

Celia It's quite bizarre. This is presumably the most romantic few moments I'm ever going to have in my life and I'm feeling faintly sick. Well, what plans have you got then? What are our plans? Are we going ahead with the bakery?

Lionel Bakery?

Celia Yes, we did discuss it once, didn't we? You were hoping to buy the old bakery.

Lionel Well, I've been inquiring around a bit and I'm not so sure the demand's there.

Celia You aren't?

Lionel No. You see, your old style traditional master baker, I'm afraid he's a dying breed.

Celia I see.

Lionel I was really meaning more short-term plans, Mrs Teasdale. Like when can you get away from him?

Celia Yes, well. (*She swallows*) Excuse me.

Lionel Drink some tea. I mean, how about tonight?

Celia Yes, well, if you don't mind, I would like to look a little further ahead than that. Say a month or so. I mean, how has the bottom suddenly dropped out of baking? A few weeks ago it seemed to be the "in" thing.

Lionel Ah, well.

Celia Anything's got to be better than this bread. You are a master baker, aren't you? You weren't making that up?

Lionel No, definitely. I mean, I could work anywhere. I could go around the world if I wanted to with just my hands and a piece of dough. That's the great thing about baking, you see, it's an international language. Bread knows no barriers. Bake anywhere. India, Outer Mongolia. Anywhere there's an oven.

Celia Yes. Well, let's start with the Home Counties.

Lionel Just the same, just the same. Only I don't think there's much call for it, that's my feeling.

Celia I see. Well.

Lionel I've still got plans though, don't you worry. I've still got plans.

Celia Well, what are they? Would you mind telling me. I mean, I've just agreed to throw in my lot with you, Lionel, so perhaps we could share the future together.

Lionel Well. There's a possible vague, quite vague but possible chance of ironmongery.

Celia Ironmongery?

Lionel Yes, that's the new one.

Celia Are you an ironmonger as well?

Lionel Well, let's put it this way. I'm familiar with ironmongery. I know the skills. I'm not foreign to the skills. My uncle was in the trade for a long time. And he passed it on to me before he died.

Celia Did he?

Lionel It's a verbal tradition, you see. Most of the trades are. One ironmonger passes it on to the next. (*After a pause*) Yes.

Celia (*doubtfully*) Yes.

Lionel You don't sound too keen on that.

Celia Well, possibly.

Lionel And then I had a thought. What about a greengrocer's?

Celia Yes, now that's an idea.

Lionel Now you always need a greengrocer's, don't you? That's the good thing about them. No matter what you eat, you need a greengrocer's. (*He passes Celia a sandwich*)

Celia Yes, yes. (*She accepts a sandwich from him*) Thank you.

Lionel But the snag there is that we've got two already in the village. So maybe the market's a bit full. And that's a pity because I do know quite a lot about greengrocery.

Celia Lionel, have you any plans at all?

Lionel Yes.

Celia What?

Lionel It'd take too long, Mrs Teasdale. (*He moves away from her*) I'd better clear these away. (*He starts to stack up the plates at the other table*)

Celia You haven't the first idea about anything, have you?

Lionel I have. I've got plans this high, Mrs Teasdale.

Celia All right, then. Where are we all going to live? What about a house? Supposing my husband chucks me out which he's quite liable to do, where are we all going to live?

Lionel There's my place.

Celia Oh.

Lionel It's a bit small, mind you.

Celia Is it?

Lionel My father's there, you see. Him and his wheelchair.

Celia Yes.

Lionel He's a wonderful old man, you know. He taught me all I know.

Celia Did he?

Lionel He's a poet.

Celia Yes, the point is there's no room.

Lionel Not really, that's what I'm saying.

Celia So. We'll have to find somewhere. I'm not complaining. I just want to know what the position is.

Lionel I was thinking. The other thing, you know, that did occur to me is of possibly becoming an estate agent. Then we'd be more or less guaranteed a house.

Celia Yes?

Lionel I mean, all you have to do basically, and I know a little about this, is you open up your office, you see, and you sit there and you wait for someone to come in who wants to sell. Then you add a bit to what he's asking, stick it on your board and pocket the profit. That's estate agency.

Celia I think that's the broad principle, Lionel.

Lionel There's plenty open to me. I'm not depressed.

Celia Good.

Lionel It's just the choice really. It's all at my feet. I mean, I've got qualifications. I've got my City and Guilds. And my certificates. I'm fully documented. In fact, I found it doesn't pay to wave them around too much because there's such a thing as being over-qualified, did you know that? That was certainly the case with the Air Force.

Celia The Air Force.

Lionel Yes. I went and did myself out of a job as a pilot a couple of years ago waving my certificates about. They said you can do better than this, son. Kicked me out.

Celia Did they?

Lionel Same with the Police Force. Same old story.

Celia Really.

Pause

Lionel That and the helmet.

Celia Helmet?

Lionel Yes. I've got a special skull, you see. The weight of the helmet would have pressed down on it.

Celia Oh, I see.

Lionel Given me my headaches. Can't stand those.

Celia Do you—do you get a lot of headaches, Lionel?

Lionel Not really. A couple of times a week sometimes. I just lie down for a bit. They wear off. I could always stop in the hotel trade, I suppose.

Celia Yes, maybe you should.

Lionel I have a feeling that they've got their eye on me for something bigger here.

Celia Do you?

Lionel I get that feeling. Nothing specific, you know. I just catch them now and again. Looking at me, you know. Weighing me up. I mean, you don't rush into making someone manager, do you? Not without observing them for a bit. You know, Mrs Teasdale, I feel like—like Goliath, you know. All my options open, you by my side. I knew this was going to be the day, Mrs Teasdale. I just knew it. I feel—God, I feel like I just got a cup winner's medal, you know.

Celia Lovely.

Lionel What's the matter then?

Slight pause

Celia (*with difficulty*) It really isn't going to work, is it, Lionel?

Lionel How do you mean?

Celia I think—I think the sort of woman you need—

Lionel —is you.

Celia No. Is someone uncluttered. Able to face things with you without—
slowing you down. I'm a born worrier, Lionel, you see. I can't get as
excited as I know I should be getting about—not knowing what's going to
happen tomorrow. I have to know, you see, roughly what I'm going to be
doing at this time tomorrow. Maybe it's age. Maybe it's the children, I
don't know. I think I'm looking for a little excitement possibly but I don't
think I could face an adventure.

Lionel No, that's good. That's good. I think you're right. You ought to
know. You need to know. A woman particularly needs to know.

Celia No, I don't think it's women particularly. Just me. My friend, Mrs
Coombes, for instance—she'd join you at the drop of a hat. My father
was a chemist, he had to be rather careful. I think I'm part of that
particular verbal tradition.

Lionel I could be a chemist. There's not a lot to that.

Celia No, I'm sorry. That is something I do know something about. You
have to be very highly qualified to be a chemist. Very highly qualified
indeed.

Lionel I'm not saying you don't need to be qualified but with all my "A"
Levels, surely. . . . (*He picks up the plate of cakes and hands it to Celia*)
Would you mind?

Celia (*gloomily taking one*) No.

Lionel I take it you'd like a bit of security then?

Celia Yes.

Lionel Right. I'll set that in motion. I'll get that organized right away. (*He
moves to the door with the tray*) Whoops. I can see he's looking round for
me. Mr Hobjay.

Celia You'd better go.

Lionel Er—will you be telling him before this evening? Your husband.

Celia I don't think so, Lionel. No.

Lionel Well, I'll be standing by. I'll keep an eye on you. Give me the nod.
Only it's my day off tomorrow. We could have had a look round at some
properties. (*He backs through the door*) Farm's a possibility. We could
possibly start farming.

Celia Yes.

Lionel That'd be nice for the kids.

Celia Yes.

Lionel Well, enjoy your tea.

Celia Thank you.

Lionel goes into the hotel

*Celia sits for a moment. She starts to cry to herself. She is deeply unhappy and
disappointed, and angry with herself for being either of these. Halfway through
a sob, she hiccups*

Oh, God. All I need are hiccups. (*She sits with her hands in the air, her
thumbs and little fingers of each hand pressed together in an attempt at a
hiccup cure. In between spasms, she continues crying softly*)

In a moment, Toby returns

Toby stops and stares at Celia, hiccupping and weeping and sat, so far as he is concerned at yet another table full of food

Hallo.

Toby Hallo. (*He looks at the other tables and back at her but decides, in view of her present state, not to comment*) Well, that was a walk and a half. Well, more of a half really. The promenade they have here stretches for all of a hundred and fifty yards. Breathtaking. And it's well worth the walk. Once you get to the other end, they've created one of the most striking examples of twentieth-century redbrick toilet building I've ever set eyes on. It's worth picking your way through the rubbish just to look at it.

Celia hiccups

Well, you've obviously been hard at it in my absence. You've left a few cakes here. Have you noticed? Or are you just getting your fourth wind?

Celia hiccups

Fifth wind. Well, what else can I tell you about my walk. Nobody's hat blew off, I'm afraid. Very little excitement. Look, we've always had a rather separate—a rather arm's-length relationship, haven't we?

Celia hiccups

Yes. And that seems to have suited us both quite well, in the main. You've always chosen to undress in the bathroom and I've always cut my toenails privately and that's perfectly acceptable.

Celia hiccups

I'm glad you agree. But it does occur to me, without in any way wanting to shatter that reassuring, sliding glass patio door we have between us, that you appear to be in a bit of a state. Is there anything I can do to help you? Anything at all? That doesn't entail going upstairs again. (*After a pause*) Can I help you out with some of the cakes?

Celia hiccups

No, thank heaven for that.

Celia sniffs

Handkerchief. That I can do for you. Just a tick. (*He opens her handbag, takes out her handkerchief and hands it to her*)

Celia (*taking it from him*) Thank you.

Toby Your bag is full of sandwiches, did you know?

Celia nods

Toby Oh, you do. Afters, are they?

Celia (*suddenly*) Dear God, what a stupid ass of a woman I am. Honestly. (*She hiccups, then says furiously*) Bloody hiccups, go away.

Toby I could go and get our room key, if you like. Drop it down your neck.

Celia hiccups

I think the thing is, you just change tables too much. Confused your stomach.

Celia Toby, I have to tell you, there's no point in trying to hide it. The point is I've just met——(*She hiccups*)

Toby Who?

Celia Lionel.

Toby Lionel who?

Celia Lionel—(*She hiccups*)

Toby God, this is an appallingly difficult conversation. It's like chatting to the Dead Sea Scrolls.

Celia (*in a rush*) I've just met Lionel Hepplewick. He followed us here somehow, he found out where we were staying and he's working here as a waiter.

Silence

EITHER he says:

Toby And that's the cause of all this, is it?

Celia Yes.

Toby Lionel Hepplewick.

Celia Yes.

Toby Would you mind telling me what's been happening?

Celia He—I—oh, it's too complicated. (*She hiccups*)

Toby Right. You say he's working here as a waiter?

Celia Yes, now, Toby, please don't——

Toby (*rising*) Just a minute.

Celia I didn't want to tell you in case you—

Toby I'll be back. (*He moves off towards the hotel*)

Celia Where are you going?

Toby I'm going to find the manager of this place. I'm going to inform him that he has a lunatic on his staff masquerading as a waiter who has been intimidating my wife and reducing her to a hiccupping ruin.

Celia Please don't do anything—(*She hiccups*)

Toby I'm also asking for compensation. And if that doesn't work——(*He turns round to the hotel window*) What are you all staring at? Mind your own bloody business, you bunch of withered old wombats. And if that doesn't work, I'm going to personally poison him with one of his own revolting cream teas.

Toby goes off

(*Off*) And stop that God-awful din.

The piano stops playing for the first time

Celia (*half following him*) Toby, do be careful. Toby. (*She starts after him but, unable to face going through the lounge without at least checking her appearance, returns for her bag. She opens it and reaches for her mirror. She reaches in again for a tissue but produces instead a handful of sandwiches. She dabs her nose with these before she realizes what they are*) Oh. (*Irritably, she dumps them on the table. She produces some tissues and checks her face*) Oh, look at me, look at me. (*She straightens her hair and dabs at her face with a tissue*) He mustn't get into these states, he really mustn't. (*Satisfied at last, she moves to the door to hurry after Toby*)

Lionel comes running out

Lionel Excuse me, Mrs Teasdale, your husband's just had a bit of a collapse.
Celia Oh, no.
Lionel He's all right, he's all right.
Celia He's all right?
Lionel Yes. It's just he came running through there. I wasn't expecting him and he caught sight of me, you see, and he sort of went peculiar. He tried to pick up Mr Hobjay's trolley. He's all right though. He seems OK.
Celia Oh, no.

Celia goes in to the hotel

Lionel (*calling after her*) I had a quick look myself. I've had a little medical training as it happens. I'll wait to hear from you then, Mrs Teasdale. I'll wait to hear. (*He moves away towards her table to clear it*) Yes. I'll wait to hear. (*Cheerfully, he pops a sandwich into his mouth*) I can wait, Mrs Teasdale. I can wait.

Lionel starts to clear the table

The Lights fade to a Black-out

To: A FUNERAL (page 95)

OR he says:

Toby And that's the cause of all this, is it?
Celia Yes.
Toby Lionel Hepplewick.
Celia Yes.
Toby I see.

Silence. Celia hiccups

Well, I told you he was mad.
Celia You were right. I never realized. (*Slight pause*) You're being very calm.
Toby Am I?

Celia Yes, that's good. You mustn't get excited. That's the main—(*She hiccups*)

Toby I have to tell you that I'm fairly excited inside. Inside I'm greatly tempted to go in there and beat him senseless. Very luckily for him I have the wrong shoes on.

Celia Toby, I am sorry. I'm as much to blame as he was. I have to admit it, I did encourage him a little. (*She hiccups*)

Toby Celia, I'm prepared to forgive you practically anything. . . .

Celia You are?

Toby If only you'll promise to stop hiccupping.

Celia I'm trying. I can't help them.

Toby Anyway, I don't think we want to start blaming each other. If you encouraged him, it was probably because I did very little to encourage you not to. I'll try and be a bit more understanding. I promise.

Celia Thank you. (*She hiccups*)

Toby It's just it's difficult—(*He screams at her*)—STOP IT!

Celia jumps in her seat with shock

(*Calmly*) That done the trick?

Celia Yes, I think it has. Thank you.

Toby To break a lifetime habit, though.

Celia Yes, it has. Done the trick.

Toby I've never really understood you, Celia. It's going to be extremely hard to start now. But I'll have a go. Are you going to plough on with this Tea Festival of yours or have you finished?

Celia I've had quite enough, thank you.

Toby Hooray. Right. (*He rises*) Coming in then? I'll need you to carry me upstairs.

Celia (*picking up her handbag*) Just a minute. I can't go in there looking like this.

Toby I don't know why not. I'm going in there looking like this.

Celia Yes, but you always look like that. Go on, I won't be a minute.

Toby I'll get the room key. Just don't order any more tea.

Celia No.

Toby goes in

Celia opens her bag and reaches for her mirror. She reaches in again for a tissue but produces instead a handful of sandwiches. She dabs her nose with these before she realizes what they are

Oh. (*Irritably, she dumps them on the table. She produces some tissues*) Oh, look at me, look at me. (*She straightens her hair and stabs at her face with a tissue*) Stupid woman. (*She moves to go in to the hotel*)

Lionel passes her, coming out on to the terrace with an empty tray

Lionel Have you finished, Mrs Teasdale?

Celia (*alarmed*) Lionel, he didn't see you?

Lionel No. I hid behind the trolley. Mr Hobjay's trolley.

Celia Good.

Lionel I bet you never had a tea like that before, Mrs Teasdale.

Celia No, never.

Lionel (*confidentially*) It's all right. I'm spreading the cost round. Nobody'll notice. I'm very good with figures. That's another possibility. Accountancy.

Celia Yes.

Lionel Have you told him yet?

Celia No. Not yet. Lionel, it may be some time. Some considerable time.

Lionel Right. Right.

Celia No, I mean, ages, Lionel. Literally ages and ages. All right?

Lionel Right.

Celia You do understand?

Lionel I do.

Celia Well, I hope you do. (*As she goes*) Ages.

Celia goes inside

Lionel (*cheerfully*) Right. (*He moves away and starts to clear the tea-table*) I can wait, Mrs Teasdale. I can wait.

The Lights fade to a Black-out

To: A SERVICE OF THANKSGIVING (page 99)

A FUNERAL

A Churchyard. This year

The church door is closed. A gravel path leads away from it to an unseen road. A variety of gravestones border the path

We hear a church bell signifying a funeral and, in the silence that follows, only a few rooks from the vicarage trees

After a short pause, Celia, dressed in black, comes round the side of the church. She stands alone for a minute, thoughtful and silent

Shortly after, Miles, a rather sad-looking man of about the same age as Celia, comes anxiously after her. He is also dressed in black. Seeing Celia, he stops and respectfully waits for her to finish her sojourn. After a while, he realizes she is not going to and decides to speak

Miles Celia . . . Celia . . .

Celia Oh, Miles. I'm sorry. I was just thinking.

Miles I didn't mean to disturb you. I—it's just that Rowena's taking all the kids, your lot as well as ours, back round to our place. If that's OK. We'll bring them home later.

Celia Oh, that's lovely. Thank you.

Miles Give you a bit of time to yourself, anyway. I'll—er—be sitting in the car. I'm ready to run you home whenever you want.

Celia No, it's all right. You don't have to wait. I'm coming in a moment.

Miles It's entirely up to you, Celia. Really, you take as long as you like.

Celia Miles, you're being so kind, both of you.

Miles Well. (*He shrugs*)

Celia Toby was your best friend. You'd known him longer than I had. You must be just as upset as I am.

Miles Yes. Still I wasn't married to him, was I?

Celia No, you weren't. (*After a slight pause*) I suppose you were quite fortunate in that respect.

Miles (*laughing rather awkwardly*) Yes.

Celia Oh, I suppose I shouldn't say that. But it really was hell, Miles, some of it. Especially these last few years. Him being virtually an invalid. No school for him to go to. Nothing to occupy him. Not even able to drink. I used to hate it when he got drunk but he was even worse sober all the time. I suppose he needed someone who would stand up to him more. I never stood up to him, Miles. I just let him stand on me. It was as if every time he needed a soap box, he stood on me.

Miles Yes, I suppose he did tend to do that a bit to people. We were thinking, that is the School Governors, we had a meeting and we were thinking it might be rather nice to put up a small plaque for him somewhere. Bronze, you know. We thought the cricket pavilion might be a good place. He was pretty keen.

Celia How nice. That's lovely.

Miles What are—what are your plans now, Celia? Have you had time to think about them yet?

Celia Well, I've had masses of time really. I mean, one was sort of prepared. One suspected this might happen. I suppose if he'd controlled his temper, he'd probably be alive today. Then you couldn't keep everything away from Toby that might have caused him to get angry.

Miles Hardly.

Celia I do blame myself, though, a little for this last time.

Miles Oh, come on.

Celia Yes, I do. I knew Dr Burgess was on holiday and I usually made special arrangements to ensure that dear old Bill Windsor didn't come round while he was away because if there was one thing guaranteed to make Toby lose his temper it was the sight of Bill Windsor scattering his medical equipment all over the floor.

Miles Yes, he's a very nervous man, isn't he, Bill? A good doctor but a bit jumpy. I mean, when I'm ill, I always find myself reassuring him. Promising him I'll get better and he's not to worry. I suppose it's quite a good technique of his really.

Celia Not for Toby. He actually got up and tried to throttle him.

Miles Oh, dear. Ah, well. So what will you do?

Celia Me? I'll go back to work, I think. I'd like to. I've been an unpaid nurse for five years. I might as well do something now and get paid for it.

Miles Quite.

Celia I'm not getting married again, I tell you that.

Miles Very sensible. Have an affair.

Celia No, no. I don't think I'll even do that. At least, nothing serious. I'm entering now what I sincerely hope will be the second half of my life. For this bit, I think I'd just like to concentrate on being me. The past fifteen or twenty years I've always found myself serving as an extension of whoever I've been with. Toby mainly. I must say, over the years I served him very well.

Miles You did. You've got delightful kids and your house is——

Celia No, I meant more as his stooge, actually. I served him well as that. I mean, he got an awful lot of laughs at my expense over the years.

Miles Did he? I never noticed.

Celia Oh, Miles, come on. You know he did. You always laughed the loudest.

Miles Did I? I don't—I don't think I ever laughed at you, Celia.

Celia You did, you know. Whenever Toby asked you to. Don't worry. I don't think you realized you were doing it half the time. It became second nature. People tended to greet us like Stan and Ollie.

Miles Maybe. Maybe I laughed, but it wasn't *at* you, Celia.

Celia Well, it was.

Miles Yes, I suppose it was. Sorry. I suppose it was a case of "he laughed wisely but not well".

Celia Yes.

Miles Perhaps we should have put that on his headstone.

Celia Possibly.

Miles Oh, yes. I meant to ask. What does that mean? On his headstone. I think a lot of people were puzzled. The bit that's carved on it. I didn't understand it. About animals or something.

Celia No, it says: Toby—a husband who will be sadly missed by all baboons and dumb animals.

Miles Extraordinary. I mean, I didn't even know he liked animals.

Celia Oh, he liked them around.

Miles Did he?

Celia Especially dumb ones.

Miles Ah. I still don't think I understand it. Look, I'm going to be in the car. All right?

Celia I'll come in a moment.

Miles Take your time.

Miles exits

Celia Well, Toby, I'm going to have to make my own decisions, aren't I? Could be quite fun. For a change. I'll be able to cook ravioli which you never allowed me to have in the house and moussaka and play Sibelius and that other man, Carl Thing. There's a lot I'll miss and a lot I won't. Funny thing is, the thing I'll probably miss most is being called a stuffed puffin. Silly really. (*She turns to follow Miles*)

As Celia turns, from across the graveyard, Lionel appears. He is muddy, has obviously been working and still carries his spade

Lionel Mrs—Mrs Teasdale.

Celia Oh, dear God, Lionel.

Lionel Afternoon, Mrs Teasdale.

Celia What are you—Oh, I see what you're doing.

Lionel I'm just—I got a job working for the church, Mrs Teasdale. Just temporary. I'm just——

Celia Yes, I can see what you're doing, Lionel.

Lionel Your husband.

Celia Yes, Lionel, please.

Lionel Oh, I'm sorry. I'm sorry, Mrs Teasdale.

Celia I thought—I thought I heard you'd gone away, Lionel.

Lionel Yes, yes. I did, Mrs Teasdale. You see, after we talked that time and then your husband was ill, well, I sort of waited and then I waited for you and you didn't get in touch and I waited some more and then—er—then I wasn't very well. I had to be—er—I had to be—in hospital.

Celia Yes.

Lionel For a bit. But I'm out again now and I got this job as a way in, you see.

Celia A way in to what?

Lionel For taking the cloth. I'm thinking of being ordained.

Celia Oh.

Lionel But the point is this—before I say to the bishop and so on—because they're pretty keen to have me—they've been pushing me very hard to say yes. . . .

Celia Yes, I see.

Lionel I wanted to talk to you first. The thing is, would you fancy being a vicar's wife, Mrs Teasdale?

Celia Er——

Lionel You be honest now, Mrs Teasdale. Don't say yes just because of me. Not if you don't mean it. We'll do what you want.

Celia Well, no. I don't actually, Lionel. I don't think I really want to be a vicar's wife.

Lionel Fair enough, fair enough. I'll turn them down then. I'll tell them no. Fair enough.

Celia Yes, look, I must go now, Lionel.

Lionel (*loping after her*) You see what I'm planning to do, Mrs Teasdale— this is appreciating your need for security—what I'm going to do is I'm not going to trouble you unnecessarily but whenever I'm offered a new job, like, or just before I take one, I'll just come round and check with you. See if it's something that interests you. And if it is, if it is, then we can go ahead. And if not, well then I'll just keep looking, that's all.

Celia (*backing away from him*) Good. Good.

Lionel We'll find something, don't worry. So long as you can wait, Mrs Teasdale. So long as you don't mind waiting.

Celia No, I can wait, thank you, Lionel. Goodbye.

Celia hurries away behind the church

Lionel Goodbye, Mrs Teasdale. (*He watches her move away. He turns, smiling, satisfied*) Any day now. Any day now.

Lionel goes back to his grave

The Lights fade to a Black-out

A SERVICE OF THANKSGIVING

A Churchyard. This year

The church door is closed. A gravel path leads away from it to an unseen road. A variety of gravestones border the path

We hear church bells signifying a happy occasion, followed by the sound of singing within the church. A Service of Thanksgiving for Bilbury Lodge's fifty year's existence is being celebrated

The church door opens and Toby comes out. He stands in the churchyard taking a few deep breaths. The service continues behind him

In a second or so, Celia follows him out, closing the door behind her. They are both dressed for the rather formal festive occasion

Celia You all right?

Toby Of course I am.

Celia You suddenly got up and went out.

Toby I just felt like some air, that's all.

Celia You felt peculiar again, didn't you? Admit it. You felt ill.

Toby Celia, I have not felt ill in five years. Now stop fussing round me, woman.

Celia You felt dizzy.

Toby Dizzy is not ill. Dizzy is dizzy which is something totally different. One might describe you as dizzy. But I don't think you're ill. I wanted to come out. I got up very discreetly in the midst of that appalling cacophony and crept out.

Celia You cannot creep out if you're Headmaster. The whole school saw you. Everyone turning round wondering where you were going. I thought you must be seriously ill.

Toby Well, I'm not. So stop standing there lke a piebald parakeet and go back in again.

Celia All right. (*She lingers at the door*) It's quite a nice service, Toby, it really is.

Toby It's all right.

Celia It's quite touching. Fifty years of the school. Since it was founded. Not bad.

Toby Not bad.

Celia And there are three ex-headmasters there. Isn't that lovely?

Toby That's not so good. Looking at that trio lined up there, you wonder how the hell the place lasted fifty years.

Celia They're all charming men. Great characters.

Toby I wouldn't trust any of them to park my car. Pasty, wishy-washy pastel Liberals to a man.

Celia Balanced men. I prefer to call them balanced.

Toby What the hell is the point of having a balanced man as a teacher? The whole point of education, surely, is to teach children a few prejudices. Like not liking dishonesty or people who cheat you. Or people who use force for the sake of it. Those three are so bloody busy understanding everyone they wouldn't recognize good from evil if it came up and hit them in the face like a garden rake.

Celia Toby, we are in church.

Toby We are not in a church. We are in a churchyard. Standing among a lot of dead people. None of whom can hear me. But if they could hear me, they would all stand up and agree with me. Because most of them are down there because of people like those three in there.

Celia I'm going back in. I'm not going to bother arguing with you.

Toby You? You wouldn't know how to argue with me.

Celia Well, I might just surprise you one day.

Toby You might. I doubt it. Parrots don't argue. They just repeat themselves.

Celia You have such contempt for me these days, haven't you? It's just sheer contempt. Maybe you've always had it. I don't know. But now you don't even bother to hide it. You think I'm a fool. You think I'm just a comic turn, someone you can use for your stupid jokes and sarcastic remarks and whenever you want to show off. You're so busy scoring off me, belittling me, making me look that high in front of people, well, I'm sick and tired of it, Toby. I'm just sick to death of it and I'm not having it.

Toby (*soothingly*) All right, quietly, quietly, quietly.

Celia No, not quietly, Toby. To hell with you. I'm very sorry this is a churchyard but to hell with you. You can make your stupid, bigotted cruel jokes on someone else. I'm finished. That's it. Finished. Goodbye.

Celia walks off down the path

Toby (*with more amusement than alarm*) Celia. Celia. (*He shrugs*) Oh, she'll be back.

Toby opens the church door and goes inside

Celia appears again and watches it close. She begins to walk about the churchyard agitatedly

Celia I'm not going back. I'm not going back this time, I'm really not. Every time he—talks me round or he's ill or something. . . . Well, this time . . . this time—it'll be different. Wait and see. The next time somebody asks me to run away with them, I won't be so loyal. I'll go. Like a shot. I'll go and start a bakery. Or an ironmonger's or whatever. See how you cope on your own. (*She stops and lights a cigarette*) And I smoke far too many of these. It's all his fault.

As she stands there smoking, from the direction of the road, Lionel appears. He is smartly dressed in a suit

Lionel Mrs Teasdale?

Celia (*startled, turning*) Er—hallo.

Lionel It's Lionel, Mrs Teasdale. Lionel Hepplewick.

Celia Lio—Lionel? So it is. I didn't recognize you.

Lionel Well, I—it's been a long time.

Celia Yes. Five years.

Lionel Right. I meant to arrive for the service, only the traffic's very bad.

Celia Oh, was it? Have you had to come far?

Lionel North London.

Celia Oh, I see.

Lionel I didn't want to miss the service because—well, I still feel a little bit part of the school somehow. And, of course, for my dad. He was ten, fifteen years, of course.

Celia Yes, indeed he was. I'm sorry, he . . .

Lionel Yes. For the best though. (*He points*) Buried just over there.

Celia Yes. (*After a slight pause*) So obviously a lot's been happening to you.

Lionel Quite a bit.

Celia It looks as if you're doing quite well.

Lionel Yes, yes, can't complain. I—well—after I last saw you, that time at the hotel, I think you made me realize, Mrs Teasdale, that I needed to do some thinking. About myself.

Celia Yes.

Lionel Half of me wanted to carry on hoping you'd, you know, change your mind. But—but I saw you and your husband were a lot closer really than I thought you were. It's very easy to read things into people's relationships, isn't it, if you're on the outside. Specially if you want those things to be there. But, of course, it wasn't like that. You were both perfectly happy. No way were you going to leave him for me. Why should you? You know, when he had the heart thing, Mrs Teasdale, I wanted him to die. Isn't that terrible? I really wanted him to.

Celia Well, he's very much alive.

Lionel I'm glad for you. So anyway, I met this—other fellow who was a waiter with me at the hotel and he suggested we set up this taxi firm together because he knew we could grab the hotel trade, you see. So we got this car between us, got a licence and off we went. Drove it twenty-four hours a day between us. Couple of years, we had three or four people and then we started a van. Little bit of moving here, little bit of moving there, you know. Got a few more vans. Now we're in rental. Just this year. Got a couple of dozen of them. We keep growing.

Celia Heavens.

Lionel Moves fast, my partner.

Celia I'm—well, I'm very impressed.

Lionel I'm really glad to see you, Mrs Teasdale.

Celia (*smiling*) I'm pleased to see you, Lionel.

Lionel You haven't changed.

Celia You have.

Lionel (*smiling*) I should hope so. (*He remembers something*) Oh, I did bring you something—(*He reaches in the inside pocket of his suit*) I suddenly saw this. And I thought, who'd like this? Here. (*He hands her a small paper bag*)

Celia takes it. She looks inside

It's a cassette.

Celia Oh, thank you. Thank you.

Lionel Hope you've got something to play it on.

Celia Er—yes. . . . Yes, I think I can get hold of something.

Lionel It's Symphony Number Four by Carl Nielsen. You remember?

Celia Oh, yes. Yes, I do.

Lionel He called it *The Inextinguishable*. Sort of reminded me of you, you know. Inextinguishable.

Celia Looks lovely. Thank you. (*She smiles at him*)

Lionel (*smiling back*) I'd have brought the wife down, only she's not feeling too well today.

Celia Wife?

Lionel Yes, she's seven months pregnant and she didn't feel like the journey.

Celia Oh, I see.

Lionel This'll be our second. We got one little girl. Cheryl Jean.

Celia Lovely.

Lionel I'd have driven them down for the ride but the car, you know. Makes her feel a bit sick when she's expecting.

Celia Oh.

Lionel She's very nice. I think you'd like her. She was an air stewardess. She was.

Celia Oh.

Lionel She's Norwegian.

Celia Ah.

Lionel I'll bring her down next time.

Celia Yes.

Lionel Have to keep an eye on her if I do. All the lads round here. I know what they're like with big tall blondes. Falling over themselves.

Celia Yes.

Lionel Well, I suppose I had better go in. Catch the end. I parked the car there. Be all right, will it?

Celia Yes. It should be. (*She strains to see*) Looks a nice car.

Lionel Yes. BMW. Nice, isn't it? New.

Celia Yes.

Lionel Are you coming in?

Celia In a moment. I'm just going to finish my cigarette.

Lionel Right. See you after perhaps.

Celia Right.

Lionel Good to meet you again, Mrs Teasdale.

Lionel goes into the church and closes the door behind him.

Celia stands for a moment, then throws down her cigarette and grinds it out

Celia (*looking at the cassette*) Oh dear. You stupid, stupid woman. . . . Oh, dear.

Celia goes back inside the church

The Lights fade to a Black-out

INTIMATE EXCHANGES is a related series of plays totalling eight scripts

This is the Third

A GARDEN FÊTE
preceded by *How It Began* (page 3)
and
A Gardener Calls (page 5)

CHARACTERS
APPEARING IN THIS SERIES OF SCENES

Celia
Lionel
Sylvie
Toby
Joe Hepplewick

THE SELF-IMPROVING WOMAN

The same. Five days later. The morning of Saturday, June 19th. It is sunny

Lionel is at work in the garden or to be more precise, in the garden shed which he is in the process of clearing out. He comes to and fro regularly, dumping rubbish he has found into a growing pile of old tins, boxes, bits of rope and broken garden tools. He works, as is his manner, slowly but consistently

In a moment Celia comes from the house. She is dressed smartly in a hat and coat

Lionel apparently does not see her

Celia (*watching Lionel*) I'm just going out then, Lionel.
Lionel (*straightening from his exertions*) Pardon?
Celia I said I'm just off out.
Lionel Right you are.
Celia Sylvie's here if anyone calls so don't worry about any bells.
Lionel Right, Mrs Teasdale.
Celia The children are round at their friends so they shouldn't bother you either. How are you getting on?
Lionel All right.
Celia Dreadful mess.
Lionel Yes.
Celia (*inspecting the shed*) Heavens, you are doing well. Jolly good.
Lionel 'K you.

Pause

Celia (*staring at the debris*) Yes, this is absolutely splendid. Well done.

Pause. They both stand there

　　Yes, jolly well done. (*She claps*)
Lionel Yep.
Celia Er—we're having a small dinner party tonight. ...
Lionel (*grateful for the invitation*) Oh, well now—that's——
Celia And we were rather hoping to have it out here so I wonder if you'd mind leaving it all nice and tidy.
Lionel Oh. Yes. Right, I will.
Celia I hope it'll stay fine. We always mean to eat out here and we never do. Well, I'm afraid I'm off to a dreary coffee morning.
Lionel You look very nice, Mrs Teasdale, if you don't mind my saying so.
Celia Thank you, Lionel. I don't mind you saying that at all. Thank you.
Lionel Nice to see a lady looking elegant.

Celia Well, fairly elegant anyway.

Lionel I think many women these days are a disgrace to themselves. They walk around as if they was ashamed of what they are. I like a woman who's not ashamed to be a woman and shows she is.

Celia (*a little taken aback by this long speech*) Yes. I suppose there are several ways you can show you're a woman.

Lionel Only one proper way in my view. You dress like one and you display your physiology with a pride.

Celia Yes. Well, I'd love to stay and talk to you about this but—whoops— (*She topples slightly as she turns to go in*)

Lionel (*springing forward*) Can you manage, Mrs Teasdale?

Celia Yes. These shoes. Not made for gardens like ours. If you want any tea, I'm sure Sylvie will make you some. Well, carry on. Jolly good. Splendid. Well done.

Celia goes indoors

Lionel stares after her in some admiration. After a moment, he continues his task. He brings more stuff from the shed including a woman's very old battered straw sun hat. Also an old football. Lionel throws down the sun hat and lays the football at his feet. He stares at it for a moment, a dreamlike gleam in his eye

Lionel (*softly*) . . . and the ball's across to Hepplewick and Hepplewick's past his man. He's passed a second. There's absolutely no stopping this golden boy and there goes the big right foot—(*He kicks the ball back into the shed*) And it's a goal. It has got to be the Goal of the Month. Lionel Hepplewick has done it again. Kiss, kiss. kiss. (*He hugs himself from all angles. He pauses, takes a cigarette from his jacket, lights it and sits on the debris, thoughtful*)

Sylvie comes out of the house. She's in the midst of more housework. She has a bag of rubbish for the dustbins

Sylvie Good to see someone's working.

Lionel I need a break.

Sylvie Oh, yes? She's gone out anyway.

Lionel I know.

Sylvie He was having another bout last night from all the signs, Mr Teasdale. Whole place stinks of whisky, empty bottles. He don't half put it away. Don't know how she puts up with it sometimes.

Lionel seems uninterested by this

What time you get home last night?

Lionel 'bout half three.

Sylvie My sister heard us, you know.

Lionel Hope she enjoyed it.

Sylvie I got all those snide remarks over breakfast.

Lionel What remarks?

Sylvie She kept saying things like, "Mum, is it true that only virgins can eat Grapenuts without crunching because if so, hark at Sylvie". If she tells my mum about us, I'll strangle her. I'll strangle her anyway. Sitting there trying to swallow Grapenuts, I was.

Lionel She won't tell, will she?

Sylvie You never know with her. (*After a slight pause*) It were good though, wasn't it? Be great when we got our own bed. Our own place. Won't have to worry then. (*Pause*) Really great, wasn't it? I thought it was great. (*Pause*) Did you think it was great?

Lionel It was great, yes.

Sylvie It was great for me. Was it great for you?

Lionel Yes, you weren't bad for a beginner.

Sylvie Beginner. Just because you're so old. Don't call me a beginner. (*She sits apart from him*) Look at all this junk, eh? It'll be great with a place of our own, won't it? We don't need anything very big. Just somewhere we can shut the door on ourselves. We could make it look nice whatever it was. Us two. Between us, couldn't we? I wouldn't want anywhere too big, anyway. I think people with big houses are unnecessary. That Colonel Malton, he's got a house with thirty-four rooms in it. He only lives in two of them. Mrs Hetherington told me. If we had children we might need a bit bigger but that wouldn't be straightaway. Be a year or two, I expect, wouldn't it? I mean, I wouldn't even mind one of those little houses on your estate. You know, one of the smaller ones at the back. By the railway. They're all right. They don't get the view but they got nice little gardens. Not much smaller than this. I think they'd be all right. They'd suit me. (*After a pause*) It were great last night, weren't it?

Lionel gets up

What are you thinking about then? All broody there.

Lionel I'm thinking you're a woman with a very narrow and limited viewpoint.

Sylvie What do you mean?

Lionel I mean, you're hardly what you call visionary, are you?

Sylvie What?

Lionel You've got as much drive and ambition as this bloody shed, haven't you?

Sylvie (*hurt*) Don't say that to me. No call for that. Why do you say that?

Lionel You're a small person, Sylvie. You think small, you dream small. People like that finish up small.

Sylvie I don't know why you're saying this all of a sudden.

Lionel Because. (*He goes into the shed*)

Sylvie What?

Lionel comes out of the shed

Lionel You really want to live and die on that estate, do you? The Greenfield Road Estate. You had a quick look at the rest of the world, did you? You've had a bit of a think, have you? After careful consideration, you've rejected Florida, Bermuda, the Greek Islands—no, thank you very much. What? When I can live on the Greenfield Road Estate. You must be joking.

Sylvie What are you talking about, Bermuda? How the hell are we going to live in Bermuda.

Lionel You get on a plane, that's all.

Sylvie You're barmy. You ought to come down out of the clouds, you.

Lionel I'll tell you one thing. You want to spend your life with me, you'd better start expanding your horizons.

Sylvie What are you talking about?

Lionel Think about it.

Lionel goes round the back of the shed

Sylvie Just because I'm practical. Responsible. I can't help being responsible. I was brought up responsible. Anyway it's a good thing to be responsible, people told me.

Lionel returns with a paving stone

Lionel And you'd better smarten yourself up and all.

Sylvie What now?

Lionel Get yourself straightened up.

Sylvie I can't, I'm working.

Lionel When you're not working, you can.

Sylvie I do, when I'm not, I do. I did last night. When we went out, I dressed up then. Didn't I? I did.

Lionel You call that dressed up? Like going out with a lime green skydiver. All you needed was a parachute and a crash helmet.

Sylvie You didn't look so good. That old suit looked like your grandad's.

Lionel No way. Less than a year old, that suit. Slap in fashion that suit.

Sylvie Didn't look it.

Lionel That's your ignorance. You look in Burton's window.

Slight pause

Sylvie That was new that outfit, too.

Lionel Bloody iced lolly with legs.

Sylvie Well, that's it. I'm not standing here listening to this. I'm off.

Lionel Suit yourself. Can't stand home truths, off you go.

Sylvie (*tearful*) I bought that specially. It wasn't lime green. It was applemint green. Applemint. It was the only one my size. I wanted pink. Why did you let me go out, then, if I looked so awful? I'm going in. I'm not standing here to be insulted. (*After a pause*) I'm off. (*After a pause*) Right.

Sylvie goes indoors

Lionel works on silently, apparently unaware of her departure

Sylvie returns slowly

Silence

Sylvie sniffs a bit and watches Lionel, waiting for him to notice her. He doesn't

(*At length*) If you knew so much about it, what should I have worn then?

You know so much about it, Lionel? (*Angrily and loudly*) Lionel, I'm talking to you.

Lionel (*calmly*) Sylvie, here a moment.

Sylvie (*suspiciously*) What?

Lionel Come on, come here. I'm not going to do anything to you. Come on.

Sylvie (*moving towards him cautiously*) What?

Lionel Sit down a minute.

Sylvie Why?

Lionel Sit down.

Sylvie Why should I?

Lionel (*moving away*) All right.

Sylvie (*hastily*) All right. (*She sits*) What?

Lionel Now listen. Don't say anything. Just for a moment, you listen. Are you listening? You've got to start to raise your own opinion of yourself, Sylvie. That way it's just possible you might raise other people's opinions of you.

Sylvie I——

Lionel Now wait, I haven't finished. Now who are the people you most admire? Is there anybody you most admire? Any woman particularly.

Sylvie (*striving to think*) Well …

Lionel Nobody at all? No woman you admire?

Sylvie Amy Johnson.

Lionel Amy Johnson?

Sylvie That aeroplane woman. I quite admired her.

Lionel Well, you dress like her. No, I was thinking of someone a little nearer to home, Sylvie.

Sylvie I don't know. Can't think of anyone.

Lionel What about Mrs Teasdale. Do you admire her?

Sylvie Well …

Lionel The way she looks. Do you like the way she looks?

Sylvie Oh, yes. She looks very nice. She can do.

Lionel Right. Now how do you suppose she gets to look as good as that? Because she takes trouble, Sylvie. She has a style. She has a dignity.

Sylvie She's got money.

Lionel That's not everything.

Sylvie It helps.

Lionel But it's not everything. Just stand up a minute.

Sylvie What?

Lionel Stand up, go on.

Sylvie stands

Now, would you say it took a lot of money to be able to stand up straight?

Sylvie To what?

Lionel To stand up straight. Does that cost a lot?

Sylvie 'Course it doesn't.

Lionel You don't need a private income?

Sylvie What are you talking about?

Lionel Then why the hell aren't you standing up straight, then?

Sylvie I am.
Lionel You're not. You're like an angle bracket. Here. (*He moves towards her*)

Sylvie flinches

Here, all right. I'm not going to hurt you. Now—(*He puts a hand either side of Sylvie's head*) I want you to imagine there's a string attached to the top of your head here that's suspending you. Know what I mean? You're just hanging from this string, all right?
Sylvie Ow!
Lionel (*lifting her gently by her head*) Come on, that's it. That's it.

Sylvie is now on tip-toe, her neck and body stretched

That's better.
Sylvie (*speaking with difficulty*) Feels peculiar.
Lionel It will do. You've never stood up properly before, have you?
Sylvie I can't stand like this.
Lionel Yes, you can.
Sylvie I can't see where I'm going. I feel like I've got my neck in plaster.
Lionel Now, you don't have to go stiff. Relax. Relax. Let your arms swing as you walk around. That's it. Walk around.

Sylvie walks around, her arms flapping wildly

That's it. That's it. (*He yells*) No, keep your head up.
Sylvie I keep walking into things.
Lionel Well, glance down. Glance down then. You don't have to peer at the ground like a gundog. You see the Queen on television, she isn't crawling around on her hands and knees, is she, looking for the red carpet?
Sylvie (*still walking with difficulty*) Is this what Mrs Teasdale looks like, then?
Lionel Not unlike. Not unlike. She's had a bit more practice, that's all. Good. Now you're beginning to look like a woman to be reckoned with.
Sylvie I feel like a tortoise on its hind legs.
Lionel (*snatching up the straw hat from the pile of rubbish*) Here, put that on.
Sylvie It's dirty.
Lionel Put it on.

Sylvie does so

No, not like that. (*He adjusts it to give it more of an appearance of Ascot*) There.
Sylvie That all right? How's that look?
Lionel Not bad.
Sylvie Feels daft. Are my arms supposed to hang in front of me or behind me?
Lionel They're not supposed to hang at all. Here. (*He picks up an empty paint tin and hands it to her*)
Sylvie What's this for?
Lionel That's your handbag.

Sylvie Oh, yes. Very nice. (*In a refined voice*) How do you do? I'm just going out shopping, Sylvie, to buy some more booze for my husband. He's going on a piss-up tonight.

Lionel Now, come on. You do it properly. How do you do?

Sylvie How do you do? I feel like that *My Fair Lady*.

Lionel She done all right, didn't she? How do you do, then.

Sylvie How do you do?

Lionel Look at me, look at me.

Sylvie I am.

Lionel No, you're not, you're looking at my feet. How do you do?

Sylvie How do you do. I prefer your feet.

Lionel That's better.

Sylvie Stupid.

Lionel Now, how do you do? My name is Sylvie Bell.

Sylvie How do you do? What a coincidence, so is mine. (*She stands on the patio declaring in a plummy voice*) It gives me great, great, great, great pleasure to open this instant coffee morning. I'm talking like this to you today because unfortunately I have run out of glue and I'm having to hold in my dentures with my tongue. On behalf of all the women here today with bugger all else to do with ourselves, may I thank you for coming and say it's for a very worthy cause. All proceeds will be used in order to restock my husband's drinks cabinet. I must dash now as I need to find a loo. Thank you.

Lionel (*in appreciation*) There you are. Great. That's your first lesson. That'll be five quid. (*He returns to moving his paving stones*)

Sylvie Great help that is. Get me thrown out of everywhere that will. Going around with that hat on and swinging a tin of paint. (*She tosses both these items back on the pile*) I must get on too.

Lionel But you understand what I meant, Sylvie.

Sylvie No.

Lionel Yes, you do. What I'm saying is, you're a beautiful woman and I'd very much like to see your face occasionally if you wouldn't mind tilting it up in my direction.

Sylvie All right.

Lionel And don't walk around like something out of Notre Dame.

Sylvie You're terrible you are, you know. You could destroy someone, you keep on like that. I'll never be able to wear my applemint now.

Lionel That's good news.

Sylvie I'll have to give them away now.

Lionel Good. (*After a pause*) Enjoy watching people working, do you?

Pause

Sylvie (*ignoring Lionel's comment*) You really think I'm beautiful?

Lionel When you put your mind to it.

Sylvie That's nice. (*She considers*) I don't think I am really. Not beautiful. I suppose you can seem beautiful to people. That's the important thing, isn't it? What you seem like to them. I mean, otherwise half the people in the world would never get together, would they? Because most people, let's face it, they're horrible looking. They are round our way. I suppose as long as I am beautiful to you, that's the important thing, isn't it? I wonder if I'm beautiful to anybody else? I wonder if I'm beautiful to Pete Bartlett? I hope not. He's horrible, he doesn't deserve it. I used to look at myself in the mirror when I was very young, you know, and if I shut my eyes just a bit, like that—(*she squints to demonstrate*)—I looked really good. I looked sort of misty like those black and white women in the late night movies. But then I opened my eyes wide again and I'd be all horrible and spotty. Mind you, I had bigger eyes. I either had very big eyes and spots or very small eyes and lovely. But I could never get it quite right. I suppose if you're really beautiful you can catch yourself by surprise. I suppose if I were to be given one wish, one wish that I knew would come true, I'd wish to be as beautiful as Betty Simcock.

Lionel Betty Simcock?

Sylvie I think she's lovely.

Lionel You're thinking small again. (*He finishes his current load*) Right, I'm off now.

Sylvie Don't you want tea?

Lionel I got to mow the second-eleven field now.

Sylvie I was supposed to make you some tea.

Lionel You just practise standing up straight, go on.

Sylvie All right, all right.

Lionel You think I'm barmy, don't you? You wait. You think I'm going to do this job all my life? Mow cricket pitches for over-privileged sons and daughters of the local nobs . . .

Sylvie My sister goes there.

Lionel She's scholarship, though. She doesn't count. I'm not wasting my life here much longer. I'm just waiting for the opportunity to pounce.

Sylvie Oh, yes.

Lionel Now, if you want to come along with me that's fine. But I want someone who's quick and fit in her head and ready to move at a moment's notice. I want a woman who's ready for a challenge, ready for the unknown. That's what I'm looking for.

Sylvie Are you proposing or recruiting for the SAS?

Lionel You think about it, Sylvie. I'm not joking. I'm really not. I'll see you later then. (*He moves away*)

Sylvie Lionel.

Lionel (*turning*) Yes?

Sylvie It was good last night, though, wasn't it?

Lionel Good. Glad you enjoyed it.

Lionel exits

Sylvie (*a little feebly, after him*) Bye then. (*She practises her new walk. She puts on the hat again and tries various tones and voices*) Hallo. Oh, hallo. Hallo there. Hallo. How are you? (*She practises walking and getting taken by surprise*) Oh, hallo. (*She tries it again*) Hallo, it's you. (*She does it again, in a sexier voice*) Hallo. (*She giggles*) Dynamite, aren't I? Hallo. Oh, hallo there. Hallo. (*She continues "hallo-ing"*)

Toby comes from the house. He carries his newspaper

Toby (*answering her*) Hallo.
Sylvie Oh. (*Resuming her old self*) Hallo, Mr Teasdale.
Toby Is that Sylvie?
Sylvie Yes, Mr Teasdale.
Toby Who were you saying hallo to?
Sylvie No one, Mr Teasdale.
Toby No one?
Sylvie No, I was just practising.
Toby Practising.
Sylvie Saying hallo.
Toby Were you? Well, yes. It does take a bit of getting the hang of. Is the hat part of it?
Sylvie Oh. No, I was just trying it on.
Toby Yes, I see. You know, I have the distinct impression, Sylvie, that Mrs Teasdale pays you to do some work, doesn't she?
Sylvie Yes, Mr Teasdale.
Toby Then I suggest you get on with it.
Sylvie Yes, Mr Teasdale. Would you like some tea, Mr Teasdale? (*She giggles*)
Toby No, thank you. My wife is out, I take it?
Sylvie Yes, she went to the coffee morning. Mrs Coombes's Oxfam.
Toby Jolly good. Right. (*He sits*)

Sylvie goes in

(*Muttering*) Practising saying hallo. Girl's completely round the bend. (*He reads his paper*)

Sylvie comes out with some rubbish

Sylvie (*as she passes*) Lovely day, Mr Teasdale.
Toby Lovely day, yes, Sylvie. Lovely. (*He glances down the garden*) What's going on there?
Sylvie (*stopping to look*) Where, Mr Teasdale?
Toby What are all those stones doing there? All those bits of brick.
Sylvie I think it's crazy paving.
Toby Crazy paving?
Sylvie Mr Hepplewick, he's laying crazy paving for Mrs Teasdale.
Toby Yes, that has a certain logical ring to it. A man who has recently positioned the long jump pit so that the poor little bastards have to start their run up on the other side of the main road might well be just the chap to lay crazy paving. Tell her to try and restrict it to just the garden, will you?
Sylvie Yes, Mr Teasdale. (*She carries on towards the dustbins*)
Toby (*irritated*) Why is she wearing that hat? (*Loudly*) Why are you wearing that hat?
Sylvie Don't you like it, Mr Teasdale?
Toby No, I do not like it. I feel I'm living in the middle of a tea plantation. Now take it off.

Sylvie Yes, Mr Teasdale.

Toby reads

> *Sylvie puts her rubbish in the dustbins, returns, putting her hat back on the pile of rubbish as she comes. She reaches Toby and hovers for a moment*

Mr Teasdale.

Toby Oh, dear God, yes. (*Sharply*) Yes.

Sylvie I wonder if I could ask you something.

Toby I knew there was a good reason I went out this morning. What are you doing here on a Saturday anyway?

Sylvie I missed Wednesday.

Toby I wish I had. All right then, carry on. What is it?

Sylvie Could I ask you—well, it's a bit awkward——

Toby Sylvie, if it's about money, I don't deal with it. You must ask Mrs Teasdale, you know that. I'm sure she will review your case sympathetically once she's had a word with me. Now run along.

Sylvie No, it wasn't money.

Toby It wasn't?

Sylvie No. I wanted to ask you about me.

Toby About you?

Sylvie Yes, Mr Teasdale. You see——

Toby What's the matter with your arms?

Sylvie My arms?

Toby They're hanging in the most extraordinary way. Have you done something to them?

Sylvie No.

Toby Arms shouldn't hang like that, should they? You haven't been lifting anything too heavy, have you?

Sylvie No, Mr Teasdale.

Toby Don't, for God's sake, or we'll be liable. Have to pay you a pension for the rest of your life and keep you in surgical corsets. Do be careful.

Sylvie It's just—er—well, you see, it was about my education.

Toby Education?

Sylvie Yes, I was wondering if I could possibly get a bit more.

Toby I don't know what you're talking about.

Sylvie I wonder if you could possibly help me.

Toby What? Are you asking to enrol in the school, is that it?

Sylvie (*laughing*) No.

Toby That's as well. Because the rest of them have left at thirteen, you know.

Sylvie I know that. No. I meant, like, special coaching.

Toby Oh, I see. Why do you want that?

Sylvie I just do. I want to make up my education.

Toby Well, I think you'd probably be able to find somebody. Perhaps someone on the staff. I'll inquire if you like, by all means. They do tend to get pretty busy during term-time, some of them.

Sylvie I meant you.

Toby Me?

Sylvie Could you possibly coach me?

Toby Well, Sylvie, you see, I am extremely busy. Besides teaching, which I hardly do any of at all these days, I also have all the dreary little chores of a Headmaster—merely to stop the damned place from grinding to a halt. I honestly don't have time for special coaching, I'm sorry. I do value my leisure.

Sylvie I'd pay.

Toby No, it's really not that.

Sylvie It would only be an evening a week or something.

Toby Well, you know I really do hate to say no to you because I think what you're doing is really splendid. I do. It's always seemed to me bizarre that we try and educate people at a time in their lives when they'd far sooner be doing something else. And at the very age when they begin to get curious about things, we kick them out. It's just, sadly, you picked the wrong chap. I'm sorry.

Sylvie Oh. (*She looks very disappointed*)

Toby What did you want to learn anyway? What did you want to study?

Sylvie Everything.

Toby Yes, well, you may have to narrow that down a bit. I mean, languages? Classics? History? Biology? English literature?

Sylvie Yes, that's it. English literature, yes.

Toby Well, I'm a history man myself. So I couldn't be a lot of help to you anyway.

Sylvie I'm sure you could be. I'm sure you've read more than me.

Toby Well, that's possible. It's probably a closer thing than you realize but it's possible. I don't quite know what to say, Sylvie. I hate to—have you got taller or something?

Sylvie No.

Toby You look enormous. You see, I hate to say no to you but even if I did say yes, I'd be bound to forget and let you down.

Sylvie Oh, say yes, Mr Teasdale. Please say yes.

Toby I'd have to talk to Mrs Teasdale.

Sylvie Right, yes, right.

Toby She might not like her home help reading Virginia Woolf in the broom cupboard.

Sylvie I'll work very hard. I really will.

Toby Sylvie, why are you coming to me? I mean, what about your old school? Aren't there teachers there who'd help you?

Sylvie They're no good.

Toby How do you know?

Sylvie They can't be much good or they wouldn't be at that place, would they? I want somebody good. Someone at the top.

Toby You're really serious, aren't you?

Sylvie Yes, I am. Yes.

Toby Is there—is there a reason for this? I mean, I'm just curious. You don't have to tell me if you don't want to. I mean, were you like Saul of Tarsus on the way to the dustbins or have you been thinking about it for some time? Is there someone you're doing it for?

Sylvie Yes.

Toby Who?

Sylvie Me.

Toby With reasons like that I can't say no to you. We'll arrange a day next week, shall we?

Sylvie Thank you, Mr Teasdale, very much. I'll get on now. (*She moves away towards the house*)

Toby Oh, Sylvie. Somewhere in that bookshelf in there, you'll see a couple of books called *Tom Jones*. Supposed to be the first English novel. You'd better start at the beginning, I suppose. Did you see the film?

Sylvie No.

Toby Then read the book. I think you'll enjoy it. There are one or two people in it whom I think you might recognize. *Tom Jones*.

Sylvie *Tom Jones*. Right.

Sylvie goes into the house

Toby Well, there's a turn up for the book.

There is the distant sound of a motor mower

Now what's he doing? What's he doing with that motor mower? Hepplewick? Hepplewick? (*He moves down the garden*) Hepplewick. Ah—(*He trips on the crazy paving*) Damn piles of bricks. Like a Druid's temple out here. (*Calling*) Hepplewick. Not the pitch. Don't mow the square with the heavy mower! Just the outfield. Use the small mower for—(*he gives up*) Ah, well. It'll ginger up the wicket a bit. Be like batting on corrugated cardboard now. Make sure you put them in first, that's all. (*He starts back up the garden*)

Celia comes out from the house dressed as before

Celia Oh, you're back. That didn't take long.

Toby It never takes long to tell the PE master he's an idiot.

Celia You want some tea?

Toby I do not want tea. Why do people keep trying to give me tea?

Celia Coffee?

Toby No.

Celia All right. I'm amazed you're standing up actually. My God, how much were you drinking last night?

Toby Don't start on that, Celia, there's a dear.

Celia I mean, why do you do it, Toby, why do you do it? You're killing yourself slowly but surely. You are. (*After a slight pause*) Well, I don't know about you but I don't think I can take this for much longer.

Toby So you keep saying.

Celia I don't. What about the children? Hearing you stamping about like that in the night. Kicking the fridge. Terrifying for them.

Toby I know, I know.

Celia Well, if only you'd try. I'd help you.

Toby How was your charitable coffee morning? I presume this is the reason for this fresh burst of crusading zeal.

Celia Oh, it was all right. Rowena was at her vigorous best. As usual. I think if you won't listen to me, I think you owe it to Miles to stop drinking. You should do it for his sake.

Toby Miles?

Celia Do you realize how close you came to being sacked by the Governors? It was only Miles who saved you, you know. They were all turned against you. It's entirely thanks to Miles that you've still got a job.

Toby Thank you, Miles.

Celia I mean, those appalling letters you sent to the parents. I don't know how he explained those away.

Toby There were a considerable number of misprints in that letter.

Celia Nobody could have misprinted some of those words.

Toby It was just a gently worded suggestion that paying some school vast sums of money to take their child off their hands did not entirely exonerate them from their parental responsibilities. Only I said that more succinctly with shorter words because half the stupid bastards can't read anyway.

Celia The point is, Miles promised the Board that you'd stop drinking.

Toby My God, that's strong-willed of him. Wish I had his guts.

Celia I go round there and I see Rowena and Miles looking so happy that it makes me want to——

Toby Rowena and Miles happy? Did you say happy?

Celia Yes. Comparatively.

Toby Rowena, if you'll pardon the expression, is being serviced by every other man in the district. She's like Heathrow Airport. People are landing and taking off every seven minutes. She may well be happy. In fact, I'm sure she is. Except in fog. But that really isn't true for Miles, I can promise you that. The man is merely waiting for a suitable cut-throat razor to fall in his lap.

Celia Well, they seem happy.

Toby I'm sure we do too. To the casual outsider sprinting past the window in dark glasses on his way to a guide-dog convention, I'm sure we do too.

Pause

Ah well, as long as there is still the promise of crazy paving, all is not lost.

Celia I don't know what to do, I really don't.

Toby You could go and administer first aid to the second eleven. They're going to need it on that pitch.

Celia You've lost all your drive. All those wonderful ideas.

Toby Changing the subject mercifully, what is going on with Sylvie?

Celia Why?

Toby She asked me just now for tuition.

Celia You?

Toby Yes.

Celia How extraordinary.

Toby Well, I'm a schoolmaster. I suppose there were less suitable people she might have approached. Speedway rider, North Sea oil rig supervisor.

Celia What I meant was, how extraordinary her asking.

Toby She's a strange girl. She was practising saying hallo when I came back. Which is a fairly harmless occupation, I suppose. Unless she's standing in the middle of Liverpool docks.

Celia I think your brain's gone, actually. It's congealing.

Toby Anyway, I said I would. Give her tuition. If you don't object.

Celia Why should I object?

Toby I'll have to bring a huge nubile girl home occasionally, sit her on my knee and take her through *Lamb's Tales from Shakespeare*. You might not like it.

Celia It doesn't worry me if it stops you jumping around kicking things in the night.

Toby Only her.

Celia Yes, it's odd. She's just asked me, actually, if I could help her.

Toby French horn lessons?

Celia She wanted advice on clothes and things.

Toby Clothes? A well-dressed English literature scholar. Surely a contradiction in terms. Curiouser and curiouser.

Celia I've let her rout through those old things of mine that I was going to put out for Rowena.

Toby Does Rowena wear your old things? I never realized.

Celia No, for Oxfam. She only looks as if she does sometimes. No, I don't know what it is with Sylvie. She's probably in love, that's all.

Toby With you or me?

Celia Hepplewick, presumably.

Toby Hepplewick? Purveyor of short jump pits and crazy paving? We must save her.

Celia They're sort of engaged. He's quite attractive, isn't he?

Toby He's grotesque.

Celia Anyway, I promised to help her. She could do with some guidance. She's a little bit of a haystack, isn't she? Has she hurt her back, do you know?

Toby Apparently not. I asked her the same question.

Celia Are you in for lunch?

Toby I am.

Celia Right. So long as I know.

Toby I don't want anything though.

Celia Then why say you're in?

Toby I am in. I'm not eating.

Celia Toby, you must eat. You really must.

Toby Oh, God. (*He gets up and strides down the garden*)

Celia Where are you going now?

Toby I'm going to finish that mowing myself. I can't bear to watch him a minute longer. Carving his initials all over the pitch.

Toby goes off at the end of the garden

Celia (*rather faintly after him*) Well, don't shout at him or you'll have to get a new groundsman. Toby? Oh . . . (*She sees the sunhat*) Ah. (*She picks it* *up*) Good Lord, how extraordinary. (*She hears something from the house and moves towards it*) What's that? No, try it on if you want. It was a bit tight on me, so it might fit. (*She examines the sun hat*) Now, where did we get this? (*She calls*) Sylvie? Oh, well. I don't know why I started her on that. It looks as if I'll have to do the bedroom myself. (*She picks up Toby's newspaper and moves towards the house*)

Lionel arrives, panting, at the end of the garden

Oh, hallo. He's taken over, has he?

Lionel Seemed to want to. (*He swallows*) Excuse me. Leave me clear to get on here for an hour, anyway.

Celia Splendid.

Lionel He seems to like things mowed a special way, Mr Teasdale. Determined man. Knows his mind.

Celia Yes, he does.

Lionel I admire that.

Celia Do you? Well . . .

Lionel I do.

Celia goes into the house

(*Turning round to Toby*) You silly old bugger. You'll drive it into the ditch in a minute. Serve you right. (*He starts to bring in more paving stones and stacks them up. He stops to watch Toby again. He laughs*) I don't think he can get the brake on. I should have told him I fixed it. (*He carries on stacking the paving stones*)

Sylvie comes out on to the patio. She wears an old summer dress of Celia's. Despite her odd newfound stance, it suits her

Lionel stops and stares

Sylvie Hallo. Do you like it? It's Mrs Teasdale's. She give it to me.

Lionel continues to look her up and down

It's not lime green anyway. Do you like it?

Lionel Very nice.

Sylvie Thank you. It'll look good with my hat. (*She takes the hat off the table and puts it on*) How's that?

Lionel Terrific.

Sylvie (*shimmying down the garden towards him*) All right, is it?

Lionel I said, yes.

Sylvie Do you like me then?

Lionel Yes.

Sylvie Good. Am I standing up straight enough for you?

Lionel Yes.

Sylvie (*close to him*) Like to go to bed with me again, would you?

Lionel Yes.

Sylvie Ask me nicely.

Lionel I'm asking you nicely.

Sylvie Well, now. Let me see.

EITHER she says:

Sylvie I'll have to consider your request.
Lionel Oh, yes. (*He smiles*)
Sylvie You're right, Lionel. It's just an attitude. It's all it takes. I mean, I know I'm not going to be absolutely fantastic overnight but I could work at it. I'm going to have lessons from Mr Teasdale.
Lionel From him? What on? The history of bottle labels?
Sylvie He said he'd teach me. And Mrs Teasdale's going to help me with clothes. She's very good. She's got a good eye. So you see, I'm making the effort. So what do you say?
Lionel Good for you.
Sylvie I'm not narrow and limited then? Am I?
Lionel No.
Sylvie I'm not an angle bracket?
Lionel No.

Pause

Lionel looks at her

See you tonight then. (*They smile at each other*)
Sylvie (*flinging her arms round him*) Oh, Lionel. (*She kisses him*) Lionel the lion.
Lionel You'll get that dirty. . . .
Sylvie I love you.
Lionel Yes.
Sylvie (*looking over Lionel's shoulder*) What's that? Someone shouting, isn't it? (*They look*)
Lionel Oh, that's old Teasdale trying to stop the mower.
Sylvie It's dragging him along the ground.
Lionel Yes. I think he's got caught up in it.
Sylvie Well, go and help him.
Lionel No. It'll run out of petrol soon. I didn't fill it.
Sylvie (*insistently*) Lionel, you go and help him this minute. That's my private tutor. Go on. Or our engagement is off.
Lionel Engagement? What engagement?
Sylvie Go on.
Lionel (*leaving*) All right.

Lionel goes off to the field

Sylvie (*alone and very excited*) It's going to be great, it really is. It's going to be absolutely great.

The Lights fade to a Black-out

To: A GARDEN FÊTE (page 125)

OR she says:

Sylvie I've been giving this a bit of thought in your absence and I think you're right.

Lionel Was I?

Sylvie Yes, I am a person with a particularly narrow and limited viewpoint. I think small and I think timid. And that way I'll never finish up anything but second best. So I'm starting to change. Right now. Mr Teasdale's going to give me some lessons.

Lionel You'll need two straws then, won't you? One for him, one for you.

Sylvie English literature. And Mrs Teasdale, she's going to advise me on couture. On my clothes. Because she's got a very good eye.

Lionel (*amused*) Now what have I started?

Sylvie Oh, you just don't know. I'm chucking it all out. Starting now, everything that's second best in my life is going out the window. So the first bloody thing that's going out the window is you.

Lionel Eh?

Sylvie You can find yourself another limited angle bracket.

Lionel Come on, what's the matter with you?

Sylvie I'm growing up, that's what. I'm find out what's me, basic me and what's everybody else's fifty ps worth of wallpaper they stuck over me. And the bit that's me, even if it's only tiny, that's the bit I'm hanging on to. The rest is going. I'll tell you this, Lionel Hepplewick, you've got plans. I've got plans as well. I've got plans for me. (*She swans back to the house. On the patio she turns and says in her posh voice*) Goodbye.

Sylvie goes into the house

Lionel (*puzzled*) What plans? What plans?

The Lights fade to a Black-out

To: A PAGEANT (page 159)

A GARDEN FÊTE

The vicarage garden. Five weeks later. 2 p.m. Saturday, July 24th

A village fête is in process of preparation. This stall is at one rather obscure corner of it. It consists of a sturdy, if somewhat crudely constructed old-fashioned pillory, complete with head and armholes. This is fastened to the ground. Behind it is a protective screen, to catch any erring missiles. There is an upright folding chair lying on the ground, a length of wood, a painted hardboard sign lying face downwards and an empty tin for the money. All these appear to have been dumped in a hurry and left.

There are sounds of activity from all around as other sideshows are being completed but this particular stall is deserted

In a moment Celia enters, dressed for this social occasion. She is pushing Joe Hepplewick in his wheelchair. He is a man in his seventies with a deceptively cheering disposition

Celia They don't seem to be here, Mr Hepplewick. I don't know if Sylvie's arrived yet. I haven't seen her.

Joe Don't you worry, Mrs Teasdale, don't you worry now. I'll just wait here quietly for them. I'll just sit here quietly.

Celia Lionel's around somewhere, I've seen him.

Joe Ah, my boy's around. Yes, I know the boy's around. I've seen him. No, this is all the kindness I can expect, Mrs Teasdale. It was just a little tricky in this thing over the grass, you see. It wasn't built for grass.

Celia No, it's quite a shove.

Joe   What you should seek in women's eyes
              Is kindness. That's their greatest prize.

Celia Oh, how charming. Is that a poem?

Joe It is, it is.

Celia Who by?

Joe One of my own, Mrs Teasdale, one of my own.

Celia Yes, of course. I'm sorry, I forgot. You're our poet, aren't you? I read you every week.

Joe I contribute now and again to the local journal. Try and dissemble a little simple wisdom.
                        We spend our lives on roundabouts
                        While others choose the swings
                        But we'll all clear that playground when
                        The final schoolbell rings.

Celia Yes, yes. How true. (*She nods*) And how are your knees these days? Are they any better?

Joe I'd like to say, Mrs Teasdale, I'd love very dearly to be able to stand up and say to you in all honesty, yes. But I have to say no. No better.

Celia Oh, dear.

Joe   A ripe old age is grand I'm told
              But please don't let me grow too old. (*He chuckles*)

Celia Another of yours?

Joe Another of mine. A humorous one.

Celia Yes, you have a style, don't you? One begins to recognize it. How many verses have you actually written, Mr Hepplewick? Have you any idea?

Joe I have. I have written eight thousand nine hundred and seventeen poems, not including birthday limericks and personal Christmas cards

Celia Heavens.

Joe I write a poem every single day except on very certain days and I have done so for twenty-five years.

Celia Lord. I think you should go in the *Guinness Book of Records*.

Joe No, I don't want that. I've never been published. I've never been published except in the paper.

Celia Well, you should. Collect some together. For a book.

Joe No, no, no.

Celia I'm sure it would sell.

Joe I'm sure it would. I'm sure it would.

Celia Then why not?

Joe Well, I'll tell you what I have believed ever since I was a boy, Mrs Teasdale. A man should never try to profit from a gift that has been given to him freely by God.

Celia Ah.

Joe You think about that.

Celia Yes.

Joe Eh?

Celia Yes ... it's—I can see what you mean. I'm sure there's a flaw in that argument somewhere.

Joe With respect, I don't think there is.

Celia Wouldn't it mean, though, that no one could ever pursue any career for which they had any aptitude? So that if a man was, say, a brilliant doctor, then he'd have to become a plumber. Providing he had no natural flair for plumbing, of course. If you see what I mean.

Joe I've never been to a doctor in my life, Mrs Teasdale, so I can't argue with you there.

Celia What, never?

Joe Never.

Celia Not even for your legs?

Joe No. My legs are between me and God, Mrs Teasdale.

Celia Oh, come now. (*She mouths*) Stupid man.

Joe If He'd intended I'd still be walking, I'd still be walking.

Celia Well, I'm sure He didn't set out to put you in a wheelchair. Or He'd have given you wheels in the first place. I mean, I think He expects us to do a bit for ourselves. Not just sit there. Oh, I'm sorry. I didn't mean to say that. ...

Joe (*smiling sadly*) I'm not going to argue with the Headmaster's good lady. I know better than to do that.

Celia No. Good. Is it going to stay fine, that's the thing?

Joe I think it might. I think it might.

Celia We're generally lucky. It usually does for the fête.

Joe   I've noticed when a cause is good and true
              How often cloudy skies can turn to blue.

Celia What's that? Oh, it's another one. Wonderful. I do hope we get a good turn-out. We need a lot of money.

Joe For the church tower, this is?

Celia That's right. It's in a terrible state. It's going to cost thousands.

Joe Well, I think you'll find, Mrs Teasdale, that if God intends it to fall down ...

Celia (*rather impatiently*) Yes, well, He's probably got more important things on His mind so we're having to fix it ourselves. You must excuse me, I've got to go and organize my own stall, rolling two p pieces. It gets more expensive every year, doesn't it? I suppose when it gets to fifty, we'll have to give it up altogether. They won't roll at all. You don't mind me leaving you here?

Joe Not at all, not at all.

Celia She shouldn't be long. Oh, how do you think she's looking these days? Sylvie.

Joe Looking? How do you mean?

Celia My husband and I, we've both been working on her. No, that sounds dreadful, I didn't mean it like that. I've been advising her a little. On clothes and general things. And Toby's teaching her. A little.

Joe Yes, I heard that.

Celia You must have noticed, surely. I know Lionel has. She's looking a lot better.

Joe I'm sure the boy notices, Mrs Teasdale. He might well have done. I'm afraid, myself, I don't take a lot of notice of exterior trappings. It's the woman beneath that interests me, Mrs Teasdale, the woman beneath.

Celia (*as she goes, acidly*) Yes. Then I'm sure that makes you very similar to most men, Mr Hepplewick. See you later.

Celia exits

Joe Goodbye, Mrs Teasdale. (*He chuckles and shakes his head, looks about him and finds further amusement in what he sees. He laughs again. He shakes his head*)

                    When I survey my fellow men
                    All running here and there again
                    And then observe the smallest flower
                    What it achieves in half an hour.
                    I look at them all rushing round
                    And want to shout "Slow down, slow down".

He smiles with pleasure

Eight thousand nine hundred and eighteen. (*He spies the sign lying face downwards*) What's this then? (*With an effort, he leans over, picks it up and reads aloud*) "Pelt the varlet. Ten p for three". Ten p for three what? Pelt the varlet. (*He considers this*) Who's this varlet then?

Sylvie enters. She is dressed practically but her taste somewhat reflects Celia's influence. She has with her a plastic carrier bag

Sylvie Oh, hallo, Mr Hepplewick.

Joe Good afternoon, Sylvie.

Sylvie Let you in early, have they?

Joe I beg your pardon?

Sylvie We don't open for half an hour. The fête's due to start at two-thirty.

Joe I think I've had a little bit of special consideration. That's the privilege of age, Sylvie, the privilege of age.

Sylvie Yes, well, the other old folk are queueing up in the road.

Joe What's this then? (*He indicates the sign*) This varlet. Who's this?

Sylvie That's me.

Joe You?

Sylvie 'Sright.

Joe I didn't know they had women varlets.

Sylvie They have women everything now. Equal rights, haven't you heard?

Joe I've heard.

Sylvie I have to put my head through this and my hands through here and then they throw sponges at me.

Joe What, cakes?

Sylvie No, not cakes. Sponges. You know. What you wash with. Three for ten p. They dip them in the water and sling them at me. Aren't I the lucky one?

Joe Enjoy that, will you?

Sylvie No, we drew lots. I got this. I wanted to go on the marmalade. They sell out early and then you can go home. I'll be here till the pubs close. No, I don't mind. It's for a good cause.

Joe (*examining the pillory*) Ah, now. This'll be what Lionel was mending in our yard.

Sylvie Well, I hope he has, that's all. (*She opens and closes the pillory, checking the hinge*) Seems all right. Kept sticking before.

Joe Sylvie, I want a little private word with you if you don't mind.

Sylvie I don't want to get stuck in that.

Joe Would you spare me a little moment, Sylvie?

Sylvie I got all this to arrange.

Joe Sylvie.

Sylvie I'm rushed off my feet.

Joe   I would I'd learn the sense to stop
                  Not treat life like a china shop.

Sylvie A what?

Joe Lionel's getting anxious, Sylvie. I know the boy, you see. He's beginning to fret.

Sylvie Nothing to do with me.

Joe Tampering with the boy's feelings, Sylvie. That's wrong, you know. It's
  wrong to tamper.
Sylvie I'm not tampering. I don't know what it means even.
Joe I thought you would with all your reading lessons.
Sylvie We haven't got to T yet.
Joe He's waiting on you, Sylvie. He's waiting patiently. And that's patience
  I taught him. I said to the boy, "Boy," I said, "Wait. She'll come to you,
  boy. She's promised she'll come, she'll come."
Sylvie She might.
Joe She's promised she'll come, she'll come. A promise is a promise.
Sylvie I never promised.
Joe Oh, now, Sylvie. Be careful, girl. Did he not ask you to marry him?
Sylvie Yes, he did.
Joe A month ago, was it? More than a month.
Sylvie About a month.
Joe And did you not say yes?
Sylvie (*a little uneasily*) I said—I said maybe, I said.
Joe Sylvie, Lionel tells me you said yes.
Sylvie Well . . .
Joe You're not saying my boy's a liar now, are you, Sylvie? Are you?
Sylvie No.
Joe Then did you say yes?
Sylvie I might have said yes.
Joe You said yes.
Sylvie Yes.
Joe That's a promise.
Sylvie Well, now I'm not sure. I've changed my mind. Woman's privi-
  lege.
Joe Ah, now, now, now. We can't have that, can we? I thought you were
  telling me you were equal.
Sylvie We are. He can change his mind too, if he likes.
Joe If you're equal, then you'd better behave like a gentleman. And a
  gentleman always keeps her word, doesn't she?
Sylvie That's daft.
Joe Not daft, Sylvie, that's fair.
Sylvie I don't think you should be held to a promise like that. Not if you're
  not sure. I can't marry him just because I promised I would. I couldn't.
  It's my whole life I'm promising. I believe that bit. I believe once you go
  through with it, you go through with it. I won't walk out once I'm in. I
  just don't think I want to go in. Any rate, what's it got to do with you? It's
  between me and Lionel. He can come and talk to me.
Joe He says you won't talk to him.
Sylvie Well, when he keeps on at me I won't.
Joe The boy's made plans, Sylvie. He's made plans for you both.
Sylvie Well, that's just—What's all this "boy" bit? He's thirty-three, isn't
  he?
Joe He's still a boy, Sylvie. Till you take him. Then he'll be a man.
Sylvie (*muttering*) I think he's already qualified, don't worry.

Joe What's that?

Sylvie What are these plans of his then? Am I included?

Joe He's building an extension on the kitchen. A little conservatory for you both to sit in.

Sylvie Yes, he told me.

Joe Day and night he's been on that.

Sylvie Well, he's got plenty of time since he lost his job, hasn't he?

Joe Ah, now that was a sad business. The Headmaster in his wisdom obviously felt the boy should go. I wouldn't want to question his reasons but I don't feel he was justified.

Sylvie He was justified.

Joe The boy was following in my footsteps, learning his trade. What they call the verbal tradition. Learning the caretaking, learning the groundsman's craft. Takes time.

Sylvie He blew up the boiler. He wrecked two lawnmowers and he buggered the cricket pitch. They're hardly going to keep him on.

Joe That's a closed chapter now, Sylvie. The page has been turned. Can't hold a man to his past.

Sylvie All right, what about the present then? He had all these plans, didn't he? I don't mean conservatories. I thought he was going into business. What happened to that?

Joe He got himself a job yesterday.

Sylvie Did he? Where?

Joe It's away in the town. Means he'll have to travel.

Sylvie My God. Five miles. What's he doing?

Joe He's entered into a period of apprenticeship and training as a traffic warden.

Sylvie A traffic warden?

Joe So.

Sylvie Bit of a step down from managing director, isn't it?

Joe That's not fair, Sylvie, that's unfair. The boy's got a job. He's declared his seriousness. He went along. He was interviewed. He was accepted. Now that's not the behaviour of a man who's jocular. That's a man with serious intentions, Sylvie. Now it is incumbent upon you to take him seriously. You owe him that.

Sylvie I don't see why.

Joe It's your duty, Sylvie, it's your duty.

Sylvie Oh yes?

Joe You go to Church at all, Sylvie?

Sylvie Not much, no. Why?

Joe I suggest you might find it worthwhile to pay a visit. You know what they say about Church? Church is the place where a woman learns her duty and man learns his responsibilities. You think about that. Oh, you can quote all this equal varlet business and all that but that's not for you, Sylvie. That's for a load of middle-class women with nothing better to think about. You're a woman, Sylvie, and that's the end of it. You're never going to be equal. And you're never going to be unequal. You're yourself. You've got a woman's duties to perform and a woman's responsibilities. That's got nothing to do with politics or sociologists. That's basic God-given biological. You known what I'm saying?

Sylvie (*impressed by his seriousness, but confused*) Well, I'm ... I don't know.

Joe You know I wouldn't lie to you, Sylvie. The boy needs you badly. He needs your strength, Sylvie. He needs your woman's strength.

Sylvie Well, I. ... Well. ...It's not—I don't want to hurt him. I just think that I should—I don't know what I feel really. I mean, he's full of rubbish half the time, isn't he?

Joe That's another job then, isn't it? Get rid of the rubbish in him.

Sylvie I don't think that's my job.

Joe A man and a wife, Sylvie, each moulds the other. That's in a good relationship. Gently they alter the other's image moving it closer to the ideal they hold in their own eyes. I moulded his mother.

Sylvie I bet you did.

Joe She probably moulded me, I don't know.

Sylvie She's dead now, isn't she?

Joe Well, that's another story.

Sylvie You see, I've been—I've been having these lessons with Mr Teasdale over the past few weeks and he's been telling me a lot. Really friendly. I mean, nothing ... just friendly, you know. He's told me so much. It's amazing. Because I thought he was a bit of an old twit, really. But he's very interesting.

Joe He's a Headmaster. He would be interesting, Sylvie, he would be.

Sylvie Well, I don't know about that. Mine wasn't. Anyway, Tobe—Mr Teasdale, he's got a lot of ideas. You know, to talk about. And he's been—if I'd had him at school instead of old Sykes, I'd have been brilliant. And I think in a funny sort of way, I've helped him too. Mr Teasdale. I mean, he used to drink a lot but he doesn't seem so bad lately. So. You know. There's a lot of new things happening, that's all. New concepts. It's like before I was just looking through the letter-box but now, somebody's opened the front door a bit. I don't know where I'm going but I can see there's more than one direction. I mean, five weeks ago I had one choice really. Should I marry Lionel or shouldn't I? And if I didn't marry Lionel or he didn't ask me, who was I going to marry. It's a bit more complicated now. I'm not sure I want to marry anybody. I still don't know anything but I'm beginning to know how much I don't know anyway.

Pause

Joe Yes, well, that's marvellous. Marvellous for you. (*After a pause*) So far as it goes.

Sylvie How do you mean?

Joe You're like a fish, Sylvie, that's jumped up out of the water for a second. Caught a glimpse of dry land and thought, hallo, that looks interesting. I think I might like that. And then, one day, you take the plunge out of the water on to the bank and suddenly you're dying. And you're longing to be back in that water where you belong but it's too late. You're a dead fish who jumped too far for its own good.

Sylvie You mean, I don't belong?

Joe No, Sylvie, you don't.

Sylvie Because I'm a woman.

Joe Partly. Partly because of your upbringing. Partly because of yourself. Put all those together, Sylvie, and you belong to part of a team looking after a man who works for you and who gives you that precious gift of children. (*He pauses*)

Sylvie stands unhappily

Still, I'm not going to try and persuade you against your will. It's your life, Sylvie. You can choose to take the natural course or you can choose to take the unnatural course. It's a child's duty to kneel before its mother, it's a woman's duty to kneel before a man and it's a man's duty to kneel before God. Those are unfashionable words these days, Sylvie, but you think about it. You think about it.

Pause

Sylvie (*unhappily*) I'm going to go and get my sponges.

Sylvie exits

Joe (*smiling after her*) Good girl, good girl. (*He murmurs, satisfied*) I think we got her for you, boy, I think we got her.
        Who can deny it is the case
        That all of nature has its place
        And woe betide the——

Sylvie returns. She carries a large tin bath full of water with several ancient foam rubber sponges in it

Sylvie (*interrupting Joe*) You won't be able to sit there, you know. You're right in the firing line.

Joe Ah, now, yes. Well, perhaps you could give me a little push, would you, Sylvie?

Sylvie Yes, where to?

Joe Just over there. I want a word with Mrs Granary.

Sylvie Right, Mr Hepplewick.

Joe (*as she pushes him*) Joe, Sylvie, Joe. You must call me Joe, you know. You're the only person I know who calls me Mr Hepplewick.

Sylvie Yes. Over here then?

Joe That's it. Everybody calls me Joe. Afternoon, Mrs Granary. (*He laughs*) You thought I'd missed you, didn't you? No such luck.

Sylvie pushes Joe out of sight. She returns immediately still very troubled, and sorts out her sponges

Sylvie (*suddenly and loudly*) Oh, hell's bells. What am I supposed to do? (*She throws a sponge angrily at the pillory*) What am I supposed to do? They don't tell you that, do they? (*To someone nearby*) Nothing. I was just practising. ... Yes. You got the time? ... Is it? Oh, hell. (*She starts to arrange her stall. She positions the bowl of sponges at a suitable distance from the pillory. Near it, she places the chair with tin on it. She props the varlet sign up against the chair. Finally, she lays down a piece of wood to mark where the thrower should stand. She admires her handiwork. She checks the distance of the thrower from the pillory. She decides it's too close. She moves the piece of wood back a foot or two. She is more or less satisfied*)

Lionel enters. He is dressed in a gorilla skin and carries the head under his arm

Lionel Hallo, then.
Sylvie (*without enthusiasm*) Hallo.
Lionel Oh. Progress. Talking to me, then?
Sylvie Why not?
Lionel That's progress, anyway. Look.
Sylvie (*not looking*) Yes.
Lionel I'm a gorilla.
Sylvie Oh, yes.
Lionel Do I look like one?
Sylvie No.
Lionel I do.
Sylvie You look like a teddy bear.
Lionel What do you mean, a teddy bear? I don't look like a teddy bear. I won't with the head on. I'll be all right with the head on.
Sylvie I should put it on then.
Lionel I can't. It don't fit. I'm going to have to be the half Wild Man of Borneo. You fixed all right?
Sylvie Yes.
Lionel (*indicating the pillory*) I mended that for you.
Sylvie I hope you did.
Lionel You better check it's just sponges they're throwing at you. Somebody threw a beer can at the feller last year. He had seven stitches.
Sylvie Oh, thank you. Glad you told me that now.
Lionel They probably won't with you. Be glad you're a woman.
Sylvie Oh yes?

Slight pause

Lionel Just watch they don't get round the back of you.
Sylvie (*impatiently*) Yes, all right.
Lionel (*after a pause*) Saw my dad talking to you.
Sylvie He was.
Lionel Did he tell you I got a job?
Sylvie Yes.
Lionel Traffic warden.
Sylvie Yes.
Lionel Well. Could be worse. I can get you free parking.
Sylvie I haven't got a car.

Lionel If you had, I could. They have a lot of sway, traffic wardens. You'd
be surprised. My uncle told me. I'm not doing it for long. I've got a few
ideas floating. You fancy an ironmonger's?

Sylvie An ironmonger's?

Lionel Just a thought. Keep it dark.

Sylvie The last time I talked to you, you were going to open a bakery.

Lionel (*mysteriously*) You have to move with the times, don't you? (*He
watches her for a second*) How's your education coming along then? Got
your degree yet, have you?

Sylvie (*sharply*) All right.

Lionel What?

Sylvie You're always sneering, aren't you? Why do you do that all the time?
Make you feel better, does it?

Lionel No.

Sylvie Then why do you do it? I mean, you started it, you know.

Lionel I did not.

Sylvie You did, telling me I was narrow. I've been broadening.

Lionel I didn't mean like that.

Sylvie What?

Lionel Not like that. Not like you're doing. What's the point of that?

Sylvie What?

Lionel All this reading and all that. You're never going to use it. It's not
useful.

Sylvie How do you know?

Lionel When have you ever used anything like that? It's like all that stuff at
school. Geometry. You ever use geometry?

Sylvie No, but . . .

Lionel You learn algebra, you ever use that?

Sylvie No.

Lionel Useless.

Sylvie I learnt to read at school.

Lionel Then read something useful.

Sylvie I am. I'm reading *Great Expectations*.

Lionel That's not useful. I meant something practical. Like accountancy or
joinery.

Sylvie Joinery?

Lionel Why not?

Sylvie Because I'm not interested in joinery.

Lionel Well, whatever. Needlework then.

Sylvie I'm not interested in doing needlework either.

Lionel Well, what are you interested in?

Sylvie I'm interested in reading.

Lionel What, just reading?

Sylvie Yes.

Lionel That's useless.

Sylvie All right. Maybe it is. Why does everything have to be useful?

Lionel Because in this world, there's no room for the useless, that's why.
We've got enough of them as it is without having middle-aged women

with surgical stockings and flat feet with three kids standing in the middle of the supermarket spouting Shakespeare.

Sylvie Oh, that's me, is it? Surgical stockings and flat feet.

Lionel Could be. If you turn me down.

Sylvie And how are you going to stop that happening?

Lionel Because I'm going somewhere better.

Sylvie You're going to give parking tickets out in Bermuda, are you?

Lionel That's only temporary.

Sylvie Everything's temporary.

Lionel I know where I'm going, don't you worry.

Sylvie You're taking your time.

Lionel Your sun lounge looks good. Nearly finished it. You should come round and have a look.

Sylvie It isn't my sun lounge.

Lionel Choose a colour.

Sylvie You built it, I didn't ask for it.

Lionel You'll like it. You can sit out there in the sun even in the wind.

Sylvie In my surgical stockings resting my flat feet.

Pause

Lionel Still on then, is it?

Sylvie What?

Lionel Us two. Still on, is it?

Sylvie I don't know, Lionel.

Lionel Come on, Sylvie.

Sylvie Oh, go away. You and him between you, I don't know if I'm—go away.

Lionel I'll be back. It's nearly half past. You'd better get your head in there.

Sylvie So had you.

Lionel Want a hand?

Sylvie I can manage.

Lionel See you later then.

Lionel exits

Sylvie fetches her carrier bag. From it, she unpacks her protective clothing. This consists of a waterproof cape and a shower cap which is decorated with a piece of ribbon in an attempt to make it seem faintly historical. She decides, before putting these on, to test out the pillory. She attempts to get herself into it but it proves more difficult than she imagined, unassisted. She gets first her head and one hand in, then her head and the other hand in. The hand that is closing it always contrives to be left outside. On her third attempt, she triumphantly manages to get both her hands in but leaves her head out. She then finds she is trapped. The device appears to have jammed. She stands very angry with herself. She is anxious not to summon help and draw attention to herself

Sylvie Oh, hell. Bloody Hepplewick.

Toby strolls on. He seems somehow brighter and fitter

Toby Aha, what does this say? Pelt the varlet. Ten p for three. Good afternoon, Sylvie. Are you a varlet?

Sylvie Yes. Could you give me a hand, please. I'm stuck.

Toby Isn't that the point? Aren't you supposed to be?

Sylvie Not like this.

Toby Oh, no. Your head's wrong, isn't it?

Sylvie I know.

Toby I think your head wants to go in there.

Sylvie I know it does. Can you help me out, please. Then I can get my head in.

Toby Yes, righto. I must say you look a bit like a sort of punk Punch and Judy show at the moment. (*He releases her*) There you are.

Sylvie Thank you. (*She examines the hinge suspiciously*)

Toby (*looking into the tin bath*) What are we supposed to throw at you? These things?

Sylvie Yes.

Toby Oh, well. Fairly harmless. A couple of hundred years ago, they'd have thrown everything. Eggs, bricks, bottles, you name it.

Sylvie Times haven't changed that much, then. (*She starts to put on her hat*)

Toby What's that?

Sylvie It's a shower hat. I stitched this round the top to make it look old-fashioned.

Toby Very clever. What's that bit? (*He indicates the cape*)

Sylvie It's a cycling cape. It's Mrs Bateman's brother's. Only he's in Portugal.

Toby Where presumably it doesn't rain. Or maybe they just don't have any bicycles.

Sylvie What are you on about? You're woffling again, aren't you?

Toby Sorry.

Sylvie (*smiling*) That's all right. I like you woffling.

Toby I just came to check with you before the hordes rush in to pelt you, I've got Sunday afternoon clear, tomorrow. Do you want to pop round? See how far you've got with it. How are you finding it? Dickens. A bit heavy going, is he?

Sylvie No.

Toby Really?

Sylvie Great.

Toby Yes. You sound as if you're having a whale of a time. Want to try something else? (*After a pause*) Sylvie? What's the matter?

Sylvie I'm thinking perhaps I'd better stop it all really.

Toby Stop it?

Sylvie Yes.

Toby Your classes?

Sylvie Yes.

Toby I see. (*After a pause*) Why's that then?

Sylvie Well. Bit stupid really, isn't it? At my age. Starting all that.

Toby I thought we'd got over that one.

Sylvie Well, I thought about it. It's stupid really. Bit useless as far as I'm concerned. Not much use to me.

Toby Depends what you think's useful.

Sylvie You know, useful.

Toby Were you enjoying the books?

Sylvie Yes. I was enjoying them.

Toby Then it can't have been useless.

Sylvie I don't mean it in that way.

Toby Even at their simplest level if all the books were giving you was pleasure, no fresh ideas or perspectives, no new thoughts, they still can't have been useless.

Sylvie I mean, useless in a useful way, you know. I mean—I don't know the bloody word, do I?

Toby If you finished the books, you probably would.

Sylvie I'm not arguing. I'm not arguing with you. I'm stopping, that's all.

Pause

Toby (*quietly*) All right.

Sylvie (*who has finished dressing*) Could you help me, please?

Toby Has someone been getting at you?

Sylvie How do you mean?

Toby Persuading you to give up. Lionel?

Sylvie No.

Toby I think he has.

Sylvie He just thinks it's useless, that's all.

Toby Oh, he's the one who thinks it's useless.

Sylvie Yes.

Toby And what about you? You're the one I'm interested in. Do you think it's useless, that's the point?

Sylvie I don't know.

Toby (*loudly*) I'm just asking you, do you think it's useless?

Sylvie (*louder*) Don't shout at me.

Toby (*quietly*) Sorry.

Sylvie Everybody's shouting at me. All these men shouting at me.

Toby Well, I'm sorry you think you've wasted your time with our classes.

Sylvie Yes, I do. I think they were useless and I think they were boring. Now leave me alone.

Toby (*after a pause*) I'm sorry. I don't believe that.

Sylvie Believe what you like.

Toby I've never taught anyone who looked more interested.

Sylvie Well, I'm not now.

Toby No, I'm sorry. I'm not going to give up that easily, you know. Oh, no. I'm sorry. I can see what's in operation here. This is what I term the first great sod's law of teaching, this is. About once every five years, if you're lucky—ten, if you're not—fifteen, if you're me—you get one pupil, one student with an actual cast iron interest in what you're trying to teach them, a fractional inkling of what the hell you're talking about. Who doesn't gaze at you with his jaw banging his desk with incomprehension. Or reach his academic peak merely struggling to master the indefinite article. Occasionally, God willing, there is one, one pupil who makes it worthwhile. And wouldn't you know it—and this is where the law comes in—that's the one that has to get expelled for assaulting the matron or taking heroin during Confirmation classes or riding his motorbike round the inside of the chapel roof. It always has to be him. Not the other lot. Never them. They sit on, year after year, yawning and belching and farting and smirking until you would pay, willingly pay, to make them go away. But, oh no, it has to be this one. Well, I don't give a monkey's what you want quite honestly, you're being educated whether you like it or not.

Sylvie leans against the pillory unable to argue

Sylvie? Do you hear what I'm saying?

Sylvie (*shaking her head*) It's no good.

Toby I'll decide that.

Sylvie Will you help me in, please?

Toby I hope that's clearly understood.

Sylvie Would you help me into this, please? I can't get in on my own.

Toby helps Sylvie into the pillory

Toby So. I'll see you tomorrow then.

Sylvie does not reply

Comfy?

Sylvie Yes.

Toby (*closing the pillory on her*) Bloody silly way to spend the afternoon, isn't it?

Sylvie It's in a good cause.

Toby I'm not so sure. I think they should let it fall down anyway. It's a hideous building. I still haven't had an answer. You'll be round tomorrow, then?

Sylvie No, I won't.

Toby Oh yes, you will.

Sylvie If you want to talk to me, you'll have to buy some sponges.

Toby Listen, you're an extremely bright, intelligent woman. It would be absolutely criminal to abandon your learning at this stage.

Sylvie Ten p for three.

Toby God knows, it's not much to ask, is it? Three sessions a week, dabbling in the shallows of English fiction.

Sylvie (*shouting*) Come and pelt the varlet. Ten p for three sponges. Come on then.

Toby ⎫   ⎧ I mean, it's not as if I'm asking you to read Dos-
     ⎬ (*together*) ⎨   toyevsky.
Sylvie ⎭   ⎩ (*yelling*) Come along, now. It's all in a good cause.

Toby (*delving into his pocket*) Oh, to hell with it. There you are. Ten p. (*He drops it into the tin*) Now listen, I'm not suggesting you give up the rest of your life. You can still get married, you can still have your children . . .

Sylvie You'd better take your sponges.

Toby		(*picking up a sponge*) But that doesn't mean you have to throw your brain out of the window, does it? Or does it? Is that what you want to do?
	(*together*)	
Sylvie		Throw it at me. You're supposed to throw it at me.
Toby	(*together*)	Just retire and become a child-bearing turnip.
Sylvie		Come on.

Toby You have been given a brain, Sylvie, and it is your duty to use it—oh, what the hell. (*He tosses the sponge lamely at her feet*)

Sylvie That wasn't much good. I thought you played cricket.

Toby You're not even listening, are you?

Sylvie (*shouting anew*) Come along now, any more for any more? Pelt this vile varlet most foul. This way, roll up. Ten p.

Toby Oh, my God. (*He picks up a couple more sponges*) Sylvie, please. Will you listen to what I'm saying? Or do I have to come over there and kick you. (*He throws another sponge*)

Sylvie That's not allowed. You keep behind the line.

Toby Sylvie.

Sylvie You only want to carry on for you. You don't care about me. Gives you and your wife something to do, doesn't it? She dresses me up, you try and teach me things. I'm a Barbie doll with pop-out brains.

Toby That is totally untrue. You know that.

Sylvie Throw your sponges. There may be others waiting.

Toby There aren't. (*He throws a third sponge*)

Sylvie (*yelling*) Roll up! Roll up!

Toby drops another coin in the tin and takes a sponge

Toby All right. There's a certain amount, I admit, of self-interest but only as there is with any teacher and his pupil. He wants the pupil to succeed. There's a certain gratification if she does.

Sylvie Couldn't teach sponge throwing, could you?

Toby (*hurling a sponge on the ground angrily*) That's the whole bloody point of teaching in the first place. Because you feel you have something to give, something—God-given, if you like.

Sylvie Old Mr Hepplewick says you shouldn't charge money for gifts from God, that's wrong.

Toby Old Mr Hepplewick should be punted off the roof of St Paul's Cathedral. His pallid poetry has set the whole English language back two thousand years.

Sylvie Keep throwing your sponges.

Toby (*taking two more sponges*) Sylvie. All right, I do. I admit it, I need you. I need you because I want to help you. Because by helping you, it does something for me. Look, you know all this, I know you do. You're not stupid. And I refuse to stand here pelting you with wet sponges pleading my case like this. What do I have to say? Sylvie. (*He throws another sponge*) I wish to God you'd come out of there. It's like trying to hold a conversation with a moose's head. Sylvie. Listen, to hell with the regulation distance, if you don't answer me I'm stepping over this piece of wood, I am coming over there and I'm going to do unmentionable things with this sponge, I'm warning you.

Sylvie All right. If you must know. I've been asked not to come round any more.

Toby Who by? Lionel?

Sylvie No.

Toby Who then? His father? The poisonous poet?

Sylvie No.

Toby Who?

Sylvie By your wife.

Toby Celia?

Sylvie Yes.

Toby Why?

Sylvie I think she—I think she's a bit jealous. She thought I was getting—you know—close.

Toby Nonsense. She's perfectly happy. She welcomed the arrangement. Thoroughly approved.

Sylvie She did at first. Not now.

Toby Since when?

Sylvie Couple of days.

Toby Nonsense.

Sylvie She was very nice. She just said she thought it was unhealthy and that sooner or later, one of us was going to do something stupid. Bound to. And I was to stop coming round. She was very nice.

Toby All right. I think I'm going over there to ask her, right now, if this is true.

Sylvie Go ahead. She'll deny it. She said she would. She doesn't want any trouble, does she? (*After a pause*) I shouldn't have told you.

Toby Well, it's the first explanation that's made any sense, anyway. I'm rather glad you did tell me. That would appear to be that, then. (*He dries his hands on his handkerchief*) Thank you. You were quite right. I'd have hated to have gone away thinking it was my fault. I'd have hated that.

Sylvie (*gently*) Oh, it's not your fault. It was never your fault. Ever.

Pause

Toby Well, old varlet, I shall no doubt pass you in the village.

Sylvie Yes.

Toby You're still coming to us to help Celia, are you?

Sylvie No. Better not.

Toby Right.

Sylvie Yes.

Toby Goodbye.

Sylvie Goodbye, Mr Teasdale.

Toby Sylvie, just promise me something. Whatever you do, don't waste your brain, will you? It's a good brain.

Toby exits sadly

Sylvie (*with delayed afterthought*) I'll let you have your Dickens back . . .

(*more quietly*) ... when I've finished it. (*She yells*) Come along, roll up there! Come and throw sponges at this varlet now. Three for ten p. Come and sling 'em at her because she's bloody miserable and could do with a few nice sponges to cheer her up. Come on then. ... (*She gives up*) Oh, to hell with this. This is no life for a woman. I'm getting out of this. (*She tries unsuccessfully to release herself*) Oh, hell. I'm stuck and all. Get me out of this. Somebody. Get this blasted varlet out of here.

Lionel enters, still in his skin and carrying his head

Lionel Hallo. You shouting?
Sylvie Am I shouting? Of course I'm shouting.
Lionel (*cheerfully*) Got a problem, have you?
Sylvie Yes, I can't get out.
Lionel You're not supposed to.
Sylvie No, come on, Lionel. It's stuck again. You didn't mend it at all. It keeps jamming.

Lionel examines the pillory but makes no effort to release her

Lionel Oh, yes. I see.
Sylvie (*dangerously*) Lionel.
Lionel You've only been in there ten minutes.
Sylvie Now I want to get out. (*She struggles*) Lionel.
Lionel Got me an answer yet, have you?
Sylvie Bugger off.
Lionel (*moving away*) No, I don't think I like that one.
Sylvie Lionel, please.
Lionel What?
Sylvie Please, I'm getting—panicky. I can't bear being trapped like this— please, Please.
Lionel You're not in a very good position to argue then, are you?
Sylvie You bastard. You're a real bastard, aren't you?
Lionel Dear, dear, dear. (*He moves away from her*)

EITHER she says:

Sylvie All right. It's yes, then. Is that what you want to hear? Yes.
Lionel Yes what?
Sylvie I will.
Lionel You'll what?
Sylvie Marry you, if that's what you want. Got no options, anyway.
Lionel Not pregnant, are you?
Sylvie No, I'm not pregnant, you great hairy fool.

Lionel comes back and leans on the pillory

Lionel Well, this is nice. Nice and romantic. Be able to tell the grandkids this. This is your grandma accepting your grandpa.

Sylvie (*groaning*) Oh, God.
Lionel (*moving to release her*) Right, out you come then.
Sylvie No, don't bother now.
Lionel You stopping in then?
Sylvie Yes.
Lionel Right.
Sylvie Might as well.
Lionel Sling a sponge at you, shall I?
Sylvie Yes, that would be terrific, Lionel. That would just about round it all off, I think.

Lionel gathers up the sponges with enthusiasm, dunking them back in the water

Lionel Here I come then. I'll have fifty p's worth. I'll owe you for it. Are you ready? I warn you I'm a good shot. Dead Eye Dick.
Sylvie Yes, I reckoned you would be, Lionel.
Lionel Here we go. One. (*He hurls a sponge hitting Sylvie full in the face*) Bull's eye.
Sylvie (*closing her eye and gritting her teeth*) Oh, God.
Lionel Two ... (*He continues to hurl sponges at her with devastating and somewhat malicious accuracy*)

The Lights fade to a Black-out

To: A CHRISTENING (page 145)

OR she says:

Sylvie (*plaintively*) Please, Lionel, please.
Lionel (*relenting*) All right. Just a minute. (*He releases her*) All right?
Sylvie (*greatly relieved*) Yes. It was horrible. I was trapped.
Lionel So.
Sylvie Like being strangled. Must have been terrible in those days.
Lionel Well?
Sylvie What?
Lionel What about it? My answer. What about it?
Sylvie Well. (*She starts to remove her costume*)
Lionel Yes?
Sylvie I've discussed it with interested parties and considered it and—er ...
Lionel Yes?
Sylvie No.
Lionel No? What do you mean, no?
Sylvie I don't want to. I don't want to get married.
Lionel What else are you going to do?
Sylvie I don't know.
Lionel You're going on with your lessons instead, are you?
Sylvie No.
Lionel Oh yes.

Sylvie I've given them up, too.
Lionel Have you?
Sylvie Yes.
Lionel What're you going to do?
Sylvie I've got plans.
Lionel (*shrugging*) Get on. You'll be changing your mind again. I'm not bothered. You'll be round. You wait till you see your sun lounge. Your little eyes will pop out. (*He looks in the tin*) You haven't done much business either, have you? The Wild Man of Borneo isn't going so well. Kids don't find him very convincing with no head. Damn thing sort of catches on my nose, you see. I can get it on to here—(*he pulls it half way over his head*)—it's getting it over my nose.
Sylvie Here, let me.
Lionel (*allowing her to do so*) I bet you, you'll be round to see me by the end of the week. Well, if not the end of this week, then the——

Sylvie pulls the head down sharply over Lionel's face

Ow-oy! That's gone right over. (*In a muffled voice*) That's better. How's it look?
Sylvie Great improvement. I'm changing my mind already.
Lionel Yes, it just needed—(*He raises his paws to his head*) I can't get it off.
Sylvie Don't be daft.
Lionel I can't. Sylvie, help, please. Please help, I'm stuck.
Sylvie Here. Let me. Hold still, hold still. (*She tugs in vain*) Yes, you are. You're stuck.
Lionel Yes, I know I'm stuck, you stupid cow. I'm stuck.
Sylvie All right, all right. Don't panic, don't panic. Here, come here. Come on. (*She pulls him towards the pillory*)
Lionel What's happening?
Sylvie Here. Just a minute, put your head here.
Lionel What're you doing?
Sylvie I'm going to lever it off. Put your head here.

Lionel puts his head on the pillory

Now grab hard. Go on, grab on.
Lionel Right. (*He grabs the pillory*)

Sylvie closes it, so Lionel is trapped head and hands

Sylvie There you are.
Lionel What are you——? Sylvie!
Sylvie The Wild Varlet of Borneo. Bye-bye then. Hope they don't throw beer tins. (*She takes off her hat and cape*)
Lionel You can't leave me here, Sylvie. Where are you going?
Sylvie I'm off, Lionel. I'm away. I'm off to do something really useless. The most useless thing I can think of. I'm just going to keep moving. From now on, my life's going to be one huge, marvellous, glorious china shop, so there. You can stick that in your sun lounge. (*She throws a sponge at Lionel*)

Sylvie exits

Lionel mutters indecipherable things inside his gorilla's head as he tries to release himself

Black-out

To: RETURN OF THE PRODIGAL (page 151)

A CHRISTENING

A Churchyard. This year

The church door is open. A gravel path leads away from it to an unseen road. A variety of gravestones border the path

We hear church bells signifying a happy occasion, then as the Lights come up, the sound of children and several babies crying from within the church

Lionel appears in the doorway in his best suit. He seems rather harassed

Lionel (*speaking to someone small behind him*) Charlie, you come out here now. Come on. You come and look after Henry. (*He turns and looks off into the churchyard*) Henry, don't you run away too far now. (*He talks back into the church*) Now, you do as your dad tells you. You come out here. Come on, Charlie. You get down off there. If you swing on that it'll break, then you'll have the vicar after you, won't you? Charlie. (*He turns back to the churchyard*) Henry, I can see you.

Celia arrives in the church doorway dressed in her hat and coat

Celia Would you like me to look after them for you, Lionel?
Lionel Oh no, thank you, Mrs Teasdale. That's all right.
Celia If you wanted to see the christening. I think it's your turn next.
Lionel No, that's all right. (*He speaks back into the church*) All right, you sit there with your sweeties then. And don't throw them papers down.
Celia They're little terrors at that age, aren't they?
Lionel He is. He's a terror. (*He looks back into the churchyard*) That one's not much better. (*He calls*) All right. You play round there then. Won't do a thing I tell them. My dad used to have his belt off to me at that age.
Celia Did he?
Lionel He said, a little cruelty could spread a lot of kindness later.
Celia Yes, that sounds like him.
Lionel She won't let me do that though, Sylvie.
Celia Well, no, it's not the best solution. It's sort of self-perpetuating, isn't it? He'll grow up and do the same thing to his children and so on and so on.
Lionel Unless he marries someone like her, then he won't.
Celia (*laughing*) Oh dear. Is she giving all the orders, is she?
Lionel She knows what she wants.
Celia Ah, well.
Lionel Usually she gets it. If you want to go back in, don't let me ...
Celia No, I just thought I'd have a quick cigarette actually. (*She takes one from her bag*) You don't, do you?

Lionel No, thank you. One too many luxuries, I'm afraid.

Celia Yes, I should really stop but. . . . There's a dreadful din in there, isn't there? I don't know why he can't christen them one at a time. Have an appointment system. I mean, all those babies there at once just set each other off. Can't hear yourself think. I'm sure half of them go away with the wrong name.

Lionel I hope ours does. Anne Charlotte Emily Branwell Hepplewick. That's a hell of a mouthful, isn't it? That was her idea. I wanted to call her Lily. After my mum. She wasn't having that.

Celia Still, they've all got rather quaint names, haven't they? (*She indicates in the direction of the child in the churchyard*) What's that one? Henry . . .?

Lionel Henry Tom Tristram.

Celia Heavens.

Lionel And him in there, he's Charles Oliver Nicholas Magwitch. I don't know where she digs them up half the time.

Pause

Celia No. . . . We haven't seen either of you for ages, have we?

Lionel No, 'fraid we haven't.

Celia Considering we live so close.

Lionel True.

Pause

Celia By the way, it was very sweet of you to ask us both to be godparents.

Lionel Oh, well. Sylvie thought that——

Celia Toby, I know, was thrilled to bits. Very touched. I hope you understood why I couldn't . . .

Lionel No, no, that's quite all right.

Celia I mean, normally I'd have said yes like a shot but I'm so rushed off my feet at the moment that I don't honestly feel I could have done the thing justice. And I do think one has to do these things properly, don't you? No point in putting your name to something just for the sake of it.

Lionel No, we both quite understood——(*He looks out into the churchyard*) Where's he gone to?

Celia It's all right, he's behind the tombstone.

Lionel Oh, yes.

Pause

Celia You're still with the corporation, are you?

Lionel Oh, yes. Parks department.

Celia Is that interesting?

Lionel Very interesting indeed. Always something new to tackle. Always coming up with fresh ideas.

Celia Oh, yes. Weren't you—didn't I read about that business with the clock? That was you, wasn't it?

Lionel It was, it was. The flower clock, you mean? By the Town Hall.

Celia Yes, what was all that?

Lionel Well, a little altercation with the councillors. I wanted to modernize it, you see.

Celia Modernize it?

Lionel I wanted to make it digital. Be the first digital flower clock.

Celia Heavens, how complicated.

Lionel Yes, it needed a bit of working out. Basically quite simple though. You have these two revolving discs, you see—like this—(*he demonstrates*)—about twelve foot in diameter and then there's this shutter that comes across over the top so that only the numbers you want to see are being revealed.

Celia How ingenious.

Lionel It was. Only trouble was the flowers kept dying. Didn't get any light.

Celia Yes, that would have been a drawback. A dead flower clock wouldn't be very attractive.

Lionel I could have licked it given time. Anyway, I'm on with the bowling green at the moment. Getting it level before the season starts. Do you know, it's been there eighty-seven years on a slant and nobody noticed.

Celia Really?

Lionel Till I pointed it out. (*After a pause, he indicates*) Dad's grave there, you see.

Celia Yes. Nearly two years now, isn't it?

Lionel Yes. The winter finally got him. I think he got a bit cold sitting in that sun lounge. There were one or two draughts.

Celia Shame. (*She glances into the church*)

Lionel He all right, is he?

Celia Yes, he's eating a bar of something.

Pause

Lionel Mr Teasdale's looking well.

Celia Yes. He's feeling a lot better since he gave up teaching. The responsibility really did weigh him down a bit, I'm afraid. Fortunately our friend, Miles Coombes, has stepped in to help yet again. So my husband's now joined his firm as a senior executive. Back to industry where he started. He looks a bit better anyway.

Lionel glances back inside the church

Have they finished?

Lionel Yes, I think just about. (*With indecision*) I'll—er——

Celia I'll keep an eye on that one if you want to pop back in.

Lionel Would you mind? I'll just see if she needs a hand. Won't be a minute.

Lionel goes back into the church

Celia Right. (*She speaks to the child in the churchyard*) What are you doing, Henry? I wouldn't play with those, dear. They're not your flowers. Put them down. Put them down. (*Sharply*) Down. That's better. Well, haven't you got a funny face? Yes. Quite hideous. Yes. You're worse than your brother who's covered in chocolate. Peep-bo. Yes. Peep-bo. (*She glances up at the church tower*) It's still falling down this place. We've spent

thousands on it. (*She moves to Joe's grave and reads aloud*) "In memory of
Joseph John Hepplewick aged seventy-five."

"This will not be the last of him you've seen.
His poetry will linger evergreen."

He appears to have passed on the gift. Peep-bo ... yes ... peep-bo. Dear
God. ... Oh, now you've walked into it, haven't you? No, well that's
stupid, isn't it? You look where you're going. I'm not feeling sorry for
people who walk into tombstones. That's just plain silly.

Toby comes out of the church

Toby Oh, there you are.

Celia Yes.

Toby Couldn't you have even sat in for the service?

Celia I couldn't bear it in there. It was like a maternity ward at feeding time.

Toby Would have been a nice gesture.

Celia So you're now a godfather.

Toby Yes.

Celia I hope you'll take it seriously.

Toby Of course I will.

Celia Don't just send it pound notes. Like mine did. I never saw her.

Toby I don't think I even had any.

Celia Of course you did. Everybody has godparents.

Toby I didn't. No, I intend to take it very seriously. I shall take a personal
interest in her education.

Celia Oh yes? I thought you'd given all that up. Teaching.

Toby Well, maybe one exception.

Celia I see.

Toby That's if you don't have any objections.

Celia Me? Why should I?

Toby You did before.

Celia Oh, Toby, don't start all that again. How many more times. I never
said a word to Sylvie. I did feel on occasions you were getting—well, it
wasn't good for her. She was very young but I never said a word to her. I
promise. I wouldn't be that stupid.

Toby Ah, well.

Celia You still don't believe me, do you?

Toby (*jumping suddenly in fright*) Oh, dear God.

Celia What's the matter?

Toby I just thought I saw something. Awful gnome thing. Popped out of a
tombstone. ... God, there it is again. What is it?

Celia It's a Hepplewick.

Toby Is that what it is?

Celia Keep an eye on it a minute, will you?

Toby Me?

Celia I just want to say goodbye to Sylvie.

Toby Are we going?

Celia We might as well. Unless you want to be godfather to any more of
them.

Celia goes into the church

Toby (*staring after Celia thoughtfully*) Yes. (*He turns towards the child in the churchyard*) Where's it gone then? Oh, there you are. (*He feigns shock as the child jumps out at him*) Whoo, don't do that. Frightened me. (*After a pause*) Whoo. He's done it again. (*After a pause*) Whoo. Yes, right. We've had that one. I'll give myself a heart attack otherwise. (*He sits*) May I give you a word of advice ... yes, boo to you ... when you grow up ... whoops, careful ... if you grow up and if you decide to get married, do marry a woman with sense of humour, won't you? Two reasons for this. First, it's intolerable living with a woman without one and second, looking at you, she's going to need it. Boo. Boo. Frankly, the way things are going at present, I very much doubt if either of these problems are going to concern you. Every time I hear a jet plane these days, I think it's a rocket. No way to live, is it? Cowering under the kitchen table. Bloody lunatics, all of them. They're all lunatics. God, I could do with a drink.

Sylvie comes from the church. She is rather stouter than before and slightly more staid

Sylvie Is he out there?
Toby Yes.
Sylvie Come on, then. Come on, Henry. Don't do that now, come on. (*To Toby*) Your wife says you're leaving.
Toby Apparently.
Sylvie Right, well. Thank you very much for——
Toby No. Thank you. For asking me.
Sylvie You don't need to do anything, you know. It's just we wanted someone and——
Toby No, I intend to fulfil my duties. Celia's been giving me a lecture.
Sylvie You don't have to.
Toby I insist. Anne Charlotte Emily Branwell's education will shortly be continuing where yours left off.
Sylvie Oh. Well, I'm sure that'll be very nice for her. (*She calls*) Henry, I'll come over and get you in a minute. Now you come here. Before I get cross. (*To Toby*) I thought you weren't teaching any more. I thought you were a managing director or something.
Toby I'm certainly not that.
Sylvie Well, whatever.
Toby I'm a supervisor in the packing department. Which is about the most responsibility I can handle. We are busily despatching micro-computer parts all over the globe in an attempt to make the business of killing each other off that much easier. Since most of the stuff's so tiny you can hardly see it anyway, it's doubly rewarding. Like packing nerve gas.
Sylvie I shouldn't do it then, if you don't like it.
Toby One has to make a contribution, you know. You see, the cunning thing is because I'm often drunk, generally incompetent and never give a damn, most of the stuff gets put in the wrong boxes anyway so the Arabs get the stuff that's meant for Israel and the Americans get the Russian

bits. I'm probably singlehandedly holding up World War Three. As soon as they've sorted out the right bits, off they'll go.

Sylvie You ought to stop drinking.

Toby Oh, don't you start.

Sylvie You once told me not to waste my brain. God knows what you've done to yours. Right, I'm coming over there now, Henry. (*She starts to move*) I shouldn't have worn these shoes. When I get home, I'm putting my feet up, I don't care. (*She calls*) Come on.

Toby You still read, Sylvie?

Sylvie When I get a minute. Not many of those at the moment.

Toby Sylvie.

Sylvie What?

Toby Tell me something, would you? Just out of curiosity. I mean, it can't make any difference now. Was it really true Celia asked you to stop your lessons? (*After a pause*) Was it?

Sylvie Can't remember now. Five years ago, wasn't it?

Toby It wasn't true? Was it?

Sylvie Well, maybe she didn't ask me. But she would have done sooner or later.

Toby I don't think she would have done. For one thing, she'd have had no grounds. And I'd have told her so. Absolutely none. My attitude to you, as I'm sure you'll agree, was always entirely that of a teacher to his pupil, wasn't it?

Sylvie Oh, yes.

Toby Well then. No grounds, no case.

Sylvie I don't think it was you she was worried about. (*She calls*) Come on. Last time.

Toby (*startled*) What? You mean——? She can't have. . . . Well. Then she's completely off her head, isn't she? If she thought that.

Sylvie (*softly*) She's not a fool, you know. Your wife. Don't underestimate her.

Toby (*lost for words*) Ah.

Sylvie (*moving away*) Come on now. I'm taking you home for tea, Henry. Look at those hands. Come on, home for tea. Teatime.

Sylvie exits across the churchyard

Toby watches her for a second

Toby (*recovering*) Yes. So it is. Time for tea.

Toby goes into the church

The Lights fade to a Black-out

RETURN OF THE PRODIGAL

A Churchyard. This year

The church door is closed. A gravel path leads away from it to an unseen road. A variety of gravestones border the path

We hear church bells signifying a happy occasion, followed by the sound of singing within the church. A service of Thanksgiving for Bilbury Lodge's fifty year existence is being celebrated

The church door bursts open and Toby staggers out, looking slightly the worse for wear

After a moment Celia follows anxiously, closing the door behind her

Toby breathes deeply

Celia (*watching him for a second*) Are you all right?

Toby Yes, yes.

Celia This is getting too much of a good thing, you know, Toby. This is the third time this has happened.

Toby Indigestion.

Celia It's not indigestion. Sit down.

Toby I don't want to sit down.

Celia All right, stand up then.

Toby (*still feeling queasy*) Oh, God. (*He sits down*)

Celia I wish you'd have a check up. It's so embarrassing. They all turned round to stare.

Toby They wouldn't notice, that lot.

Celia Oh, yes, they did. The Headmaster can't walk out in the middle of a service without being noticed. I wouldn't mind but it has to be this service. All the Governors, the parents, those ex-headmasters. Then there are the visiting headmasters. . . .

Toby Yes, all right, Celia, I don't want the bloody guest list.

Celia It's supposed to be a fifty-year celebration for the school. I think the least you could have done was to try and—control yourself.

Toby Just tell them I started celebrating earlier, that's all. Never mind. We've got the Staff production of *Charley's Aunt* tonight. That'll cheer us all up. If it's anything like *Ruddigore* last year, it'll close us down for good.

Celia It sounds great fun. I'm going.

Toby I'm not. I'm going to the cinema.

Celia What to see?

Toby Nothing. I'm going to play Bingo.

Celia I wouldn't put it past you, I really wouldn't. Do you feel up to talking to this woman?

Toby What woman?

Celia The woman you're supposed to be talking to.

Toby My darling, you are talking in riddles. I see no woman, only you, my love. Is this woman invisible? Or is she buried somewhere round here? Have we got to start digging her up?

Celia Toby.

Toby Yes.

Celia You agreed you would talk to a journalist.

Toby I did?

Celia Yes.

Toby When did I?

Celia Weeks ago. You said you would. It's some magazine for women. I don't know. The editor wrote, then she rang and you said yes and they've sent someone.

Toby I said yes?

Celia Yes.

Toby Why? Why should I say yes?

Celia Probably because I told you to say no. Anything I suggest, you do the reverse. Well, she's here now. I don't know what you're going to say. It sounds like some terrible radical thing.

Toby What is it? A magazine?

Celia Yes, I told you at the time. It's called—I don't know—"Plastic Brides" or something.

Toby "Plastic Brides"?

Celia Something like that. It's woman's jargon. It's feminist and all that business.

Toby Feminist?

Celia Yes.

Toby Dear God. Well, I'm not talking to them.

Celia Well, she's here now.

Toby Where?

Celia In church. Somebody pointed her out to me.

Toby A religious feminist. It gets worse. What's she like?

Celia I don't know. I only saw her from the back.

Toby Young?

Celia She looks it.

Toby Oh, for heaven's sake. This is too much. I loathe all young people, you know that.

Celia Good. Well, you can use that as the opening to the interview. I loathe all young people, said the Headmaster. . . .

Toby What does this "Plastic Brides"—it can't possibly be called that— what does it want with me?

Celia Well, they want to talk about the fiftieth anniversary of the school and you and private education. I suspect probably in a very denigrating manner—they don't sound as if they're all in favour of the system.

Toby What am I going to say to her?

Celia I don't know.

Toby I shall probably punch her in the nose.

Celia Yes, well, I expect you'll be your usual tactful self. (*She starts to move back towards the church*)

Toby (*agitatedly*) No, wait, wait, wait. Celia, Celia.

Celia We've got to go back in.

Toby What am I going to say?

Celia Toby, I don't know. Tell her you're strongly in favour of hanging and bringing back the birch and child chimney sweeps and taking the vote away from women.

Toby Don't be ridiculous. I don't believe that. Well, the last one perhaps but not the rest of it. I don't believe all that.

Celia It never stopped you saying it, did it? You just say the worst things you can think of. You told the man from the *Church Times* that the body of the Church was maggot-ridden. That looked rather good in print, I thought.

Toby Oh, God.

Celia Toby, you agreed to talk to her. You will have to talk to her. She's coming to the house this afternoon. Now if you've changed your mind and you don't want to see her, you will have to tell her so. I'm not doing it for you. Now come back inside, please.

Toby In a minute.

Celia Toby, please.

Toby (*snarling*) In a minute.

Celia All right. (*She is suddenly tearful*) Why do you do this to me, Toby . . .

Celia goes back inside the church and closes the door

Toby (*muttering*) "Plastic Brides". (*Loudly to himself*) You're not to drink any more, Teasdale, do you hear me? You've had your limit. (*In a female voice*) How do you view the woman's role in modern society today, Mr Teasdale? (*In his normal voice*) Well, personally MIZZZ Jones, I think you should all be rounded up, put into a sheep pen and dipped regularly. (*In a female voice*) Oh, how interesting, Mr Teasdale. . . . (*He wanders as far as Hepplewick's tombstone and reads aloud*) "In memory of Joseph John Hepplewick aged seventy-five."

"This will not be the last of him you've seen.
His poetry will linger evergreen."

I hope they buried his poems with him. I bet he's still writing them down there. Aren't you, Hepplewick? If you listen very carefully, you can probably hear him. Like this . . . (*He kneels and then lies on the ground*) I bet you can hear his disposable ballpoint pen scratching away. Yes, there he goes. Further immortal stanzas. Still trying to think of a good rhyme for garbage. Oh, dear God, I'm tired. That's better. Keep going, Joe. Keep going, lad. By the law of averages you've got to write a decent line of poetry eventually. (*He dozes on the ground*)

The church door opens and Sylvie comes out. It is a new trimline Sylvie. Her hair's been cut and she is altogether more urbanized

Sylvie (*looking round*) Mr Teasdale? Mr Teasdale?

Toby (*with his eyes still closed*) Hallo, there, Joe. How are you?

Sylvie (*seeing him, alarmed*) Mr Teasdale, are you all right?

Toby (*opening his eyes with a start*) Oh, good heavens. Yes, I do. I mean, I am. (*He stares at her*) Sylvie? It's not Sylvie, is it?

Sylvie Hallo, Mr Teasdale.

Toby Dear God, it's Sylvie. I thought you'd vanished for good. Where have you been all these years?

Sylvie Do you want a hand?

Toby Thank you.

Sylvie helps Toby to his feet

Sylvie What were you doing down there?

Toby I was just having a quiet word with Joe Hepplewick.

Sylvie Oh, I see. Has he got any less objectionable since he died?

Toby No, he's worse still. Much worse.

Sylvie That figures.

Toby How long's it been? Five years, isn't it?

Sylvie Yes.

Toby You've changed.

Sylvie Well. Had my hair cut.

Toby Oh yes, so you have.

Sylvie I saw you running out in the middle. I wondered if you were all right.

Toby Indigestion, that's all.

Sylvie (*disbelievingly*) Oh yes.

Toby Why didn't you say you were coming?

Sylvie Surprise.

Toby What brings you back, anyway? I thought you'd fled for good.

Sylvie Well, business really.

Toby Oh yes? What's that?

Sylvie You.

Toby Me?

Sylvie I've come to interview you.

Toby You've come to——Oh, my God. You're not this "Plastic Brides" woman, are you?

Sylvie Plastic what?

Toby What's your magazine called?

Sylvie *Drastic Strides.*

Toby That's the one. You haven't gone and joined all that lot, have you?

Sylvie All what?

Toby All that bunch. That aggressive business.

Sylvie I'm not aggressive.

Toby Thank God.

Sylvie Nor's the magazine.

Toby Isn't it?

Sylvie No. It just puts the woman's point of view about things. That's all. It's very small. There's only about five of us.

Toby I see. What do you do? Sell it in public lavatories and things, do you?

Sylvie No, we don't. (*She smiles*) Honestly. You've got worse not better, haven't you?

Toby Probably. There's nothing to stop me now Joe Hepplewick's dead. The whole moral climate's shot to ribbons. What do you want to talk to me about?

Sylvie I'm coming to see you at three o'clock. We'll talk then.

Toby What about?

Sylvie About you. About the school.

Toby So you can tell them what a rotten corrupt establishment it is. Run by a middle-aged reactionary.

Sylvie No. I hope I can write better than that.

Toby Really?

Sylvie I'll say what I think are the good things and what I think are the bad things, that's all. How are you?

Toby I'm tremendously well. A hundred and fifty per cent fit.

Sylvie (*drily*) You look it.

Toby I haven't had my hair cut, that's all.

Sylvie I hear Lionel's married.

Toby Yes. He married another traffic warden. A female one, I think. They must have collided, both trying to book the same vehicle. A flurry of notebooks and plastic bags, until their rubber bands became inseparably entangled.

Sylvie smiles

Pause

You fixed up with someone?

Sylvie Sort of.

Toby OK?

Sylvie (*smiling*) Great. Absolutely great.

Toby Good. I'm glad you haven't given up men altogether.

Sylvie Who said it was a man?

Toby (*flummoxed*) Isn't it? It isn't a——It's a man, isn't it? Isn't it?

Sylvie (*smiling*) Yes, course it is. (*She laughs*) Your face. That was wonderful. When I bring my camera up there this afternoon, I'll try and catch that expression again.

Toby You're not taking pictures of me, I can tell you.

Sylvie We'd better go back in. It's nearly over.

Toby Oh, Lord. I suppose so.

They start to move back towards the church slowly

Sylvie (*laughing*) "Plastic Brides".

Toby You're not married?

Sylvie No, I'm bloody not.

Toby Right.

Sylvie (*stopping*) Hey, just before we go in ...

Toby Mm?

Sylvie Here. In case I don't get a chance later. (*She kisses Toby on the mouth*) Thank you.

Toby What for?

Sylvie For opening the door for me. Helping me escape.

Toby (*quite moved by this*) I didn't do very much.

Sylvie You did, you know. Anyway, to say thank you.

Toby (*recovering*) I thought you women rather objected to doors being opened for you.

Sylvie (*smiling*) Well, there's some doors we don't mind ... (*She opens the church door*) After you, then.

Toby Thank you.

Toby goes into the church

Sylvie takes a last look round the churchyard, smiles and follows him inside

As she closes the door, the Lights fade to a Black-out

INTIMATE EXCHANGES is a related series of plays totalling eight scripts

This is the Fourth

A PAGEANT

preceded by *How It Began* (page 3);
A Gardener Calls (page 5) and *The Self-
Improving Woman* (page 107)

CHARACTERS
APPEARING IN THIS SERIES OF SCENES

Celia
Lionel
Sylvie
Toby

A PAGEANT

A meadow. Five weeks later. 2 p.m. Saturday, July 24th

In one corner there is a raised platform stage, extremely simple and crude in design. It has two uprights at the back suspending a horizontal curtain pole. On this hangs a cloth backdrop of light material with a centre and two side openings. The stage itself is filled in around the front and sides by a valance of similar material. It is thus possible to crawl in under this from all sides

In a moment, Lionel enters carrying a bag of tools and a couple of planks. He appears in no hurry. He puts his tool kit on the stage and stops for a moment to enjoy the day. After a while, he turns his attention to the stage, grips hold of it and attempts to rock it. He nods thoughtfully. He takes a hammer and nails from his tool kit, lifts the valance and crawls underneath the stage

Lionel (*off*) Ah. Now then. Sort this bugger out.

After a pause Celia enters from the other direction. She appears to be in search of somebody but seeing no one around stops rather irritably. She is carrying a looseleaf folder

Celia Oh. (*She opens the folder and flips through a few pages*) Yes. . . . (*She starts to mutter almost inaudibly to herself, concentrating on a page of dialogue that she has only imperfectly learnt*)

> Come ye, Britons, know ye that I speak
> Not as a mighty woman born . . .

(*She glances at the script*) . . . No——

> Not as a woman born of mighty men . . .

She brandishes one arm rather ineffectually, stepping on to the platform as she does so

> Not the wife of King thing . . .

What's the wretched man's name—(*She looks at the script*)—Prasutugus.

> Not once the wife of King Prasutugas
> Oh, people of Iceni now behold

She gestures

> Plain Boadicea . . .

Sound of a burst of hammering from under the platform

(*Alarmed*) Oh, dear heaven.

Sound of more hammering

> Who is that there? What are you doing down there? Who is that? This is the Headmaster's wife. Who is it?

Lionel (*off*) Afternoon.

Celia Who is that?

Lionel (*off*) Afternoon, Mrs Teasdale. It's Lionel.

Celia Lionel? What are you doing?

Lionel (*off*) Just making this safe, Mrs Teasdale.

Celia Isn't it safe?

Lionel Not quite.

Celia Oh. (*She steps off the platform*)

Lionel (*off*) Needs another support or two.

Celia You should put a notice on it, Lionel.

Lionel (*off*) Ah.

Celia (*studying the platform with fresh interest*) Have you—have you built things like this before, Lionel?

Lionel (*off*) Sorry, like what?

Celia Platforms. And things.

Lionel (*off*) Oh, yes.

Celia Ah. I didn't realize.

Lionel (*off*) I'm building a conservatory at the moment.

Celia Oh.

Lionel (*off*) For my dad.

Celia Lovely.

Lionel (*off*) I'm a trained cabinet maker.

Celia Really?

Lionel (*off*) Had to jack it in though.

Celia Oh, dear.

Lionel (*off*) No call for it.

Celia Oh, I don't know. I'd have thought there would have been.

Lionel (*off*) When did you last need a cabinet?

Celia No, true. (*She looks puzzled*)

Lionel (*off*) It's all two ply veneer and polyfilla these days.

Celia Yes.

Lionel (*off*) No pride.

Celia No.

Sound of burst of hammering

> Lionel.

The hammering stops

Lionel (*off*) Hallo.

Celia You won't be making too much noise, will you?

Lionel (*off*) No.

Celia It's just that I need to rehearse, you see.

Lionel (*off*) Right.

Celia Boadicea's speech to her people on the eve of battle. Very inspiring. (*She declaims*)

> Come ye, Britons, know ye that I speak
> Not as a woman . . .

The hammering restarts

Oh, God. (*She tries to speak over the noise*)

> Know ye that I speak
> Not as a woman born of mighty . . .

Oh, this is impossible——

> mighty . . .

The hammering stops

> . . . men.

Oh, thank heavens. (*She stands and regains her breath, ready to start again*)

Toby enters carrying a script and a loudhailer

Celia At last.
Toby Oh, hallo.
Celia I've been here for ages.
Toby Have you?
Celia Yes. Where have you been?
Toby I'm looking for Hepplewick.
Celia He's under there.
Toby What the hell's he doing under there?
Celia Apparently mending it.
Toby (*lifting the corner of the valance*) Hepplewick, I say?

Sound of a burst of hammering

What the hell is he doing? (*He crawls under the valance*) Hepplewick?

The hammering stops

Lionel (*off*) Afternoon, Mr Teasdale.
Toby (*off*) Have you finished that chariot yet?
Lionel (*off*) Nearly done.
Toby (*off*) Well, we need it this afternoon.
Lionel (*off*) Right, I'll get on with that then.
Toby (*off*) You'd better. Tomorrow morning's a dress rehearsal and the show's in the afternoon. Get on with it.
Lionel (*off, cheerfully*) Right you are, Mr Teasdale.
Toby Right. (*He starts to reverse out*)
Lionel (*off, muttering*) Stupid old bugger.
Toby (*moving under the valance*) What was that?
Lionel (*off*) Nothing, Mr Teasdale.
Toby (*emerging*) Yes. Just watch yourself, Hepplewick.

Sound of more hammering

Toby straightens up with difficulty

The hammering stops

He was supposed to have finished this weeks ago.

Celia So long as he does. I don't fancy standing on it otherwise.

Toby No, neither would I. (*He looks at his watch*)

Celia Well.

Toby Mm?

Celia Let's get on with it then.

Toby On with what?

Celia The rehearsal. I thought we were supposed to be rehearsing.

Toby Are we?

Celia Oh, Toby, don't be so obtuse. We're desperately short of time, now let's get on with it.

Toby I'm sorry, Celia, I'm completely lost. What are you talking about?

Celia The pageant.

Toby The pageant, yes.

Celia For tomorrow afternoon.

Toby Yes.

Celia Boadicea and the Romans. Remember?

Toby Boudicca, yes.

Celia Oh, good. Some part of your brain still works, anyway.

Toby The brain's working splendidly, Celia. I still don't know what you're talking about.

Celia Here I am.

Toby Jolly good.

Celia To rehearse.

Toby Rehearse?

Celia My part.

Toby What part?

Celia Boadicea.

Toby Boudicca.

Celia Boudicca, then.

Toby You?

Celia Yes.

Toby Oh, come off it.

Celia What?

Toby You're not playing Boudicca.

Celia Oh, yes I am.

Toby Who said?

Celia Basil Pickup.

Toby Basil Pickup.

Celia Yes. He phoned me last night. While you were at—at the pub.

Toby At the monthly cricket club committee meeting.

Celia At the pub.

Toby Which is regularly held in the pub. What the hell's all this got to do with Basil Pickup?

Celia I said, he phoned me. In the middle of a very good television play so I'll never know whether it was her fault or whether the son was deliberately lying because he knew that the girl was already in love with his friend. . . .

Toby Celia, what are you saying?

Celia I'm saying he asked me—perhaps they'll repeat it—he begged me to play Boadicea. He said you were both at your wits' end. And that Janet Mallet had broken her wrist. And I was the only one. And I said yes—well, I was very busy but yes—and he said splendid. Come and rehearse this afternoon. Only he wouldn't be here because he was away with the First Eleven. So here I am.

Toby (*taking all this in*) Hell's bells. What the blazes did he do that for?

Celia He said you were desperate.

Toby (*muttering*) Not that desperate.

Celia Well, thank you very much.

Toby Why doesn't Basil tell me before he does these things? Why didn't you tell me?

Celia Because you didn't get home till heaven knows when and you wouldn't wake up this morning. I had to be off out. I have a lot to do. Particularly if I'm going to give my afternoon up.

Toby Basil Pickup should mind his own damn business.

Celia It is his business. He's the author.

Toby Well, I'm the producer. Casting is my job, not his. It's my job to cast it and to try and kick his bloody awful pentameters into some semblance of civilized language.

Celia I don't know why you want to do it at all. You're not a producer. You hate the theatre. Why didn't you leave it to Simon Fognorth?

Toby No damn fear.

Celia He was very hurt not to be asked again.

Toby Good.

Celia Last year's play was delightful.

Toby What—"Comus"?

Celia Quite charming.

Toby It was teeth-scrapingly boring. It had the same effect as sucking powdered pumice stone.

Celia I enjoyed it. Lovely little frocks the girls had.

Toby Well, I had enough of it. I wanted something with a bit more—beef dripping to it. I'd seen enough eight year olds tripping round the lawn in yards of grubby tulle. Time we livened things up.

Celia You'll certainly do that. I mean, reading it, it does seem rather violent.

Toby It is violent.

Celia That's horrid.

Toby Reflection of our times, Celia. Art should reflect life.

Celia On the contrary, surely art should lead us into something more beautiful. Serene. Calm. Restful.

Toby A sort of spiritual Horlicks.

Celia Nonsense.

Toby I'm sorry, I prefer a drop of something stronger in mine.

Celia Well, we won't argue. We haven't time. Where do you want me to stand?

Toby I don't care where you stand, just don't get in my way.

Celia Toby, where do you want Boadicea—Boudicca to stand?

Toby I want Boudicca to stand on the platform.

Celia Thank you. Then I shall do so.

Toby On the other hand I do not want you to stand on the platform, Celia.

Celia What do you mean?

Toby Because if you stand there, there will be no room for Boudicca.

A slight pause

Celia Do I take it from that that I'm not playing Boudicca?

Toby Sorry. No. It's already cast.

Celia (*icily*) And may I ask who is?

Toby The part of Boudicca is being played by Sylvie Bell.

Celia Sylvie Bell?

Toby Sorry.

Celia What nonsense.

Toby We went for a younger woman.

Celia What absolute rubbish. I mean—she can—I mean—she can hardly read.

Toby Oh, she can read.

Celia She's er—she's so—well. She's——

Toby She's perfect.

Celia Toby, you—are you seriously preferring Sylvie Bell to me?

Toby In this instance, I'm afraid I am, Celia. I hope you're not too upset. I went round to see her last night on the way to the meeting. I asked her to do it for me as a huge last-minute favour. To take over from Janet Mallet. She agreed.

Celia I'm sure she did. With alacrity no doubt.

Toby Oh, now, Celia. . . .

Celia So. I'm not wanted.

Toby Celia, don't get dramatic.

Celia No. No. (*After a pause*) The fact that I've sat up half the night trying to learn those terrible lines—rushed round this morning amidst everything else, Jimmy's cubs for one—trying to put together some sort of costume—arranging to have my hair done for tomorrow when she was absolutely booked solid, only to be told by my own husband that he doesn't want me. He'd prefer some little—thing—that he's apparently become totally obsessed with—to the exclusion of his family—his children—his work—me. . . .

Toby Have you finished?

Celia Yes. Yes. Yes. Yes.

Slight pause

Toby How long have you been bottling all this up?

Celia I've seen you, Toby, don't try and. . . . I know you. You're besotted with this girl. You're both in there in the dining-room, night after night, laughing and—reading—and God knows what else and I have to carry on my life as if I hadn't noticed. Everybody smiling at me sympathetically. Poor Mrs Teasdale. It's too much, Toby. Now you've even given her—(*She weeps*)—Boadicea.

Toby (*gently*) Celia, you couldn't—you couldn't possibly play Boudicca.

Celia (*snuffling*) Of course I could.

Toby Celia. She was—er—she was a wild, primitive, uninhibited woman who was responsible for the massacre of over seventy thousand crack Roman soldiers whilst clad only in three bits of fur and some blue paint.

Celia So that's why you want Sylvie Bell to play it.

Toby No, no, I'm exaggerating. I don't think the parents are quite ready for that. The point I'm making, Celia, is that Boudicca—although very little is known about her really, except through Tacitus who was somewhat prejudiced—none the less, she was a woman of the earth, shall we say?

Celia She was a queen.

Toby (*dubiously*) Well. Not in the sense you mean. Tribal leader.

Celia She was. She was royal. And, with respect, Sylvie Bell—well, she's hardly what you'd call blue-blooded, is she?

Toby Neither are you.

Celia I'm a good deal bluer than she is, I can tell you. My great, great, great, great, great grandfather was a falconer.

Toby So what? My grandfather kept pigeons. That's not what I'm saying.

Celia I know what you're saying. You're saying you prefer Sylvie Bell to me.

Toby Celia, why are you doing this? What is the point of getting jealous of a girl who means—well, practically nothing to me.

Celia Practically?

Toby Practically. Anyway, you don't have the qualities, Celia, and that's it. I'm the producer. I know what I'm looking for. I'm sorry, you're dead wrong. Thanks for coming along. Leave your phone number. Maybe next year.

Celia sobs

Oh, God.

Celia It's no good, Toby, I'm going to have to leave you.

Toby Yes. Well, we'll talk about it later, shall we?

Celia No, now. It has to be now.

Toby Look, Sylvie's due here in a minute. Where the hell is she?

Celia It's her or me, Toby.

Toby I'm sorry, Celia, I'm not going into this.

Celia You can't have us both.

Toby I don't want you both.

Celia Well, then, choose.

Toby It's not a question of choosing. I don't have the choice. I can't have her whom I get on with quite well because the whole thing would be quite ludicrous and I've got you whom I don't like and I'm stuck with it.

Pause

Celia (*muted*) Oh, well . . .

Toby I'm sorry, I didn't mean that.

Celia Oh, yes you did.

Toby No. You know me, Celia. I—bounce words around sometimes just for the hell of it.

Celia Well. The trouble is they hit people, Toby. That's the trouble. (*After a pause*) Do you know, I think I might fight this one.

Toby Fight?

Celia Yes.

Toby What?

Celia Why should I give up everything for her? Everything I—we've worked for.

Toby I don't know what you're talking about.

Pause

Celia I never thought you'd be so conventional, Toby. A middle-aged man and a young girl. Not like you. So conventional. (*After a pause*) What are you thinking about?

Toby Nothing.

Celia Her?

Toby Oh, Celia . . .

Celia Her.

Toby I was actually thinking of you.

Celia Well. Surprise.

Toby I was just thinking, you know, this isn't a criticism but I've never ever seen you without your clothes on. Isn't that extraordinary? Not in, what is it, eleven years?

Celia Twelve.

Toby Twelve years. Isn't that odd? I mean, I'm not complaining. It's just extraordinary. People probably wouldn't believe it.

Celia Well. I never—you never seemed that interested. You were always reading a book. What do you want me to do? Paint myself blue?

Toby It's just odd. I mean, these days you see so many bodies, particularly women's. Women you'll never meet. But the one woman I do know—will have known best of all in my life when I die—I've never seen.

Celia I was—it's nothing very special. Never was.

Toby Perhaps I should have been the judge of that. I'm pretty bloody odd as well come to that.

Celia I don't know why we're suddenly talking about bodies.

Toby (*gloomily*) Must be the warm weather.

Celia It never interested you before. Well, not that much.

Toby We've had two children.

Celia Yes. Just. (*After a pause*) Oh, dear God. I'm terribly unhappy, Toby.

Toby Sorry.

Sound of a sudden hammering

Celia (*appalled*) Has he been there all this time?

Toby Must have been.

Celia But that's awful. That's awful.

Toby What's it matter.

Celia I forgot all about him. We've been talking about our whole—most private—life.

Toby Who cares?

Celia (*mouthing*) Our sex life.

Toby Oh, come on, Celia. Rip 'em off. Rip off all those layers of thermal interlocked inhibitions. Let the air get to you.

Celia You're at it again. It's that Bell girl. It really is. You're like some awful old dead tree that's suddenly burst into leaf. It's quite horrifying.

Toby Tremendous.

Celia I shall be back.

Toby Really.

Celia With or without my inhibitions. I'm going to fight this, Toby. I intend to fight. We'll soon see which one of us is the true Boadicea.

Celia exits

Toby (*calling after her, without much energy*) Boudicca. (*After a pause*) I hope you enjoyed all that, Hepplewick.

Sound of more hammering

Right. The Roman Legions are over there. The audience are over there. The Britons'll start off here. And then march up there. That'll do it. (*He lifts a corner of the stage valance*) Hepplewick, are you there? (*He sticks his head under*) Hepplewick?

Lionel (*muffled*) Yes, Mr Teasdale.

Toby (*still under the valance*) What are you doing under there? Are you tunnelling out of there?

Lionel (*off*) I think it might just need another brace here, Mr Teasdale.

Toby (*still under the valance*) Well, put it in and then get the bloody chariot. I need the chariot to rehearse with.

Lionel (*off*) Right, I'll just——

Another burst of hammering

Toby emerges

Toby (*glancing at his watch*) Where the hell is she? (*He sees someone in the distance*) Oh, there she is. (*He hails*) Sylvie! Come on, hurry up. Come on.

Sylvie enters breathless. She carries her costume in a carrier bag

Sylvie Sorry, Mr Teasdale.

Toby You're terribly late, Sylvie.

Sylvie Sorry. Last minute panic. I had to change Leroy. He'd thrown up his dinner.

Toby Oh. Is he ill?

Sylvie No. He's always throwing up. He's one of those babies. Some do, some don't. Jeannine kept it down. So did Rachel. Marcie threw up.

Toby Yes.

Sylvie As for Gerald. Both ends all the time.

Toby Yes, right. Ready to go, are we?

Sylvie Brought my costume. I'll change somewhere here.

Toby Good.

Sylvie Wasn't going to walk through the village in it.

Toby Something wrong, is there?

Sylvie Well. She's a funny shape, isn't she? That Mrs Mallet. All bottom and no top. Is that what they used to wear then?

Toby Er—yes. Probably less than that actually.

Sylvie Less?

Toby Yes.

Sylvie God. I'm keeping my pants on.

Toby Yes, yes. Do.

Sylvie Want me to change now?

Toby No, let's go through the speech first. Then we'll do it all properly.

Sylvie Right. Woo. Nervous. Very difficult to learn, this Bowdyker. She's difficult.

Toby Boudicca.

Sylvie Boudicca, is it? Who was she then?

Toby She was the wife of Prasutugus, king of the Iceni and she was a queen.

Sylvie Yes, I gathered that. Was she, you know, like that other one? Boadicea?

Toby It's the same person.

Sylvie Why are we calling her Boudicca then?

Toby That's her proper name. Boadicea was a bastardization. She was probably called either Boudicca or Bodicca.

Sylvie Wasn't she sure then?

Toby She was. We aren't.

Sylvie I wonder if they'll say that about me. She was either Sylvie Bell or Slyvie Ball. We're not sure.

Toby Oh, God love us.

Sylvie Maybe even Silver Ball. Who can tell?

Toby You are the most extraordinary pupil I have ever come across.

Sylvie Am I?

Toby The more I teach you, the more stupid you become.

Sylvie Ah well, as my dad used to say, it's only the learning that stops us from understanding each other.

Toby Yes, very shrewd. Means bugger all but it sounds good.

Sylvie Didn't work with him. He was pig ignorant and you still couldn't understand him.

Toby Ah.

Sylvie Mind you, I think that was because of his teeth mostly.

Toby Ah.

Sylvie They worked loose. You want to get on then?

Toby If you don't mind.

Sylvie (*smiling*) Slave driver.

Toby You want to learn, you have to work.

Sylvie Non-stop. Did Mr Pickup write this then? (*She takes her script from her bag*)

Toby Yes.

Sylvie Not much good, is it?

Toby Ah, so you are learning.

Sylvie Not as good as Shakespeare.

Toby No. True. Come on, then.

Sylvie Do I have to say it without looking?

Toby If you can.

Sylvie I'll try. You want the long bit?

Toby Yes.

Sylvie Oh, mother.

Toby (*indicating the platform*) Stand up there and do it.

Sylvie Up there?

Toby That's where you'll be. And you'll be talking, remember, to all your troops. There were actually probably about a hundred thousand of them but you'll have to make do with the third and fourth forms. Then over there's your cavalry, that's the fifth and upper fifth and, last of all, your generals over here. That's your sixth form.

Sylvie I'll have to shout a bit then.

Toby Yes, you'll need to sing it out. But you see, the glory of this place is— you see that grass bank curving round—well, that's where the audience will be and it forms a natural amphitheatre. Almost Greek. When we've done it once, I'll go right to the back there and prove it to you.

Sylvie How many audience?

Toby I don't know. Couple of hundred.

Sylvie Oh, God.

Toby If it doesn't rain.

Sylvie I can't do this.

Toby Yes, you can.

Sylvie You know me. I can't even order a cup of tea.

Toby Come on, come on. Off you go.

Sylvie (*getting into position*) Right. (*After a pause*) Want me to start?

Toby (*irritably*) Yes.

Sylvie Right. (*After a pause*) I've forgotten it.

Toby Come on. Come ye, Britons——

Sylvie Oh, yes.

Come ye, Britons . . .

Pause

What's the next bit?

Toby Come ye, Britons, know——

Sylvie Come ye, Britons, no . . . (*pause*) . . . no what?

Toby Know ye that I speak——

Sylvie That's right.

Know ye that I speak.

What's the next?

Toby Oh, God. Read it for now. Go on, read it.
Sylvie Now, don't get angry with me.
Toby I'm sorry.
Sylvie There's no point in getting angry.
Toby No.
Sylvie I won't do it if you get angry.
Toby I'm sorry. I've said I'm sorry.
Sylvie Right. (*She reads softly*)

> Come ye, Britons ...

Toby What?
Sylvie What?
Toby What did you say?
Sylvie I said.

> Come ye, Britons ...

Toby Well, you're going to have to speak louder than that, Sylvie, you really are.
Sylvie (*louder*)

> Come ye, Britons.

Is that better?
Toby A bit.
Sylvie Know ye that I speak not as a woman born of mighty men——
Toby Now come on, Sylvie. (*He corrects her intonation*)

> ... I speak not as a woman born of mighty men.

Sylvie That's what I said.
Toby Read the sense, girl, read the sense.
Sylvie It doesn't make any blood sense, that's the trouble. I think he was pissed out of his mind when he wrote this.
Toby Come on.

Sylvie   ... Mighty men.

> Nor once——

Is that a nor?
Toby Yes, nor once, come on.

Sylvie   Nor once the wife of King Pras—Pru—Prasle—Pralu—Pr—
>   Prlus——

Oh bloody hell, why isn't he called George?
Toby Prasutagus.

Sylvie   ... Prasutagus.

> Oh, people of ICI.

Toby Iceni.
Sylvie Iceni. I looked out my window and Iceni going down the road.
Toby Come on. Now behold——

Sylvie Good that.

> ... Now behold
> Plain Boudicca, a woman of your tribe
> Whose body has by Roman whips been scourged ...

Awful, isn't it, that?

> ... her daughters outraged ...

Does that mean ...
Toby Yes.
Sylvie God, that's worse—

> ... all her freedoms curbed
> Be not dismayed I lead you in this fight.
> Remember we are used to woman's rule—

That all right?
Toby Good, good.

Sylvie   Recall triumphant Ver—Veru—Vermuluwaluum——

Oh, here we go again.
Toby Verulamium.
Sylvie Who's he?
Toby It's a name of a place.
Sylvie Oh.

> Which shared the fate of Camul—camel—

Oh, God.
Toby Camulodinum.
Sylvie I'll never be able to say all this.
Toby Yes, you will.
Sylvie I thought they were Britons.
Toby They are.
Sylvie Well, where are all these funny damn places then? Camul thing.
   Where's that then?
Toby It's the name for Colchester.
Sylvie Colchester.
Toby Yes.
Sylvie I can say that. Colchester.
Toby Well, Camulodinum was the Roman name for it.
Sylvie Roman.
Toby Yes.
Sylvie Rotten bunch they were.
Toby They had their moments.
Sylvie Going around whipping people. And changing all the names.
Toby Do let's get on, Sylvie.

Sylvie   Fear not the force of——

Here's another bloody one—Suet something ...

Toby Suetonius.
Sylvie Where's that? Basingstoke?
Toby It's the name of the Roman Governor. Suetonius Paulinus.
Sylvie Suet. Good name for a bloke, Suet.
Toby Sylvie, I'm going to get angry in a minute.
Sylvie Sorry, Mr Teasdale.
Toby Either take this seriously or go home.
Sylvie Yes, Mr Teasdale.
Toby Otherwise you'll just have everyone laughing at you.
Sylvie Yes, Mr Teasdale.
Toby And at me.
Sylvie Yes, Mr Teasdale.
Toby Now, be serious.
Sylvie Yes, Mr Teasdale.
Toby Come on.

Sylvie   ... Suetonius whose cowed divisions shun our British——

(*She dissolves into giggles*) I'm sorry.
Toby Sylvie.
Sylvie I'm sorry, Mr Teasdale. Does he keep cows?

              Whose cowed divisions shun our British might.
              Cursed be my sex this day who lie abed——

He's nicked that——
Toby Yes, Henry the Fifth. Get on with it.

Sylvie   Let men stay slaves but be it known that I
              Mere woman do intend to fight——

Sound of violent hammering

The sharpened end of a nail appears between Sylvie's feet

Bloody hell, what's that?
Toby It's only Lionel.
Sylvie Lionel? Is he under here?
Toby He's finishing it off.
Sylvie Did he build it then?
Toby Yes.
Sylvie Help, I'm getting off.
Toby That's all right. You do at this point anyway. You come down off there and you leap into your chariot——
Sylvie Chariot?
Toby Which will be there waiting, drawn by anyone with a total of twenty-five or more minus marks up to and including half term—and away you go.
Sylvie Drawn by delinquent slaves.
Toby Right.
Sylvie This chariot. Did Lionel Hepplewick build that too?
Toby Yes, when he's finished it.

Sylvie I demand danger money.

Toby You'll be all right.

Sylvie What do you mean? He's maimed thousands, he has. He's Mr DIY himself. Dead inefficent and useless.

Sound of more hammering

Toby All right, I'm going up the top of the bank now. I want you to come out through the curtains there, stop as you see your troops, quieten them down and then address them. And then at the end of your speech, you jump down and imagine your chariot there. Then off you go.

Sylvie Right.

Toby They'll gallop you and your army over to those trees there where the Roman troops are gathered.

Sylvie Who are the Romans then?

Toby St Catherine's.

Sylvie Hey, they're a tough lot. I don't fancy a punch up with them.

Toby It's not a punch up. It's all been rehearsed. It's all been choreographed very carefully. No one need get hurt.

Sylvie What do I do?

Toby You just stand in your chariot exhorting your troops. The minute you see you've lost, they'll gallop you back here. You take poison and drop dead.

Sylvie Cheerful, isn't it? I think I liked last year's better with the fairies.

Toby Oh, God.

Sylvie Lovely dresses.

Toby You just learn your lines.

Sylvie Right.

Toby picks up his loudhailer

What's that?

Toby So I can talk to you.

Sylvie I thought this was a natural amphitheatre.

Toby It is. Only works one way though. I'll be able to hear you but you'd never hear me without this. I'll give you a shout.

Toby exits

Sylvie (*picking up the script*) Impossible. I'll never learn that. I'll write it on the inside of my shield. That's a good idea. If I get a shield. (*She reads*)

Come ye, Britons, know ye that I speak——

Right. (*She moves forward and repeats the line without the book*)

Come ye, Britons, know ye that I speak——

Right. (*She moves back and looks at the book again*)

Not as a woman born of mighty men——

Right. (*She moves away*)

Come ye, Britons, know ye that I speak
Not as a woman born of mighty men——

Right. (*She hurries back and reads another line*)

> Nor once the wife of King Prawoolly-wooly.

I'll write him on my shield and all. Right. (*She moves forward*)

> Come ye, women, know ye that I born not as a Briton——
> Mighty——

Oh, God. Once the King Thing. Wife. Men. Something. I can get all the words. I can't get the right order. (*She looks again*)

> Oh, people of Icicles, now behold a woman of your tribe
> Whose body has by Roman whips been scourged——

I'm glad we're not doing that bit.

Lionel emerges from under the platform.

Oh, hallo.

Lionel ignores her

Still not talking then?

Lionel, by way of reply, bangs the protruding nail back through the stage

Honestly, Lionel. Five weeks. Daft. Just pride, that's all it is. Because I didn't say you were wonderful, marvellous, knock-out. Sensational. My king, my master ...

Lionel takes one of the planks he has brought with him and starts to measure off a length of it, first marking it with a pencil and then with the help of a set square

(*Watching him*) Lionel. It's stupid, isn't it? We can still be friends, can't we? I'm not doing anything with Mr Teasdale. It's nothing like that. Lionel?

Toby (*off, through the loudhailer*) All right then, Sylvie. Ready when you are.

Sylvie Sorry, what was that?

Toby (*off, through the loudhailer*) Ready when you are.

Sylvie Right, Mr Teasdale, right. I'll start behind the curtains. Just a second. (*To Lionel*) Don't you laugh neither.

Sylvie goes behind the curtains

(*Off*) Right, I'm coming out.

Sylvie comes onto the stage

Mr Teasdale, should I look surprised to see them here?

Toby (*off, through the loudhailer*) Of course not, you blithering idiot. There are a hundred thousand of them.

Sylvie Oh, yes. I suppose she would, wouldn't she? Right.

Sylvie goes behind the curtain

(*Off*) Here I come.

Sylvie comes onto the stage

Come ye, Britons, know ye that I——

Lionel, meanwhile, having finished marking his wood picks up his saw and starts attacking the piece of timber vigorously, using the edge of the stage as a saw-bench

Look, will you shut up, you Lionel-bloody-Hepplewick. Lionel.

Toby (*off, through the loudhailer*) What the hell's going on down there?

Sylvie What? Well, it's him here. (*She approaches Lionel*) Look, shut up. (*She kicks his piece of wood*) Did you hear me?

Lionel What?

Sylvie I said shut up.

Lionel Why should I?

Sylvie Because I'm trying to act, that's why, and I can't do it with you sawing and banging.

Lionel Who told you you could get up there anyway?

Sylvie Nobody. Mr Teasdale.

Lionel Did he?

Sylvie What's it to you? I don't need permission.

Lionel Oh, yes, you do.

Sylvie Who from?

Lionel Me.

Sylvie You?

Lionel Yes.

Sylvie Why?

Lionel Because I'm the Stage Manager, that's why.

Sylvie The what?

Lionel Mr Teasdale has appointed me Stage Manager.

Sylvie I bet.

Lionel Go and ask him.

Sylvie So what? You can't stop people walking on the stage.

Lionel Oh yes, I can.

Sylvie I'm an actress. You can't stop an actress. She's more important than a Stage Manager.

Lionel No, they're not.

Sylvie They are.

Lionel Why do you think he's called a Stage Manager? Because he's the manager. He manages. He's the manager of the entire stage.

Sylvie Rubbish.

Lionel True. Same as anywhere. You're in a cafe, you don't behave yourself, the manager asks you to leave. Same as a cinema or a bingo hall. The manager, he's the one. The manager reserves the right to refuse admittance. He says who goes and who stays. So bugger off my stage.

Sylvie (*stepping off, rather bewildered*) I've got to act somewhere.

Lionel Well, go and act over there. How can I concentrate with all this talking. I'm trying to cut a straight edge here.

Toby (*off, through the loudhailer*) What the blazes are you playing at?
Sylvie He's shouting again.
Lionel Let him. His battery'll run down in a minute.
Sylvie I've got to go on, Lionel, else he'll give me an earful. Please.
Lionel Well, all right. You do it quietly then.
Sylvie I'm supposed to do it loud so he can hear.
Lionel Look, I'm the manager and I don't want it loud, I want it quiet, so keep it down.
Sylvie Oh, God.

      Plain Boudicca, a woman of your——

Lionel Ssh.
Sylvie He can't hear me.
Lionel I can. Shut up.
Sylvie (*softly*)

      Plain Boudicca, a woman of your tribe——

Toby (*off, through the loudhailer*) Sylvie, I can't hear a bloody word you're saying.
Sylvie Look, he's shouting, Lionel. He can't hear me.
Lionel You better go a bit closer then, hadn't you?
Sylvie Oh, get knotted. (*Loudly*)

      Plain Boudicca, a woman of your tribe whose body has by——

Wait a minute, don't tell me. Nobody tell me—sticks, no. Scourge something. No, wait, nobody say anything. It's coming, it's coming.

Lionel resumes sawing

Oh, oh, oh. It's on the tip of my tongue. Oh. (*With sudden fury and frustration, she seizes Lionel's piece of wood and hurls it away*) Will you shut up!
Lionel Temper.
Sylvie Well, it's hard enough.
Lionel You don't have to do it if you don't want to.
Sylvie Yes, I do.
Lionel No.
Sylvie I couldn't let him down. He's pinned his hopes on me.
Toby (*off, through the loudhailer*) Sylvie, for the last time. . . .
Sylvie (*yelling*) Won't be a minute.
Lionel He'll just find someone else if you don't want to do it.
Sylvie Who?
Lionel Mrs Teasdale's queueing up to do it.
Sylvie Never.
Lionel She is. I heard her.
Sylvie When?
Lionel Just now. When I was under there. She weren't half going off. She didn't like the idea of you doing it, you see. Said he was getting too keen on you.

Sylvie Who?

Lionel Mr Teasdale.

Sylvie That's—that's rubbish.

Lionel That's what she felt. She thinks he's getting too close to you. She said she was going to fix you good and proper and have a fight.

Sylvie A fight? She never said that.

Lionel She did.

Sylvie Against me?

Lionel Yes.

Sylvie She wouldn't fight. Not Mrs Teasdale.

Lionel Why not? You go around pinching her husband, she's got a right to come and push your face in, hasn't she?

Sylvie I'm not pinching her husband.

Lionel The way she sees it you are.

Sylvie She better not try fighting me. I could give her a few rounds.

Lionel Better get your breastplate on, hadn't you?

Sylvie I'll kick your stupid stage down in a minute.

Lionel You'll never kick that down. That's got joints in it you've never heard of. I'll be back. Got to go and fetch your chariot. He wants it. So you can practise falling out of it.

Lionel exits

Sylvie Go away.

Toby (*off, through the loudhailer*) Now, will you please get on with it.

Sylvie What's that? I'm sorry, Mr Teasdale, he kept me talking. Yes, right. Would you like me to start again?

Toby (*off, through the loudhailer*) No, I would not.

Sylvie No, right. I'll start in the middle. Here I go then. (*After a pause*) I can't remember where I was. Oh, yes.

Be not dismayed I lead you in this fight——

Just a minute—(*She hurries back to the script muttering*) I can't do it. It's no good. All those parents, I'll just panic. All looking at me. "Oh, look at her. Who does she think she is? That's that Sylvie Bell, with no tits and one "O" level. What's she doing playing Boudicca? Why isn't she at home cleaning the kitchen. (*She calls*) Mr Teasdale? I wonder if I might be better if I got the costume on. I might feel the part more. (*She speaks under her breath*) I'll feel the cold anyway. (*She calls*) Will it be all right if I put it on, Mr Teasdale?

Toby (*off, through the loudhailer*) Oh, God, all right then. Put the bloody thing on.

Sylvie Thank you. (*She speaks to herself*) Stall for time, that's the way. Whose body has by Roman whips been somethinged. Her daughters horrified. No, outraged. Her daughters outraged—(*she picks up her carrier bag*)—hell, he's coming down here again. (*She calls*) You coming down? Right. Oh, God.

Sylvie moves behind the curtains

(*Off*) All her freedoms curbed ... (*she mutters her lines to herself*)

Pause

Toby returns

Toby Either this place has lost its acoustics or you have a voice the size of a tin-whistle. I only heard a quarter of what you say.

Sylvie (*off*) I only said a quarter of it.

Toby That might explain it.

Sylvie (*off*) Are you sure you collected all the costume from Janet Mallet?

Toby How do you mean?

Sylvie (*off*) Seems there ought to be more of it. It's like there's bits missing.

Toby That's all she gave me.

Sylvie (*off*) How did she break her arm?

Toby No idea.

Sylvie (*off*) Trying this costume on probably—hell. Come ye, Britons, know ye that I—crickey! This looks more like Mrs Coombes' squash kit.

Toby Has he fixed the stage, do you know?

Sylvie (*off*) I don't know. He said he'd gone for the chariot.

Toby (*peering underneath the platform*) Ah.

Sylvie (*off*) Mr Teasdale?

Toby Hallo.

Sylvie (*off*) I'm going to have to ask you to do something.

Toby What's that?

Sylvie (*off*) Well, you have to look at this costume and say truthfully whether you think I should wear it in front of everyone. And please be honest, Mr Teasdale, because I am going to have to trust your judgement.

Toby OK.

Sylvie (*off*) Because I think I look bloody terrible.

Toby Come on, then. Let's have a look.

Sylvie (*off*) Right. Ready, here I come.

Sylvie steps from behind the curtains on to the stage. It is indeed a strange, not very flattering costume and Sylvie's judgement is undoubtedly correct. She does contrive though to look rather vulnerable, if comic

(*Anxiously*) Well?

Toby Er ...

Sylvie Be honest. I don't mind.

Toby (*slowly*) I think you look—lovely.

Sylvie (*startled*) You do?

Toby I do.

Sylvie I don't.

Toby Lovely.

Sylvie You sure?

Toby Yes.

Sylvie (*without conviction*) Well. .... (*After a pause*) Do you think Boudicca would have looked like this?

Toby It's possible. We haven't any pictures to go from.

Sylvie No. It's enough to start a riot anyway, isn't it?

Toby (*continuing to stare at her*) Lovely.

Sylvie (*rather shyly*) Thank you. (*After a pause*) I was—er—Lionel was saying he overheard you and Mrs Teasdale. Talking. About me ...

Toby Oh, yes.

Sylvie Yes. (*After a pause*) He said she was getting jealous of me.

Toby Well ...

Sylvie Is she?

Toby Maybe. She's the jealous type.

Sylvie But has she cause?

Toby I've no idea.

Sylvie Are you fond of me?

Toby Yes. Yes, I am.

Sylvie I see. (*After a pause*) And are you in love with me?

Toby That's a more—difficult question to answer, Sylvie, you know.

Sylvie It's not difficult. Yes or no.

Toby (*slight pause*) Then yes. It's bloody ridiculous and we must forget all about it.

Sylvie Must we?

Toby Yes.

Sylvie Why?

Toby Because it wouldn't work out.

Sylvie No?

Toby No. Let's do all that again, shall we?

Sylvie What?

Toby The speech.

Sylvie Oh, the speech, yes. You haven't asked me, have you?

Toby What?

Sylvie If I'm in love with you?

Toby No, I haven't, Sylvie, purposely. And I don't intend to. Come on.

Sylvie I am.

Toby No, you're not.

Sylvie I bloody am. Why do you think I'm standing up here trying to remember daft poems dressed like a shaved chimp? If that's not love, what is?

Toby I don't know.

Sylvie I wouldn't do it for Lionel, I tell you that. I wouldn't do it for anybody except for you.

Toby Come on.

	Come ye, Britons ...
Sylvie	Come ye, Britons——

I love you, Toby Teasdale, so there.

Toby

Know ye that I speak ...

Sylvie   Know ye that I speak——

I love you——
              Not as a woman born of mighty men——

love you——

              Nor once the wife of King blur—blur—blur.
              Oh, people of Iceni, now behold——
Toby (*yelling furiously*) Oh, for the love of God, Sylvie, put something into it, would you? You're standing there like a great limp sackful of rancid cottage cheese.

              Oh, people of Iceni——

Come on——

              Oh, people of Iceni——

Sylvie (*stung*) All right, all right.
Toby You've just been flogged. Your daughters have been raped. Your family have been turned into slaves. They've taken half your property and burnt the rest of it. Now get angry!
Sylvie I'm getting angry.
Toby If that doesn't make you angry, what the hell does?
Sylvie You do for one. You make me angry.
Toby (*speaking over Sylvie*) Be not dismayed I lead you in this fight . . .
Sylvie You stupid, batty old boss-eyed boot-faced bugger.

A sudden silence. Toby sits down and puts his head in his hand

Toby Oh, dear.
Sylvie (*startled*) What? (*After a pause*) Mr Teasdale? I'm sorry, I—Mr Teasdale . . . Toby? (*She moves around and sits by him*) Toby?
Toby Oh, dear. Dear Sylvie. I don't think I can cope with all this, you know.
Sylvie How do you mean?
Toby Please go away.
Sylvie Go away?
Toby Yes.
Sylvia You want me to go away?
Toby Please. I'm forty-four years old, I'm practically an alcoholic, so my friends tell me. God knows what my enemies say. There is hardly an organ or a limb in my body that is now functioning correctly due to total abuse over the past thirty years . . . I'm no possible use to you, Sylvie. None at all. It would be like purchasing a dead elephant as a pet. I urge you to go away.
Sylvie Nonsense.
Toby Please.

Slight pause

Sylvie Righto. If that's what you want. (*After a pause*) Is it because I'm no good? As a Boudicca?

Toby Of course not. You've got to be better than Janet Mallet.

Sylvie I'll get changed then.

Sylvie goes behind the curtain

(*Off*) Are you going to give it to Mrs Teasdale then? The part?

Toby Probably. She'll be much worse than Janet Mallet. How can you have a Boudicca who's just raced off to have her hair done.

Sylvie (*off*) If you want me, I'll still do it. (*After a pause*) I'm sorry I called you a boot-face. I didn't really mean that. I think you're extremely good looking. Really I do. I would never have guessed you were forty-four. I thought you were about thirty.

Toby Ah.

Sylvie (*off*) Well, thirty-two maybe. (*After a pause*) I bet there's a lot of you that is still working. I bet there is. And as for your drinking, well, you're drinking because you're unhappy, that's all. I bet if you were happy you wouldn't drink. Well, only when you were very happy. It's only because you're unhappy. Nobody to blame. It's just one of those things.

She puts her head through the curtains

Oh, God, don't send me away, Mr Teasdale, please. (*A missile apparently hits her in the back*) Ow! Who threw——?

Sylvie's head vanishes

(*Off*) Did you throw that, Lionel Hepplewick? What are you staring at anyway? Go on, buzz off, Lionel-bloody-Hepplewick. You never seen a woman before? Probably not, have you? Well, have a good look, all right? Go on. There. Seen enough, eh? Want some more? (*She laughs*) He's running. He's bloody running. (*Her voice grows fainter*) Come on, Lionel. Come back. There's more where these came from. (*Her voice fades away, whooping into the distance*)

Toby (*dejected*) It's like malaria, that's what it is. The minute you've finally congratulated yourself for having got over it, back it comes. The whole lot clobbers you again. (*He rises and picks up the script*) Ah well, it looks as if I'll have to play the damn woman myself. Even I'd be better than Janet Mallet.

Celia enters propelling her Boudicca chariot. She wears her Boudicca costume, which, in sharp contrast to Sylvie's, is both chaste and chic with only the merest of nods towards Ancient Britain

Toby What the hell . . .?

Celia Hallo. Look what I've found. Isn't it lovely?

Toby Ingenious. What is it?

Celia It's a chariot, of course.

Toby Courtesy of Lionel Hepplewick?

Celia Yes, I found it over there.

Toby That should set Rome back a bit.

Celia Aren't you rehearsing your little starlet?

Toby No, we've stopped.

Celia Finished?

Toby No.

Celia Don't say she walked out?

Toby No, I chucked her out.

Celia I see. A little quarrel.

Toby Oh, Celia, please don't be sarcastic. You're so appallingly awful at it.

Celia I'm so sorry. I don't have the benefit of personal English lessons. So. You have no Boadicea?

Toby Boudicca.

Celia Oh, that's rubbish. Everyone calls her Boadicea. Her name's Boadicea. You call her Boudicca, nobody will know who you're talking about. Where is she, Sylvie?

Toby I said, gone.

Celia Good. Well, here I am then.

Toby What?

Celia This is my costume. I think I'm now word-perfect, let's rehearse.

Toby That is your costume?

Celia Yes.

Toby My God.

Celia Do you like it?

Toby You look like a roll of liver sausage.

Celia We all try our best, Toby.

Toby I'm sure you do, Celia.

Celia Now, would you like to hear my lines? Now, you musn't stop me unless I go wrong. Right. (*She climbs on to the stage and recites in a clear ringing voice*)

> Come ye, Britons, know ye that I speak
> Not as a woman born of mighty men
> Not once the wife of King Prasutugas——

I think that should be not, don't you?

Toby No, it's nor.

Celia No, I think it's not.

> Not once the wife ...

Toby Doesn't make sense, not.

Celia Not once the wife of King Prasutugas.

Toby You mean you were twice the wife of King Prasutugas.

Celia Oh, Toby, don't be so stupid.

> Ooooh, people of Iceni, now behold
> Plain Boadicea, a woman of your tribe.

Toby Boudicca.

Celia Boadicea.

Toby You can't say Boadicea, it doesn't scan.

Celia I don't care about scanning. It's unclear. Nobody will know who I am.

Toby Nobody will know who you are anyway dressed like that.

Celia I am going to say Boadicea.

Toby Celia, listen—(*He spells it out*)—Bo-dee-cee-ah. Four syllables. Boo-dick-ah. Three syllables.

Celia What's the difference?

Toby The difference is one syllable. Poor old Basil Pickup, third rate poet that he is, has sweated nights and days in an attempt to glue together some semblance of an iambic pentameter. Fairly crudely, I agree. Nonetheless, plain Boudicca, a woman of your tribe. Tee-tum, tee-tum, tee-tum, tee-tum, tee-tum——

Celia Toby, will you kindly stop screaming?

Toby (*ploughing on*) Whereas, plain Boadicea a woman of your tribe. Tee-tum, tee-tum, tee-tee-tum, tee-tum, tee-tum. Eleven syllables. Do you understand that, you stupid, ignorant bitch, eleven syllables? You pretentious roll of potted meat.

Celia retreats from this barrage behind the curtains

Celia (*off, alarmed*) Toby, Toby, what's the matter with you?

Toby sits

It's that girl, isn't it? She's—she's done something to you.

Toby You're absolutely right. God knows what it is. All sorts of things are beginning to happen, Celia. Can you hear them? I'm like a very, very old deconsecrated church long closed. On the very point of falling down and now somebody's broken in and sat themselves down and started to play the bloody organ. And the whole damn thing'll probably fall down if they do but I don't really give a stuff.

Celia (*off*) This is madness. Just wait till I get—(*to someone behind her*)—oh, there you are, madam. I've a bone to pick with you, young lady.

Sylvie (*off*) Oh, have you?

Toby (*wearily*) Celia ...

Celia (*off*) Yes, I have. You just keep your—your ... just keep away from my husband.

Sylvie (*off*) I'm not keeping away from nobody, so there.

Celia (*off*) How dare you speak to me like that, you impudent little—brat.

Sylvie (*off*) You great snobby stuck-up madam——

The sound of a slap

(*Off*) Ow! Right.

Celia (*off*) There. That'll teach you.

Sylvie (*off*) Right, you asked for it. I warn you, I was a——

Celia (*off*) Ooooh——

Sylvie (*off*) I was a wrestler at school.

Celia (*off*) Let go.

Sylvie (*off*) Break your bloody arm I will.

Celia appears momentarily through the curtains

Celia Toby, help me. .... This girl's gone mad. She breaking my—ow——

Celia disappears

Sylvie (*off*) Up the Britons! Long live Boudicca.
Celia (*off*) Boadicea! Ow!
Sylvie (*off*) Didn't like that, did you?—ow! Don't you bite me, you nasty little Roman.
Toby Look at me. Just look at me. I don't even have the energy to stop them.

A scream from Celia

Sylvie's head appears round the curtain

Sylvie You want me to break her neck, Mr Teasdale, you just give me the thumbs down.
Toby No, thank you very much, Sylvie. No, thanks.
Sylvie I would. You've only got to—ow! Oh, we're playing those little games, are we? Right.

Sylvie's head disappears

Celia (*off*) Ah!
Toby (*singing to himself*) Seated one day at the organ ...

Sound of more thumps and bumps behind the curtain

Celia's head appears from under the curtain. Someone is apparently sitting on her

Celia Toby, please. She's breaking my leg. You have to do—ah——

Celia's head disappears

Sound of three or four grunts, then a thump, a clump and the whole platform collapses. Silence

Sylvie emerges, sucking her hand but triumphant

Sylvie I fixed her. I fixed her, Mr Teasdale.
Toby Well done, Sylvie.
Sylvie I won. Like Boudicca, eh?
Toby No. Boudicca didn't win, Sylvie, she lost. Boudicca lost.
Sylvie Oh, well. Yes. Well. (*After a pause*) I've lost then, have I?

EITHER he says:

Toby Not necessarily.
Sylvie What's that mean then? Not necessarily.
Toby It means you haven't necessarily lost.
Sylvie Ah, but have I necessarily won?
Toby Well, that depends on whether you feel it——

Sylvie (*smiling*) Necessary.
Toby Yes.
Sylvie Oh yes. I need to win. (*After a pause*) Right. Great. That's great.
Toby Had I better see to . . .?
Sylvie No, she's all right. Bang in the nose.
Toby Serious?
Sylvie No. Make her look more Roman, that's all.
Toby Ah.
Sylvie Best leave her. She's a vicious little fighter.
Toby Yes, I know. Well? What now?
Sylvie (*climbing aboard the chariot*) Carry on rehearsing, shall we?
Toby All right.
Sylvie Let's do the chariot bit. Give us a pull.
Toby Me?
Sylvie Come on. Be a sport.
Toby All right. (*He takes up the reins and pulls*) God.
Sylvie Come on, giddy-up——
Toby (*straining*) Grief. I don't think I can do a lot of this, Sylvie.
Sylvie Just as far as the Romans. Over to the trees. Here comes the queen.
     Long live the queen.
Toby (*straining*) Aaargh! (*He starts to pull her slowly*)
Sylvie   Let men stay slaves but be it known that I
                 Mere woman do intend to fight or die.

They exit

The Lights fade to a Black-out

To: A HARVEST FESTIVAL (page 189)

OR he says:

Toby I don't think it's a question of that, Sylvie. Winning or losing. Not
   quite as simple.
Sylvie No?
Toby I wish it were. I have to tell you, Sylvie, that Celia and I have together
   contracted one of the most grisly partnerships in the history of marriage
   and it has grown steadily grislier year by year. We weren't very fond of
   each other when we married. God knows why we did. I can't remember
   now. It was probably raining or something. Nonetheless, this marriage of
   ours is like a flat which you've lived in for very many years. Some
   apartment. You know where all the furniture is, you recognize where the
   draughts come from, you know the loose floorboards to avoid. It's
   familiar. And that, in the end, is what keeps most of us together.
   Familiarity. And, conversely, fear of the unfamiliar.
Sylvie (*after a pause*) I think that means I've lost.

Toby does not reply

Yes, I think that's what it means. (*After a pause*) Well. Thanks for—
everything, Mr Teasdale. I won't forget it. Never.

Sylvie exits

Toby sits silently

Toby Oh, Lord. (*After a second, he rises*) Celia? Celia? For God's sake, she
hasn't killed her, has she? (*He climbs on to the stage*) Celia? (*He opens the
curtains*) Oh, there you are.

From behind the curtains, Celia moans

All right?

Celia (*off*) She's—she's—I think she's broken my nose.

Toby Oh, dear.

Celia (*off*) If she's broken it, I shall sue. It's my only good feature. If she's
broken it, I'll——

Toby I don't think it's broken, Celia.

Celia (*off*) Vicious girl, Vicious.

Toby I rather think it was six of one, wasn't it?

Celia (*off*) She attacked me. And she's torn my dress.

Toby Oh, good-oh. (*He leaves her and climbs off the platform*) Oh, I feel
depressed.

Celia emerges, fingering her nose

Celia Well, do I get the part then? (*She indicates her dress*) Look what
she's done to this. You can hardly ask her to play it. Not after that.

Toby No, you can have the part.

Celia Good. And I can call her Boadicea?

Toby As far as I'm concerned you can call her Winifred, Celia. I'm no
longer interested.

Celia Don't be silly. Now I want you to hear the rest of my speech. See if
I've got it right.

Toby Fine.

Celia I can only breathe through one nostril. Now, where did I get to?

Toby No idea.

Celia Oh, yes.

> Be not dismayed I lead you in this fight
> Remember we are used to woman's rule
> Recall triumphant——

Try and look a little enthusiastic, Toby——

Toby Sorry.

Celia   Triumphant Verulamium
> Which shared the fate of Camulodonum——

I prefer that to Colchester. I don't know why they changed it.

Toby Probably wouldn't fit on the envelope.

Celia   Fear not the force of Suetonius——

Nasty piece of work——

> Whose cowed divisions shun our British might——

I put the cowed divisions over there.
Toby (*pointing in the other direction*) They're over there.
Celia Well, I'm putting them over there. It's a better gesture.

Toby closes his eyes

> Cursed be my sex——

Toby Hear, hear.
Celia Look, I think it would be a good idea if I stepped down on that line and leapt into the chariot.
Toby Super.
Celia You're being absolutely no help. So I can deliver my couplet on the move. So——

> Cursed be my sex who this day lie abed——

(*Leaping down off the platform*)—Whoops. (*She steps aboard the chariot*) Now, give me a pull.
Toby A pull?
Celia Yes.
Toby Me?
Celia (*impatiently*) Oh, do come on, Toby. I want to get the feel of the thing.
Toby Oh, Lord. (*He picks up the reins*)

Celia   Let men——

> Gee up, there——

Toby (*pulling*) Aaargh! I don't think I can do this for too long, Celia.
Celia Rubbish. Good for you. Just as far as the trees.

> Let men stay slaves but be it known that I
> Mere woman do intend to fight or die.

They exit

The Lights fade to a Black-out

To: A WEDDING (page 195)

A HARVEST FESTIVAL

A Churchyard. This year

The church door is closed. A gravel path leads away from it to an unseen road. A variety of gravestones border the path

We hear church bells signifying a happy occasion, followed by the sounds of a service within the church just finishing

Toby is pacing about in the churchyard

After a moment, the church door opens and Sylvie comes out

Sylvie (*closing the door*) OK?

Toby Yes.

Sylvie Right. Are we off then?

Toby Sure.

Sylvie (*as they start to move away*) There was no one in there. Well, no one you'd know.

Toby Really.

Sylvie Nice service. Harvest Festival. (*After a slight pause*) Who are you afraid of meeting?

Toby There are dozens of people living here who still know me.

Sylvie I don't know what you're complaining about. What about me? I was born here. I don't mind. (*After a pause*) I mean, your family's not here any more.

Toby No.

Sylvie Even the Coombes' have gone.

Toby Australia.

Sylvie Yes. (*She smiles*) She'll have a great time there, won't she? (*After a pause*) Why did you come back then?

Toby Mm?

Sylvie Back here with me? If it's going to make you so unhappy. I mean, I have to see my family. You don't have to come.

Toby I wanted to come.

Sylvie No, you didn't. Not really. You can't stand them. My family. You stand there on one leg, you don't know what to say to them. And they get nervous and they don't know what to say to you. Why didn't you stay in London for the weekend?

Toby I wanted to come with you.

Sylvie Or you just couldn't bear being left alone more like. You're just a great big baby, aren't you?

Toby No, I'm not.

Sylvie Yes, you are. You can't be left alone for two days, can you?

Toby I don't like you going away, that's all.

Sylvie I very rarely am. No chance.

Toby Do you want to?

Sylvie Well . . .

Toby Are you getting tired of me?

Sylvie Oh, Toby, don't start that.

Toby You want to go, just say the word. I won't hold you.

Sylvie I don't want to go. It's just—however much you love someone—you need—a little bit of time alone. (*She picks her word carefully*) That little flat, just the two rooms. Well, let's face it, we're a bit on top of each other all the time. I mean, it's two-way. I must drive you up the wall sometimes.

Toby No.

Sylvie I just need a breather. Ten days.

Toby Away from me.

Sylvie On my own. For my sake. I know how boring I get.

Toby No, you don't.

Sylvie I feel I do. I bore me rotten sometimes.

Toby I don't see you in the daytimes. You're out at work.

Sylvie Yes, that's not very interesting. Same shop, same people. Day after day.

Toby You could find something more fulfilling. You could do better than that.

Sylvie Can't be choosers. We need the money.

Toby (*uneasily*) Yes.

Sylvie We've got your family to support and mine.

Toby Well, I'm still looking around. I'm pretty sure I'll . . .

Sylvie It's all right.

Toby I should think you're getting pretty bored with me.

Sylvie No.

Toby Same old excuses. Same old rabbiting. I mean, I couldn't have carried on working in that office. I would have——

Sylvie I haven't complained. (*After a pause, gently*) You've just got to stop always . . .

Toby What?

Sylvie Well—breathing down my neck all the time.

Toby That's only because I——

Sylvie I know why it is. It's because you're frightened of something. Frightened I'll go off. Aren't you?

Toby Maybe I am.

Sylvie I'm not going anywhere. Stupid.

Toby Yes, it's ridiculous. I wake up in the morning sometimes and if I've overslept and you've gone to work, for a minute I don't know what time it is and I have this awful panic feeling you've gone off.

Sylvie Daft.

Toby It's true. And if you're late home from work, I get the shakes. Literally. Terrified. She's met somebody. She's been knocked down. I don't know. It's the most extraordinary fear. That's what it is. Fear.

Sylvie Well, it's not good. I can't even cross our road to post a letter, there you are standing on the window ledge. I mean, it's wonderful to feel you love me that much but, God, it's like being married to a secret policeman.

Toby I know.

Sylvie You must be careful you don't drive me away eventually.

Toby (*anxiously*) Am I doing that?

Sylvie No. But you might one day. I'll panic. I'll just run before I suffocate.

Toby Oh, Sylvie ...

Sylvie (*hugging him for a moment*) All right, all right. I'm here, all right.

Toby I'm sorry.

Sylvie I don't think you're that well, you know. Not really.

Toby I'm fine.

Sylvie But you're so unhappy. It can't be right being this unhappy. It was all going to be fun, wasn't it? That's what we said. That was the only way we were going to justify it. Walking out and leaving everybody. We were going to make it special.

Toby We've had fun.

Sylvie Oh, yes. But it's getting less and less frequent, Toby, it really is. Maybe you're missing your family.

Toby No. Heavens, no. Well, the kids sometimes. But I'm afraid so far as Celia's concerned I never even think of her. Isn't that awful? I behaved appallingly to her for twelve years because I didn't love her. I'm behaving badly to you because I love you too much. There must be a happy medium somewhere.

Sylvie You coming home for lunch with us then?

Toby Er ...

Sylvie Come on.

Toby No, Sylvie, I'll just walk around.

Sylvie You ought to eat. Well, don't get frozen. I'm not nursing you any more, you great baby.

Toby I'll keep moving. I'll meet you by the car.

Sylvie They'd all love to see you. Rachel—she says you were the best teacher she ever had. The minute you left the school, she went right off.

Toby Rachel? I hardly taught her.

Sylvie She remembers you. Thinks the sun shines out of your mortar-board.

Toby No, I'd just embarrass them. See you about three o'clock then?

Sylvie Well, better make it nearer four.

Toby Three-thirty?

Sylvie All right. Three-thirty.

Toby Bye.

Toby exits

Sylvie turns, on the point of leaving too, then stops

Sylvie Oh, Lord. You silly old bugger. (*She gets out a cigarette*) Started me on these as well. I never used to do this. It's his fault. (*She lights a cigarette and inhales*) That's better. Can't smoke at home. Else my Mum'll start. (*She mimicks*) I hope you know what you're doing, Sylvie. That's what killed your dad, you know. I watched him die. Filling himself with smoke day after day. . . . Till he just turned brown. (*She mutters*) I can't live in his pocket all the time. I've got to be myself occasionally. Haven't I? That's why I left this place. For a bit of freedom. What happens? I finish up a prisoner in Fulham. Fulham. That's a dump and all. I'm not spending all my life in Fulham. I'm getting old. God, I'm twenty-five. To hell with him. It's not fair on me, is it? No, it isn't. Just because I love him doesn't mean I have to lose my freedom. That's no good to anybody, is it? No, it isn't.

The church door opens. Lionel comes out, looking rather sharp and affluent

Lionel Hallo there. Thought I saw you.
Sylvie Well, look at you.
Lionel Look at yourself.
Sylvie What you doing these days?
Lionel Bit of this, bit of that.
Sylvie Oh, I see. In the Foreign Office, are you?
Lionel Not so far removed.
Sylvie Looks like things are working out.
Lionel Oh, yes. They're working out.

Pause

Sylvie I hear you married Betty Simcock.
Lionel Oh, yes.
Sylvie How is she?
Lionel I don't know. I haven't seen her.
Sylvie Why not?
Lionel She ran off after four weeks.
Sylvie Never.
Lionel With a man from the Rating Authority. Stupid cow. Anyway, she was getting fat. I didn't care.
Sylvie She was always a bit flighty. Lovely but flighty.
Lionel I don't care. It's left me a free man.
Sylvie I hear your dad died too.
Lionel Yes. He caught a chill.
Sylvie Well, they do, don't they? Old folk.
Lionel Talking of old folk, you still got old Teasdale?
Sylvie Yes.
Lionel He hasn't got a chill yet, has he?
Sylvie He's not that old.
Lionel Old enough. Still drinking?
Sylvie No.
Lionel Get on.
Sylvie Not that much. Mind your own business. I must get home for lunch. (*She starts to move off*)
Lionel How's your mum?
Sylvie Not so bad. Considering they'd written her off. Tough lot we Bells, you know.

Lionel Down here a lot, are you?

Sylvie Now and again.

Lionel Well, look me up next time. I'll buy you a drink.

Sylvie Oh, goodness gracious.

Lionel A meal too, if you like.

Sylvie Perhaps I might.

Lionel That's if you want.

Sylvie Yes.

Lionel Just give us a ring. (*He produces a card and hands it to her*) Here.

Sylvie What's this?

Lionel My business card. I'm always there. Or somebody is.

Sylvie (*reading*) Import and Export. H. and W. Ltd. What's that?

Lionel Hepple and Wick. I've gone into partnership with myself. Just for tax purposes.

Sylvie (*impressed*) Oh. Well, I might ring you. I'll see how my plans work out.

Lionel I'd—I'd like to see you, Sylvie.

Sylvie Yes. Cheerio, then.

Lionel Cheerio.

Sylvie exits

(*Watching her go*) Good. Good. I've got plans for her. I've got plans. (*He nods*)

After a moment, Lionel goes inside the church

The Lights fade to a Black-out

A WEDDING

A Churchyard. This year

The church door is closed. A gravel path leads away from it to an unseen road. A variety of gravestones border the path

We hear church bells signifying a happy occasion, followed by the distant sound of a service proceeding within the church

Celia is standing waiting in the churchyard, smoking a cigarette

After a moment, Toby sticks his head out of the church door

Toby (*urgently*) What are you doing?

Celia Nothing. I was just—I felt like a cigarette.

Toby For the love of mike, Celia, fancy walking out in the middle of a service like that.

Celia Nobody noticed.

Toby (*coming out and closing the door*) Of course they did. With this ring I thee clump, bang. What are you wearing on your feet? Auctioneers' gavels?

Celia It was frightfully oppressive. And you know I can't stand weddings anyway.

Toby I thought you liked them.

Celia Of course not. Neither do you.

Toby I don't.

Celia Then what are we doing here?

Toby It's just that they're friends and it seems——

Celia They're not friends.

Toby They are.

Celia Of course they're not. One's an ex-employee of the school whom you sacked for incompetence and one used to clean my kitchen rather badly. Hardly what I'd call friends.

Toby I regard them as friends. What do you call friends?

Celia Well. People you might might invite round for drinks. Or coffee even. I'm certainly not a friend of Lionel Hepplewick's. And you know my feelings about Sylvie Bell.

Toby That was a long, long time ago, Celia. Five years.

Celia I don't forget, Toby. I'm sorry.

Toby No.

Celia And who are all those awful people in there?

Toby Well, a significant number of them are Bells. A positive tintinnabulation of them.

Celia All with that awful ginger hair. The women in light-green suits and too much eye shadow.

Toby And the rest are Hepplewicks. They're much worse. They're the ones with the huge flowers in their buttonholes. They look as though they've arrived there by Interflora.

Celia Well, I certainly felt rather out of place.

Toby Oh, come on, it's rather fun. You mustn't be superior, Celia, you really mustn't. It's very old fashioned for one thing.

Celia Well, maybe I am. That's a village wedding between village families and we don't belong. We stood there looking like sore—what-have-you's.

Toby You should have dyed your hair.

Celia You know what I mean.

Toby It was very decent of them to ask us. I was quite touched.

Celia Super. (*After a slight pause*) Remember our wedding?

Toby Oh, you bet.

Celia Wasn't it awful?

Toby (*surprised*) Did you think so?

Celia Absolutely awful.

Toby I thought you liked it.

Celia Heavens, no.

Toby Good Lord.

Celia What?

Toby All these years I was under the impression you treasured it as the most magical day of your life.

Celia I had an awful day. I was in agony, for one thing. Mummy made me wear that ghastly dress. . . .

Toby You thought it was ghastly?

Celia Horrendous. It had bows down it.

Toby Yes, I remember. I used to wake up dreaming about it. Celia, this is an immense relief. I think I've misjudged you all these years.

Celia It was most frightfully tight as well. And the bodice, you know, the top bit. . . .

Toby Yes, yes.

Celia It was very lightly boned, you know, to keep it up. . . .

Toby Yes, yes.

Celia Only it was so terribly badly made, halfway through the service one of these dreadful bones sprang through and jabbed me under the armpit.

Toby Is that why you were holding the bouquet up there?

Celia I couldn't put my arm down. And then the pins in my headdress started sticking in my skull. I was weeping with pain.

Toby I thought that was pleasure.

Celia I was in agony.

Toby Why didn't you say so?

Celia Well, I—didn't want to spoil it for you.

Toby For me?

Celia Or mother.

Toby Oh God, that you had done, Celia. It would have got us off on the right foot, you see. As it was, all through the honeymoon, I kept thinking, she actually enjoyed it. I'm married to a woman who found that whole experience enjoyable.

Celia I had to say that. It cost a fortune.

Toby The reception was awful, too.

Celia Oh, that was worse.

Toby Tell me something else.

Celia What?

Toby Honestly.

Celia What?

Toby Did you enjoy the honeymoon?

Celia Hated every minute of it.

Toby (*moved*) Oh, Celia. If only you'd said all this.

Celia I don't quite see the point of this.

Toby Don't you realize? After seventeen years we've actually found something we've got in common. It's a very moving moment.

Celia Don't get too carried away, Toby.

Toby No.

Celia There's still an awful lot we haven't.

Toby Yes. Nonetheless, it's a start. Five minutes ago we didn't agree about anything. Now, there's a glimmer. Give us another five years, I'll come up with something else. Marzipan. You don't like marzipan, do you?

Celia No. Loathe it.

Toby Ah well, I love it. Never mind. Better luck next year.

Celia Are you coming home or going back in?

Toby We'd better go back in.

Celia You can. I'm going home.

Toby Celia . . .

Celia See you there.

Toby What if they ask after you? What am I going to tell them?

Celia Say I had a headache. Tell her my nose started hurting again.

Toby Oh, rubbish.

Celia It still does. If I wear my reading glasses for too long. Agony. She damaged a nerve. Bill Windsor was almost certain.

Celia exits

Toby Well, I'd better stay. One of us had better. You can't just walk out. She's a liability, that woman. She's getting progressively battier the older she gets. Maybe in a year or two more I might be able to get her certified. That's a cheery thought. Go and visit her at weekends with fresh supplies of raffia. Oh, well, don't get too optimistic. (*He opens the church door*) Oh, Lord, it's finished. Well, that's that. (*He waves to someone inside the church*) Hallo, there. Lovely to see you, too. How are you? Are you? Jolly good. Yes, wasn't it? Yes, lovely to see you, too. (*He mutters*) Whoever the hell you are. You look like a Bell to me. (*He sits on the bench*) Well, she's probably better off with Hepplewick than she would have been with me. Dear little Sylvie Bell. I'd have driven you nuts. And I'm almost certain you'd have driven me nuts. Or your relations would have done. (*He muses*) Would have been nice to have found out though. Ah, well.

Sylvie, in bridal dress, comes hurrying round the side of the church. She is in high spirits. She carries a carnation

Sylvie So there you are. Come on.
Toby Eh?
Sylvie Come on, we want you in this photograph.
Toby Oh, now ...
Sylvie Rachel said she'd seen you sneaking out. Where's she gone then? Celia?
Toby Oh, she had—er—she had—er——
Sylvie Another engagement.
Toby —er—no—er—headache. Backache. I don't know. Her foot fell off.
Sylvie Poor thing. Come on, we're waiting. (*She puts the flower she is carrying into his buttonhole*)
Toby No, Sylvie, you don't want me around. Not today.
Sylvie I bloody do. I need you to protect me from all them Hepplewicks. They're all horrible. I don't know where he found them. They all disapprove of drinking and smoking and keep pinching your bum. They're that sort. Dreadful. Please, I need someone.
Toby To guard your rear.
Sylvie Yes, please.
Toby All right. Five minutes or so. I mustn't——
Sylvie Here. Kiss the bride.
Toby Ah.
Sylvie Traditional. Come on.
Toby Are you sure it's——

Sylvie kisses Toby

Sylvie Ta. Still friends then?
Toby Yes, still friends.
Sylvie (*smiling*) Great. That's great. Quick.
Toby Right.

Sylvie starts to drag Toby round the side of the church

Sylvie (*yelling as she goes*) I've found him. He was hiding round here. Everybody. I want you to meet my best friend, Mr Teasdale.

Sylvie and Toby exit

As they go, the Lights fade to a Black-out

FURNITURE AND PROPERTY LIST

Affairs in a Tent

HOW IT BEGAN and A GARDENER CALLS

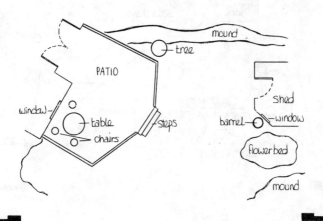

On stage: Table. *On it*: John Players cigarettes, lighter, ashtray, cup and saucer
Swing set on the tree
Shed door closed
Patio doors open
Trees set across to house
Dustbin (padded)
In shed: Half a shovel, box of weedkiller, wheelbarrow without a wheel
and an old gin bottle

Off stage: 2 mugs of tea **(Celia)**
Several old paint tins **(Sylvie)**

A GARDENER IN LOVE

Set: 2 striped garden chairs at the table
2 rubbish mounds
A shooting stick ⎫ on rubbish mounds
Gin bottle ⎭
Cup of tea and newspaper on the table

Off stage: Teapot and milk jug **(Celia)**
               Chest expander
               Polythene bag of rubbish **(Sylvie)**
               Pieces of broken paving **(Lionel)**
               Mug of tea **(Celia)**
               Cardboard box **(Celia)**

AFFAIRS IN A TENT

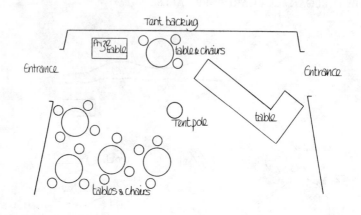

Strike: All

Set: Covered prize stand. *On it:* prizes for races to include a bottle of whisky,
            bottle of bath crystals
         5 white tables
         16 folding chairs
         Large oblong table with extension, covered with an oilcloth and white
            cloth on top
         Large gingham tablecloth
         2 large white tablecloths
         Box of vases and some small flowers
         Box of cups
         Box of saucers and spoons
         Breadboard and teatowel
         Wicker basket containing some butter, a bread knife and some jam tarts

Off stage: Box of cutlery **(Celia)**
               Box of tablecloths **(Celia)**
               Stack of sideplates **(Celia)**
               Improvised fishing rod consisting of a stick and a school tie
               Cardboard box **(Lionel)**

Strangely shaped brown loaf **(Lionel)**
Flattened and muddy handbag containing a squashed bag of tomatoes
    and a bag of cucumber **(Celia)**
Half a sliced loaf and a packet of jam tarts **(Celia)**

Personal: **Lionel:** keys

A FUNERAL

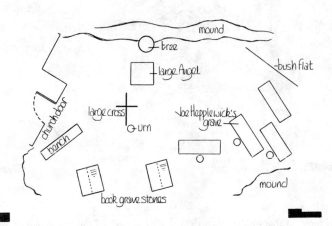

Strike: All

Set: Bench
            Several gravestones
            Large cross
            Large angel
            Urn

Offstage: Rug **(Toby)**

A NEW WOMAN

Stage plan as for A FUNERAL

Personal: **Celia:** watch, handbag containing small executive-type personal tape-
          recorder
         Lionel: chauffeur's uniform including cap

Events on a Hotel Terrace

HOW IT BEGAN and A GARDENER CALLS as previously set but with a key in
the shed door

A GARDENER IN LOVE as previously set

EVENTS ON A HOTEL TERRACE

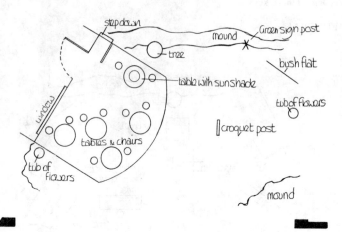

On stage: Table with sunshade. *On it:* Remains of tea for two, romantic novel at
    Celia's place, history book at **Toby**'s place
    Celia's cardigan on back of her chair
    Celia's basket and handbag containing a compact with a mirror, sun-
    glasses, notepad and pencil, cigarettes and a lighter, tissues, handker-
    chief
    5 tables
    10 chairs—2 with broken backs
    2 tubs of flowers
    Green sign post
    Net curtains to window of hotel

Off stage: Newspaper—the *Evening Chronicle* (**Toby**)
    Tray of tea for one holding a plate of sandwiches, plate of cakes, pot of
    tea, milk jug, sugar bowl and some paper napkins (**Lionel**)
    Another tea tray as above (**Lionel**)
    Empty tea tray (**Lionel**)

A FUNERAL

As previously set

Off stage: Spade (**Lionel**)

A SERVICE OF THANKSGIVING

As set for A Funeral

Personal: **Celia:** cigarettes and a lighter
             Lionel: paper bag containing a cassette

A Garden Fête

HOW IT BEGAN and A GARDENER CALLS as previously set

THE SELF-IMPROVING WOMAN

Set as above

Off stage: In the shed—rubbish including old tins, boxes, bits of rope and broken
              garden tools **(Lionel)**
              Woman's old battered straw sun hat **(Lionel)**
              Old football **(Lionel)**
              Bag of rubbish **(Sylvie)**
              Paving stones **(Lionel)**
              Another bag of rubbish **(Sylvie)**

Personal: **Lionel:** cigarettes and a lighter
             Toby: a newspaper
             Joe: wheelchair

A GARDEN FÊTE

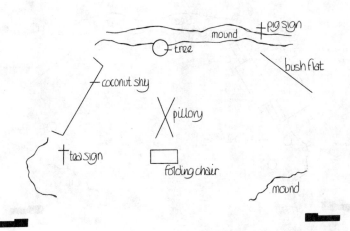

On stage: Next to pillory—folding chair, a length of wood, a painted hardboard sign
             (Pelt the Varlet), an empty tin
             Bunting in the tree
             Balloons on a stick by the bush
             Coconut shy
             Tea sign
             Pig sign

Off stage: Large tin bath full of water and foam rubber sponges **(Sylvie)**

Personal: **Sylvie:** plastic carrier bag containing a waterproof cape and a shower cap
decorated with a piece of ribbon
Lionel: a gorilla outfit with separate head piece
Toby: some ten pence coins, handkerchief

A CHRISTENING

As set for A FUNERAL but with the addition of Joe Hepplewick's gravestone

Personal: **Celia:** handbag containing cigarettes and a lighter

RETURN OF THE PRODIGAL

As set for A FUNERAL but with the addition of Joe Hepplewick's gravestone

A Pageant

HOW IT BEGAN, A GARDENER CALLS and THE SELF-IMPROVING
WOMAN as previously set

A PAGEANT

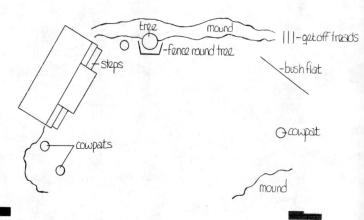

On stage: A raised platform stage with cloth backdrop and valance
Some cow pats

Off stage: Bag of tools—saw, pencil, tape, set square, hammer, 6-inch nails and 3
pieces of wood, one of which is 3 inches long **(Lionel)**
Script, loudhailer **(Toby)**
Carrier bag containing a Boudicca costume and script **(Sylvie)**
Chariot **(Celia)**

Personal: **Toby:** watch

A HARVEST FESTIVAL

As set for A FUNERAL

Personal: **Sylvie:** cigarettes and a lighter
       Lionel: a business card

A WEDDING

As set for A FUNERAL

Personal: **Celia:** a lit cigarette
       Sylvie: a carnation

LIGHTING PLOT

Affairs in a Tent

To open: Full general lighting

Cue 1	**Sylvie** exits towards the dustbins *Black-out*	(Page 13)
Cue 2	As scene A GARDENER IN LOVE opens *Full general lighting*	(Page 15)
Cue 3	**Celia** extends chest expander above her head *Black-out*	(Page 31)
Cue 4	As scene AFFAIRS IN A TENT opens *Full general lighting*	(Page 35)

Either

Cue 5	**Toby:** " ... she is the wrong way up." *Black-out*	(Page 56)
Cue 6	As scene A FUNERAL opens *Full general lighting*	(Page 59)
Cue 7	**Celia:** "All in good time ..." *The lights fade to Black-out*	(Page 64)

Or

Cue 5	The bundle clings on grimly and drags along behind *Black-out*	(Page 57)
Cue 6	As scene A NEW WOMAN opens *Full general lighting*	(Page 65)
Cue 7	**Lionel:** "Mind your step now." *The lights fade to Black-out*	(Page 69)

Events on a Hotel Terrace

To open: Full general lighting

Cue 1 and *Cue* 2 As above

Cue 3	**Celia** ... frowns, shrugs and goes back into the house again *Black-out*	(Page 33)
Cue 4	As scene EVENTS ON A HOTEL TERRACE opens *Full general lighting*	(Page 73)

Either

Cue 5	As **Lionel** starts to clear the table *Black-out*	(Page 92)

Cue 6   As scene A FUNERAL opens   (Page 95)
          Full general lighting

Cue 7   As **Lionel** goes back to his grave   (Page 98)
          The lights fade to Black-out

Or
Cue 5   **Lionel:** "I can wait."   (Page 94)
          Black-out

Cue 6   As scene A SERVICE OF THANKSGIVING opens   (Page 99)
          Full general lighting

Cue 7   As **Celia** goes back inside the church   (Page 103)
          The lights fade to Black-out

A Garden Fête

To open: Full general lighting

Cue 1   **Sylvie** moves, thoughtfully, to the dustbins with her load   (Page 14)
          Black-out

Cue 2   As scene THE SELF-IMPROVING WOMAN opens   (Page 107)
          Full general lighting

Cue 3   **Sylvie:** "It's going to be absolutely great."   (Page 122)
          Fade to Black-out

Cue 4   As scene A GARDEN FÊTE opens   (Page 125)
          Full general lighting

Either
Cue 5   As **Lionel** hurls sponges   (Page 145)
          Fade to Black-out

Cue 6   As scene A CHRISTENING opens   (Page 145)
          Full general lighting

Cue 7   As **Toby** goes back into the church   (Page 150)
          Fade to Black-out

Or
Cue 5   **Lionel** mutters as he tries to release himself   (Page 144)
          Black-out

Cue 6   As scene RETURN OF THE PRODIGAL opens   (Page 151)
          Full general lighting

Cue 7   As **Sylvie** closes the door   (Page 156)
          Fade to Black-out

A Pageant

To open: Full general lighting

Cue 1 and *Cue 2* As in A GARDEN FÊTE

Cue 3   **Lionel:** "What plans? What plans?"   (Page 123)
          Fade to Black-out

Cue 4	As scene A PAGEANT opens *Full general lighting*	(Page 159)
Cue 5	**Sylvie** and **Toby** exit *Black-out*	(Page 185)
Cue 6	As scene A HARVEST FESTIVAL opens *Full general lighting*	(Page 189)
Cue 7	**Lionel** goes back inside the church *Fade to Black-out*	(Page 193)
Or *Cue* 5	**Celia** and **Toby** exit *Black-out*	(Page 187)
Cue 6	As scene A WEDDING opens *Full general lighting*	(Page 195)
Cue 7	**Sylvie** and **Toby** exit *Fade to Black-out*	(Page 198)

EFFECTS PLOT

Affairs in a Tent

Cue 1   On opening and throughout the scene How it Began   (Page 3)
Occasional shouts of children

Cue 2   **Celia** inhales with great pleasure   (Page 5)
Door bell rings

Cue 3   **Celia:** " . . . not in the loft, Sylvie?"   (Page 5)
Door bell rings

Cue 4   On opening of scene Affairs in a Tent   (Page 35)
Play in music, then the occasional sounds of children's voices, starting pistols and the odd amplified announcement

Cue 5   **Miles:** "Excuse me, Celia, I'm sorry."   (Page 36)
Toby announcement, as script

Cue 6   **Miles:** "She's out of breath just crouching."   (Page 36)
Sound of pistol shot and race

Cue 7   **Lionel** exits   (Page 46)
Toby announcement, as script

Cue 8   **Celia:** " . . . and I must have put it down."   (Page 50)
Sound of pistol shot and race

Either
Cue 9   On opening of scene A Funeral   (Page 59)
Sound of church bell tolling for a funeral, then in the silence that follows the sound of a few rooks

Cue 10   **Celia:** "Does he ever listen . . . ?"   (Page 61)
Sound of church clock chiming

Or
Cue 9   On opening of scene A New Woman   (Page 65)
Sound of church bell tolling for a funeral, then in the silence that follows the sound of a few rooks

Cue 10   **Celia:** "Oh, what's the use?"   (Page 68)
Sound of church clock chiming

Events on a Hotel Terrace

Cue 1 to *Cue* 3 As above

Cue 4   On opening of scene Events on a Hotel Terrace   (Page 73)
Sound of distant piano music playing popular medleys from long ago operettas and the squawk from an odd seagull

Either
Cue 5   **Toby:** "And stop that God-awful din."   (Page 91)
     Piano stops playing

Cue 6   On opening of scene A FUNERAL   (Page 95)
     Sound of church bell tolling for a funeral, then in the silence that
     follows the sound of a few rooks

Or
Cue 7   On opening of scene A SERVICE OF THANKSGIVING   (Page 99)
     Sound of church bells signifying a happy occasion, followed by
     the sound of singing. This is followed by the muted sounds of a
     church service

A Garden Fête

Cue 1 to *Cue* 3 As before

Cue 4   **Toby:** " . . . there's a turn up for the book."   (Page 118)
     The distant sound of a motor mower through to the end of this
     scene

Cue 5   On opening of scene A GARDEN FÊTE."   (Page 125)
     Sounds of activity from various sideshows

Either
Cue 6   On opening of scene A CHRISTENING   (Page 145)
     Sound of church bells signifying a happy occasion, followed by
     the sounds of children and of several babies crying

     The above to be increased and reduced each time the church door
     is opened and closed throughout this scene

Or
Cue 6   On opening of the scene RETURN OF THE PRODIGAL   (Page 151)
     Sound of church bells signifying a happy occasion, followed by
     the sound of singing

A Pageant

Cue 1 to *Cue* 4 As in A GARDEN FÊTE

Cue 5   On opening of scene A PAGEANT   (Page 159)
     Sound of birds singing

Cue 6   **Sylvie:** "It's nothing like that. Lionel?"   (Page 174)
     Toby Loudhailer: "All right then, Sylvie. Ready when you are."

Cue 7   **Sylvie:** "Sorry, what was that?"   (Page 174)
     Toby Loudhailer: "Ready when you are."

Cue 8   **Sylvie:** ". . . should I look surprised to see them here?"   (Page 174)
     Toby Loudhailer: "Of course not, you blithering idiot. There are
     a hundred thousand of them."

Cue 9   **Sylvie:** ". . . shut up, you Lionel-bloody-Hepplewick. Lionel."   (Page 175)
     Toby Loudhailer: "What the hell's going on down there?"

Cue 10   **Lionel:** "I'm trying to cut a straight edge here."   (Page 176)
     Toby Loudhailer: "Sylvie, what the blazes are you playing at?"

Cue 11   **Sylvie:** "... a woman of your tribe——."   (Page 176)
            Toby Loudhailer: "Sylvie, I can't hear a bloody word you're saying."

Cue 12   **Sylvie:** "He's pinned his hopes on me."   (Page 176)
            Toby Loudhailer: "Sylvie, for the last time...."

Cue 13   **Sylvie:** "Go away."   (Page 177)
            Toby Loudhailer: "Now, will you please get on with it."

Cue 14   **Sylvie:** "Would you like me to start again?"   (Page 177)
            Toby Loudhailer: "No, I would not."

Cue 15   **Sylvie:** "Will it be all right if I put it on, Mr Teasdale?" (Page 177)
            Toby Loudhailer: "Oh, God, all right then. Put the bloody thing on."

Either
Cue 16   On opening of scene A HARVEST FESTIVAL   (Page 189)
            Sound of church bells signifying a happy occasion, followed by the sounds of a church service just finishing

Or
Cue 16   On opening of scene A WEDDING   (Page 195)
            Sound of church bells signifying a happy occasion, followed by the sound of a wedding service

MADE AND PRINTED IN GREAT BRITAIN BY
LATIMER TREND & COMPANY LTD, PLYMOUTH
MADE IN ENGLAND